MEETINGS
ON THE EDGE

For Gaylord and Beast

MEETINGS
ON THE EDGE
A HIGH-LEVEL ESCAPE FROM OFFICE ROUTINE
MAGS MACKEAN

THE IN PINN®

The In Pinn is an imprint of
Neil Wilson Publishing Ltd
o/2 19 Netherton Avenue
GLASGOW
G13 1BQ

T/F: 0141 954 8007
E: info@nwp.co.uk
W: www.nwp.co.uk

First published in May 2008.

A catalogue record of this book is
available from the British Library.

The author and publisher acknowledge that
the following brands are registered trademarks:
Coca-Cola, Gore-Tex, Hoover, Marmite, Nescafé,
Nike, Perspex, Tupperware, Walkman, Yahtzee.

ISBN: 978-1-903238-80-6

Designed by Mark Blackadder

Distributed by BookSource
50 Cambuslang Road
GLASGOW
G32 5NB

T: 0845 370 0063
F: 0845 370 0064
W: www.booksource.net

Printed and bound in Finland by WS Bookwell

CONTENTS

ACKNOWLEDGEMENTS

Writing a book is a solitary commitment. That's why an author needs inspiration and support from friends and family. I've been very fortunate in both. Throughout my life, in my travels and adventures, countless people have influenced me with their enthusiasm and quest for fulfilment.

I would like to thank Jules Fineham and Giles Trussell at Glenmore Lodge in Aviemore, who encouraged me to pursue my mountaineering dreams. The stream of practical advice at Glenmore was essential for my planning for the Pyrenees traverse. Kate Murray helped me to see maps as allies, not only as the route to understanding landscapes. My first mountain mentor, Sonam Llama, a former Bhutanese monk and guide in Nepal, inspired me with his natural wisdom and passion for climbing.

I've spent wonderful times on alpine trips and in remote, boggy places with Richard Smith, Jamie Whittle, Gavin Lang, Jamie Reid, Walter McAllister, Amanda Dengis, Ian Davidson and David Henderson. Thank you David and 'Horbs' too for planting the seed of the Pyrenees trip as we tried to think of every mountain cure for my growing unrest on the windswept Cuillin Ridge. Little did we know then how plans for the traverse would flower in the coming months! Simon Willis shared his considerable knowledge of long-distance hiking and generously offered to share all his equipment to save me expense and time. Ravi Kumar, my instructor at the US-based National Outdoor Leadership School (NOLS) has become a great friend as well as a mentor.

My thanks to the continual encouragement of Sara Hunt in the early draft of this book; her positive input and bright ideas spurred me on. My insightful readers, Franklin Ginn, Rebecca Hanley and Martin Shaw were hugely supportive. Also Heather and Hugh Carling and Margaret Howard who produced some excellent illustrations of the Pyrenees during the book's planning. Thanks too for all the love and support of Dinah Wood, Mairi Clark, Murray Shanks, Linda Little, Lou Egan, Rachita Singh, Jean Thomas, as well as my three older sisters, Sal, Liz and Jane. My editor, Morven Dooner, with her enthusiasm and sharp eye was indispensable at the final stages of the book.

Lastly, I want to pay tribute to the humour and forbearance of my parents, Tom and Muriel MacKean, to whom this book is dedicated. They never once sighed over piles of pages to be scanned there and then by their grammar-sensitive eyes. Thank you for welcoming me back home to write and take over your tower. I was relieved by your apparent pleasure when I informed you of my intention to write another book and that our routine could be faithfully observed a second time round.

Mags MacKean, Titchfield, 2008

AUTHOR'S NOTE: The height of a mountain is given in metres (m) with feet (ft) in brackets in metric parts of the world. Mountains in America are the other way round as they're measured in feet first with metres in brackets.

The camps on Mount McKinley/Denali for example, are named according to their height: Camp 11, at 11,000ft (3,353m), or Camp 14, at 14,000ft (4,267m).

PROLOGUE

Just after midnight. The cold, thin air at Kibo hut leaves everyone eager to get moving. Bulky in down, we set off slowly in staggered groups. A line of fluorescence snakes upwards as head-torches beam on the patch of scree in front. The sky, a huge canopy of stars, dwarfs the continent's highest point, Kilimanjaro's summit. I am impatient, moving so slowly; resent this throng. I strike out ahead with one of our guides, a twenty-one-year-old called Clay.

We understand with a glance when the other needs to catch breath. Every two steps up the scree, we slide back a foot. Never frustrating, only rhythmic. Up and up, scrambling fast. Everything else has stopped. There is nothing but movement. It is called 'flow', like the transcendental experience of a mind-altered state. Fully engaged in each unfolding moment we work our way upwards. The shooting stars tearing through the glittering skies drive us to move faster.

It is too cold to rest at Gillman's Point, half an hour from the top, where many turn back with altitude sickness. We scramble on over endless rocks until, at last, we reach the summit known as Uhuru. It is hard to grasp that this is the roof of Africa and that for these few moments, it is ours alone. The glacier creaks as it slowly recedes, the only movement in the stillness. Looking out at the vastness, the impressive form of Mount Kenya breaks up the thin purple arc of dawn stretching across the horizon.

Hundreds of feet below, the snake of glowing lights labours on up the long steepness. Together, alone and triumphant, the camaraderie of shared experience is exhilarating. Laughing, while grabbing my hand as if to shake it, Clay calls me 'Simba', adding for my bemused benefit, 'In Africa, we have a saying: Lion woman … you strong'.

As we race down the scree ten feet at a time, hand in hand, I know I have glimpsed a depth of life demanding to be explored.

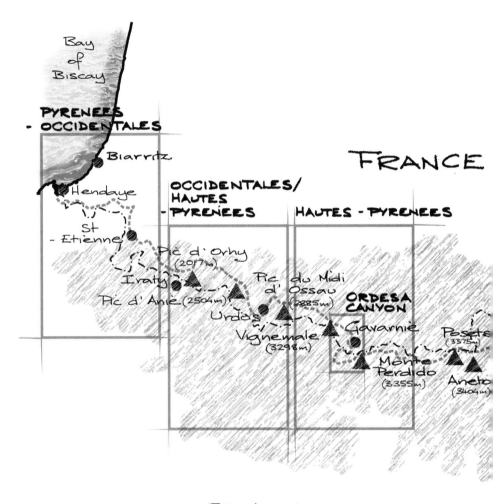

Bay
of
Biscay

PYRENEES
- OCCIDENTALES

• Biarritz

FRANCE

Hendaye

OCCIDENTALES/
HAUTES
- PYRENEES

HAUTES - PYRENEES

St
- Etienne

Pic d'Orhy
(2017m)

Iraty

Pic d'Anie (2504m)

Pic du Midi
d'Ossau
(2885m)

ORDESA
CANYON

Gavarnie

Posets
(3375m)

Urdos

Vignemale
(3298m)

Monte
Perdido
(3355m)

Aneto
(3404m)

SPAIN

KEY

········· My Route

·–·–·– Border

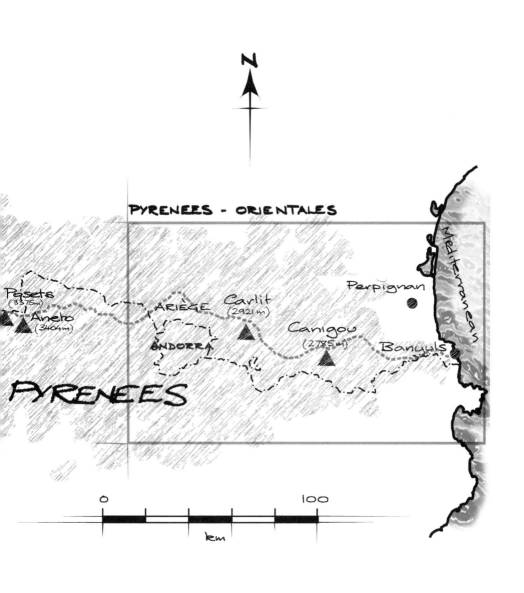

Even if you're going to live another three thousand more years, or ten times that, remember: you cannot lose another life than the one you're living now, or live another one than the one you're losing.

Marcus Aurelius,
Emperor of Rome (121–180AD)

INTRODUCTION
TRIGGER POINT: 2003

The grim report of the stalemate between the United Nations and Saddam Hussein blasts around the empty office for the second time in three hours. The Allied case against the Iraqi regime is building, as mediators try to work magic in the countdown to war. The world watches as diplomats, leaders and analysts debate on radio, television and online. Journalists in every newsroom follow the twists and turns too. During the night, news continues to roll, until the newsgathering machine cranks into life again. It's hard to figure a fresh top line for BBC Radio Scotland's 'flagship' breakfast show. As overnight editor I need to prise out the subtleties of diplomacy in deadlock. More frustrated and exhausted talking heads from both sides; more weary warnings and denials of guilt. The biggest story of the times is on a loop. As the rain lashes in the blackness outside and the bare branches of an overgrown plane tree rap against the window, I remember that my life is on a loop too.

I sift through a pile of embargoed press releases on my desk. More research linking shift working to depression and lowered life expectancy. Not for the first time I ask how I got here. A team of production helpers and presenters will soon arrive, expecting neat, crisp piles of newly printed programme scripts that they will transform into the breakfast broadcast for households around the country. Sipping strong, fresh coffee to stay awake, I glance at the tattered map of the Cold War world, taped to the wall opposite. Its shaded halves of simmering imperial tension are out-coloured by the mosaic of interwoven blues and greys, greens and oranges, which talk of oceans, continents and mountain ranges.

It is easy to forget that Scotland's wild landscape is only a short drive away from this office. So quickly the city sprawl changes into somewhere timeless. The primitive outline of the Campsie Fells to the north of the city hints at the Highlands beyond. That is what I am really here for, what drew me to this place, what took me away from the drudgery of a city at sea level and the unhealthy patterns of an all-consuming London life. All these were broken as my love of mountains and climbing became more pressing. None of my friends really understood, rolling their eyes at my latest 'holiday' venture, where gradient mattered as much as a destination's wild beauty.

Sometime between two and three in the morning, a contract cleaner, the only other night-shift worker on this floor, breezes about the empty space under the glare of strip lighting.

'How you doin' Mags, on this shift again I see. How's life treating youse?'

Maisy is a born-and-bred 'Weegie', and mother of three. Talking in her gravelly Glaswegian way, there is never a second when her attention is not partly on a duster, a cluttered desk, or on the vacuum roaring along the sticky carpet. She is always immaculate with her neat ponytail, bottle-blonde hair and figure-hugging denim.

'I'm not bad, thanks. Nothing much happening tonight.'

I remember not to complain about the rota, when this woman never moans at how her life's panned out. Her husband has been on sick leave for three years and she is the sole breadwinner. We are genuinely curious about each other, drawn together in our lonely work.

'And what about you? How is everything at home?'

'Och, no bad, no bad at all. Wee bit tired at the moment. Reckon it's the weather. It's dark when I wake up in the afternoon to begin all over again.'

'How long do you reckon you can stick this out?'

'Ah, maybe another year if I can. It pays so much more than a daytime wage … '

■   ■   ■

Tomorrow, after another programme, another prospects meeting follows. The merry-go-round of seasonal themes and 'that time of year again' events are usually enlivened by mishap, disaster or loss. It's the nature of producing news. Often it is as much a challenge in logistics to get something on air, as presenting the facts themselves. Even stories like Iraq, which speak for themselves, need planning. A decision has to be reached through the editorial hierarchy of how best they might be told. It's like peering out through Perspex glass, never really getting close to anything, as time and its ever-present pressure to reflect the world outside, ticks away to the top of the hour.

It hadn't always been like this. Once my enthusiasm made the mechanics of the job seem exciting. As a rookie reporter for Greater London Radio, as it was called then, I was only too thrilled when a story broke one Friday evening, just as we were all piling out to the pub. My editor, making sense of the squiggles jotted down during the tip-off from Scotland Yard, called me over.

'Mags – head to the Docklands! Bomb blast … suspected IRA attack. Take the radio car and call as soon as you have a signal.'

Several times I screeched to a halt in a maze of roads, asking through a wound-down window whether the Docklands *really* was this way? I was forced to park up next to a red-and-white-striped police cordon, sealing off the action a mile-and-a-half away. Press Association copy was read down the phone by a colleague. Frantic, with three minutes to go before being the BBC's on-scene authority, I spotted a solitary person on their way home from the evacuated area who gave me details of the moment of impact, the shattered glass, the panic and chaos. My faithful regurgitation of known police facts was embellished with the witness's colourful account. Finally, everything said and summed up again for emphasis, the studio presenter persisted to question, under orders to pad things out. So, leaving listeners in no doubt there really was nothing left to report, I heard myself conclude, 'Key questions are remaining unanswered here tonight in the Docklands. Who carried out this atrocity and why? Back to the studio.'

Back at the office, my editor was pleased enough. Just as I was walking out of the door, he added, 'Er, one more thing. Thank you for reminding us what we didn't know – that's exactly what we sent you there to find out.'

The years went by, stories filed, and my obsession with mountains grew. It began in Tanzania, long after a childhood of Lake District holidays. A friend and I mixed a safari trip with climbing Kilimanjaro, famed for being the highest point in Africa and one of the world's Seven Summits. It wasn't the grandeur and status of this peak, attracting hundreds of other tourists to attempt to reach its 5,896-m (19,344ft) summit, that impressed me. During the six days, we trekked through five distinct climate zones, each with its unique character and abundance of life, beginning with lush, humid rainforest, then heathery fields, upwards to a hostile landscape, almost Martian in its red dustiness, scree slopes and finally the alpine zone of glacier, towering over an extraordinary expanse of flat, dry desert.

Watching this view, I understood mountains are not simply static objects which man sets out to conquer, weather and skill permitting. The terrain that leads us further upwards has a vital identity of its own. To transfer our goal-driven values into the act of climbing them is a small part of the experience. Quite simply, I fell in love with the process of moving uphill.

Maisy busies about hoovering the carpet. As she sweeps towards my working corner, I swivel my chair, lifting my feet up to make room for her. The unfilled minutes of airtime still need to be added up before the others get here. Time, so divisible for a job like this, is hurtling by in greater chunks, as my diary becomes an interchangeable record of every passing year. It's as if I'm waiting for my life to begin – later, tomorrow, some other day. I've always been driven by curiosity for the world and what happens in it. That's why I became a journalist. But instead of engaging with life, somehow I've ended up here, in this office, processing the worn out stories of others rather than originating my own. Is this really the best life can be?

'Maisy?' She doesn't hear me above the noise of the hoover. I get up and tap her on the shoulder. She looks up and smiles, then turns it off. For a moment we stand there as the motor whines into silence.

'Maisy, you know what? I've decided to quit my job. I am going to climb mountains instead.'

PART 1 OCCIDENTAL PYRENEES

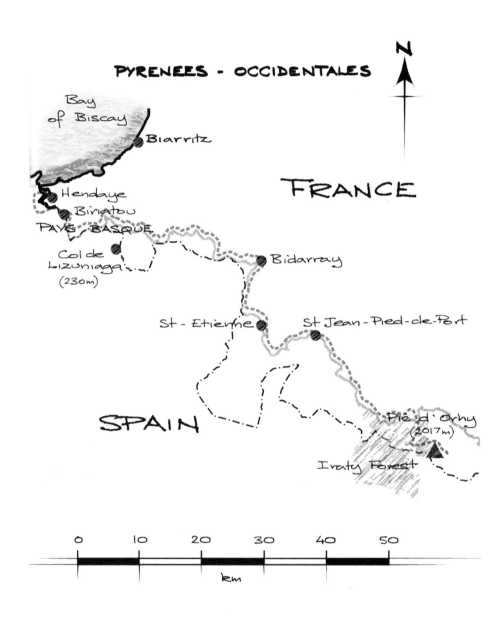

PYRENEES - OCCIDENTALES

N

Bay of Biscay

Biarritz

FRANCE

Hendaye
Biriatou
PAYS - BASQUE

Col de Lizuniaga (230m)

Bidarray

St - Etienne

St Jean - Pied - de - Port

SPAIN

Pic d'Orhy (2017m)

Iraty Forest

0   10   20   30   40   50

km

KEY

.... My Route

~~~~~ GR10 track

—·—·— Border

1 FIRST STEPS

It is two-thirty and swelteringly hot. Beyond the cool darkness of the tavern with its thick walls and worn stone flags, the heat shimmers. The noise of a *pelota* ball ricocheting across a court outside softens. The player has been a convincing match against the wall in the 'world's fastest ball game,' but sounds ready to give up. Devouring a plate of smoked ham and cheese served with baguette and butter and a slice of pickled gherkin is thirsty work and I order another ice-cold Coke. The charm of this Basque hamlet and its pervading somnolence make me ignore the pressure to get moving. I will have to make ground by nightfall. The occasional farm labourer wanders up to the bar in heavy boots to order a reviving *pression*. I listen to the murmur of polite exchange, drowsy as time stands still.

This is when the promise of adventure should spring me into life: to find my way across the Pyrenees from the grey Atlantic beginning, along hundreds of kilometres of rugged mountains towards the exotic blue finishing line of the Mediterranean. The tension between planning and uncertainty had seemed so appealing before my departure. For months, I'd been learning Spanish, pored over maps and navigation manuals, studied the science of weight economy and felt delightfully smug at saving six-hundred grams in opting for a canvas bivvy sack instead of a tent. I acquired the very lightest outdoor gear to cater for all seasons as this ten-week traverse would stray dangerously close to winter.

I wanted to savour such a culturally varied route. Exploring the valleys and their customs and comparing regions crossing the border from France to Spain would be as absorbing as finding a way through them. My limited mountaineering experience was always going to add to the excitement. Yet, after a twenty-four-hour hammering with unforeseen discomforts and testing practicalities, I am already weary and anxious.

An age has passed since my arrival in Hendaye, bordering Spain and the foothills of the Western Pyrenees. The ice-cream parlours overlooking the ocean swell had drawn me inside to cool down. As I wandered, my bulging backpack looked out of place, jarring with the serenity of wealthy leisure. Luxury apartments look out over marinas full of floating white palaces, and tanned customers with their canine accessories fuss in and out of the neat designer boutiques lining the pristine, terracotta-tiled streets. I trudge up to someone with my camera, to capture the beginning of endless blue sea without a mountain in sight.

The nearest campsite for an early night and dawn start was a long uphill slog. The sardine-style rows of canvas on scrawny patches of grass were immediately depressing and the shop stocked with mean-looking packets of dried food not at all tempting. The functional demeanour of the manageress with her finely plucked eyebrows was off putting, as she addressed me rather abruptly with a 'Seule?' The exhausted peak-season feel drove me to look at my watch. There was enough time to dash for the train to Spain. I thought about rewarding myself with an opening night in a hotel, just to ease my way into things. At once, my spirits lifted with my first change of plan, a short train ride to a fresh start.

If Hendaye lacked hospitable spirit, then Bidasoa was even more indifferent. Bigger and busier, its people weaved in and out of bars and restaurants with the focused vitality of fiesta time. There were no rooms anywhere. The eyes of the hotel reception staff were unbothered as if to say, 'It's fiesta time lady and this is Basque country. What do you expect?'

It was then dark and a taxi took me to the nearest campsite. Full up. I pleaded with the manageress, who nodded at my suggestion to pay a discounted rate for a patch of tarmac in a forlorn-looking playground. The chained-up dogs in the campsite growled and barked through the night as carloads of travellers arrived intermittently, stomping past my head in search for space. I imagined how much better it would be to sleep rough in the fields outside the compound. The first lesson had been learnt, never again to accept meagre offerings from humans when nature provides so abundantly, gracefully, and for free.

I woke up stiff and unrested. The industrial suburbs and out-of-town shopping centres stretching into the grey distance were an uninspiring start to the long way east. Not regarding the signs as encouraging this side of the border, I decided to get back to France and quickly. A short bus ride took me to a main road from where, with a bit of uphill scrambling, I could cross some fields to begin the route.

The church clock chimes, reminding me of where I am. It's just after three. The man playing *pelota* has been driven inside by the heat but I have barely covered any distance and should get moving again. I haven't decided where to camp for the night. It depends on where I can find water and how I'm adjusting to the weight. A final look at the map shows the path undulating for about two hours, passing a lake. I put on a long-sleeved lightweight layer to protect my arms, apply some more sun block and set off, aware of every bump and stone through my new, un-weathered boots.

Not yet in rhythm, my rucksack straps press into my shoulders. It is light in design, without any internal frame or support, saving around one-and-a-half kilos. I wonder about the wisdom of this now as the effect is like hauling the dead weight of a drooping sack. Tests in London parks are not a fair match for this uneven terrain. Already I'm thirsty again and knock back most of my half-litre bottle of water, glad to be rid of the best part of half a kilo. There are sources ahead – at least a stream or two before the lake.

The rolling hills and farmland are coloured with every shade of green, yellow and fawn. The sun beats down through a brilliant blue, cloudless sky. It must be 30°C – hot, even for August. Small white butterflies dart along the bushes as if to the birdsong emanating from a triangle of big oak trees. This really is rural France. Not a soul anywhere. Biriatou is already well behind me and the Atlantic a good two hours from there.

All of a sudden, through the haze, an apparently naked form in boots appears from the bushes bordering the track. I strain to see if it's a man or woman. It seems to glance at me some fifty metres away before running off, vanishing over the next rise. The vision scuffs up small clouds of dried mud. The moment is over so quickly that I wonder just for a second if it actually happened. Could it have been someone in flesh-coloured clothes? I remember the recent media exposure of Britain's naked rambler, now a tabloid treasure. The nude eccentric was at that moment walking through the UK to highlight man's connection to nature. His lone adventure was an easy filler and headline grabber for the more quiet news periods during the summer holidays, the 'silly season'. What a strange coincidence, to think that this very unpopulated area of France might have its own version! Who would believe this?

The form then reappears. It's much closer this time, less than twenty feet away. A slim man, barely taller than me, with shoulder-length hair is standing starkers beside a bush, his back to me. Could he be peeing? I scarcely have time to draw breath or size up the unusual combination of nudity and labourer's boots when he turns around. He actually falters towards me. It is at that point I understand fully what he is actually doing.

There is nothing at all innocent in this encounter. Here is someone actively enjoying the outdoors and its freedoms with an abandon usually reserved for behind locked doors. From the state of his excitement it's easy to see he is making quite an afternoon of it and I don't pick up any sense of invaded privacy. By the way he walks up to me, drinking in my open-eyed surprise, his hands busily working away a few feet below, it is clear I am an expected guest.

We look at each other for a few seconds more. He watches me watching him. A psychiatrist once told me flashers rarely attack; they're invariably lonely, reclusive people wanting to be noticed. He has my attention alright. I spring into a pantomime part and wave my sticks. My voice is deeper than usual, almost throaty:

'Monsieur, qu'est-ce-que vous faites?'

The *vous* sounds rather formal considering the apparently familiar terms we are on. He looks surprised at this, as if the fantasy has been disrupted by hearing my very real voice. He continues to hover within a few feet, swaying now. This is happening so quickly, yet at the same time each graphic moment unfolds in freeze-frame.

'Non, monsieur, *non* ... ce n'est pas acceptable!'

My surprise is overtaken by anger. He remains excited. I turn around and shout as loud as I can to an imaginary friend following faithfully: 'Alain! Vite! Alain, je t'attends!' This breaks the spell. He looks down the path, then, puzzled, he looks back at me. For the first time I notice he is clutching a scrunched up T-shirt and what looks like shorts. He turns away, as if deciding what to do next and breaks into a jog, kicking up dust as he races back towards Biriatou.

I look down the track long after he disappears. Crows pass overhead, squawking, their black wings slicing through the azure blue. Crickets and other sounds of summer are audible again. The butterflies flit and dance in pairs and a small lizard darts across a thick dried rut of mud. The stillness of this rural moment is ageless. There is nothing here that could not belong to a scene from centuries ago – except I've just had a close encounter with a solitary naked masturbator, something that's never happened during my years living in London or visiting some of the world's most flamboyant cities and their seedier haunts. There is no one here to share this with either, nowhere to channel the rising, irrepressible torrent of words ready to explode from me. My heart is beating faster. Only now I'm aware of my fear. What next? I look at my sticks, glad they have been so useful already and start walking, eyes on the track in front.

A faint murmur of voices drifts along the path long before I see anyone. A couple are packing up the remains of a picnic beneath the shade of a lone oak tree. I march over as if our meeting is inevitable and we have plenty to discuss. 'Bonjour ... salut ... excusez-moi ... j'ai ... ' I'm out of breath, in a hurry to explain. No sense of social incongruity is going to stop me now. 'J'ai rencontré un homme bizarre ... '

They look up, surprised, surrounded by picnic detritus and a tartan rug. I struggle to remember the word for naked. My O-level French didn't stretch to 'flasher' – could it be *exposeur*?

'Pardon, un homme bizarre est là-bas ... sans pantalons ... sans vêtements.' I drop the backpack for the first time since Biriatou, and my unburdened body seems to levitate.

'Comment? Vous dites que ... ,' he trails off, awkward. Silence settles over us as we search for something to say. Eventually she asks in English, 'A man who is bizarre, you say?'

'Yes, no trousers, no clothes. I am alone. Nothing really *happened* – but he was very, very *bizarre*.'

'Oh là là!'

'Oui, oh là là,' he concurs.

Strangely there is nothing left to say. They have shown suitable concern with their stupefied expressions. Who on earth is she, they must wonder? An Englishwoman, with a very English accent. Alone. Half an hour away from the village. Things like this don't really happen, and in the Basque countryside on a public path? The drama now seems absurd in my effort to share it. It's a bit like trying to recapture the mystery of a magic trick once the everyday has taken over. They want to pack up their things and I've assured them I'm OK to walk on. And so we smile and agree once more I really had encountered *un homme bizarre.*

The route persists through hilly fields. It is still very hot and I put on some more sun block. I down the last drops of water and look at the map for a source. There should have been two streams already. The sun is strong enough to vaporise anything that is not a lake or a fast-flowing river – not what I expected for late summer. The lake is another hour-and-a-half away. The vivid memory of the man is losing its grip on me as I begin to imagine bottles of clear, cold water. There is nothing to be done but continue and trust chance. I am thirsty with no prospect of relief, overloaded by a sack without support, and facing my first wild camp alone, without any idea of where that might be. Just as I start to assess whether this trip is going worse than my most pessimistic forecasts, a surge of energy overpowers my shaky resolve.

The hypnotic click of sticks sets a rhythm for the boots to follow. Far behind are hostile campgrounds, lonely men and the relentless cycle of work and play. Ahead is a boundless horizon with a promise of water.

A figure with an Alsatian strides over the next hill. He has a stick, like a staff, made from a sturdy branch. The dog bounds to my feet panting, curious, his tongue hanging out. It barks as I carry on walking. Its unshaven owner has a bandana over his head, and is making light work of walking with a big army-issue pack, as if he's been on expedition for days.

'Bonjour monsieur – j'ai soif. Où est une source d'eau?'

'Rien, rien du tout!' is the answer.

'Mais ... '

This is not what I wanted to hear. It is too hot and I am too thirsty to challenge this miserable announcement. I feel an irrational surge of contempt for this man. He throws down his pack and frees a plastic bottle wedged in a side compartment. ' 'Ere ... 'ave some.'

It's an effort not to swill back the lot. I manage to stop at five or six gulps and thank him. He reckons the lake is less than an hour from here depending how fast I walk. The issue of thirst now dealt with, my thoughts return immediately to *l'homme bizarre.*

'J'ai rencontré un homme sans pantalons, sans vêtements ... '

I try to recapture the horror but my storytelling falters without knowing key words in French and his failure to understand them in English. In fact, 'no trousers, no clothes' do not have the same impact at all. At once the man becomes intense, lowering his voice to a hoarse whisper.

'Madamoiselle, attention! Je vous implore.'

Saliva drools from the Alsatian's panting mouth. Resuming in English, to ensure there is no chance, no risk whatsoever, that I don't understand the seriousness of what he has to share, the man then warns: 'Attention. Yes. Be careful, very careful. 'Ere in France and 'ere in Pays Basque there are many maniac. Many, many maniac ... You must 've courage, be brave. At night you must camp away from ze path ... 'Ide yourself. Promise me you always camp five metres, no less, from ze path. Tell no one you are alone or where you go.'

I am stunned.

'Non, Non. Je me répète, non! Vous ne comprenez pas.' He stops, looks away and at last smiles, shaking his head at the baffled woman in front of him. 'I am 'omosexual. 'Ave no fear.'

There are no words. How could this happen, a declaration of sexuality in the middle of nowhere? How unlikely, too, to have stumbled across the strangest people I've ever met within an hour of each other, in this rural idyll! We wish each other well and the best of luck, like two socially well-adjusted people who have whiled away some time in happy exchange. We then start to walk again in opposite directions and I turn around and wave as I hear the words, 'Bon courage!'

Big boulders dot the landscape. Flourishing bush, no longer trimmed hedgerow, encroaches on the path, with looser stone underfoot. The eye-pleasing neatness of the land seems less touched by human hands. It is still uncomfortably hot and a mixture of sweat and sun cream drips into my eyes, stinging them. I run through the man's advice. Navigation and outdoor practicalities no longer top the order of challenge. Alarm bells will ring loudly now around fellow solitary walkers. And it's not just the calibre of those I might randomly meet, too far from help. It is also the camping element, amounting to at least a third of the twenty-four-hour cycle. In a couple of weeks the days will already be shorter and more time will be spent in the dark. I mustn't be at all conspicuous at night.

My mouth is dry and sticky. I can't remember ever being this thirsty. The lake will be deep, cool and fresh; a perfect spot for camping. It can't be far but I can no longer ignore the dull weight of panic. Noticing it feeds it, and it starts to spread through me in waves. Each step is getting heavier, meeting an invisible resistance. It is time to take stock. I slump on the path edge and cradle my crossed legs. Is continuing really such a good idea?

An ant is scurrying up the steep bank of a tractor rut, with a bit of shredded leaf twenty times its size. This hefty boot could crush it so easily. If I give up now I will never know what is to happen next, what is beyond the next rise; the discomforts, the rewards. My senses are infinitely more alert after the off-putting encounters with fellow man. Even the sun seems hostile as it continues to beat down with such force. All nature is thrown off balance during extremes. I will give this venture *one* more chance, *one* more.

I get up again. Everything looks as it did, carrying on as it was. There is always life and movement in nature, even on such an airless afternoon as this. The path twists for another two hundred metres and starts to climb again, where it flattens into a plateau. I set my sights on reaching that point.

The view opens up. The distant hills look higher and the area wilder, less farmed. The shade of woodland is immediately ahead; to the east the teasing blue of water, the same rich hue as the sky. The lake is an oasis in an otherwise parched land, streaked with brown. My pace steps up, my eyes on the trees, where I can trace a route to the water. My mind is on the water. Water is the only thing that matters.

Scanning the shadowy outline of the woods for somewhere to hide my pack, I realise I'm not alone. There is someone else here, sheltering from the sun, as I should be. A stick is rammed into the earth, from which a sweaty shirt hangs to dry.

'Salut,' he says. 'Comment allez-vous?

'Chaud. Soif.' Wary of conversation, I notice the striking blue eyes smiling, inspiring trust. His cropped hair is bleached almost white from the sun.

'Do you want some water? I have lots of it. Just filtered some from the lake there – a nightmare to reach.'

His English is good, with only a trace of a guttural accent. It's hard to believe what he's saying and for a moment I stare dumbly at the bottle of water in his outstretched hand. It is full and clear. I then take it, bent on drinking the lot. Never has water tasted as good. The sweet comfort of changing fortunes lifts the spirits more than a well mixed cocktail ever could. After my last sip, I stand for a moment, unwilling to move, euphoric with relief. He grins at the visible change in my morale. I then sit down next to him, glad to exchange some routine details.

He is Philippe, a Belgian, and has five weeks to reach the start of the higher mountains, known as the Haute Pyrenees. He's walked the entire 2,167-mile length (3,487 km) of the Appalachian Trail, one of America's most famous long-distance hikes, taking six months. Relaxed for the first time since leaving England, *l'homme bizarre* is described more graphically now, and the roar of his laughter makes me forget how close I was to heading back home.

His legs are covered in dried mud and scratches from the treacherously thick, silty pools surrounding the lake. It had taken him an hour to wade through it, so he settled for the muddy puddle water instead. He holds up his nifty gadget, a compact device with a tube, which transformed the brown water into the freshest drink in the world. There's no doubt that being shorter than him, I would have had more of a struggle wading to the lake and would have had no choice but to drink from the puddle. We agree that with a summer like this, water will be scarce.

It is at last a little cooler and the shadows of the trees are lengthening. Crickets are chirping in the long, springy grass, lulling me to take a nap. But we both get up at the same time, sensing the need to move on. Casually, while adjusting straps, wary of seeming too friendly, we wonder that as we're heading the same way, we might as well continue together for a bit?. Neither of us knows where we will end up for the night. Now we have water, it doesn't matter.

Philippe, half-a-foot taller and strong for a man with such a lean build, has a faster pace but the temperature is easing all the time and I am happy to work harder than I would on my own. This feels good.

2 LEARNING THE ROPES

No experience in the Pyrenees would ever be as vivid as the first day. Grasping that for the next sixty mornings, I'd be waking up in a lush wooded bedroom, made me feel wonderfully alive, ready to face whatever the day would bring. Realising that soon it would be uncomfortably hot made the stream I was washing in even fresher and more invigorating.

The track had led us through a fairyland of moss and bracken carpeting the gentle contours, past wild ponies rubbing their necks against wooden fences. Philippe strode in front, looking for suitable camping spots. We took our time feasting at a large flat rock in the fading daylight. With his penknife, Philippe made easy work of transforming a thick branch into a perfect walking stave and I was struck again by the luck of our chance meeting. As the woodland stirred more loudly in the growing darkness, I thanked my lucky stars I was not here alone. Despite being very tired, I lay awake for a long time, listening to the soothing flow of water.

The Occidental Pyrenees are a gentle prelude to the start of the higher mountains, where the landscape becomes grander and wilder. After a second day, I was feeling a bit surer of my footing, of my place in these forested hills. We found somewhere to camp on the edge of a small rural community, behind towering green plants of ripe corn, next to the banks of a river. Children shrieked as they ran about, but we could only hear them faintly from our corner. Philippe mused on how much more freedom country kids have, compared to his upbringing in Antwerp. He had always regarded the countryside as a spacious playground, somewhere to forget restraints and formalities.

After thinking ahead to supper, a matter quickly settled with our dwindling provisions of olives, cheese, tomatoes and hardening bread, we agreed I'd wash first in a plunge pool. At first glance, it was a perfect bathroom, concealed under a large willow tree, down a steep bank of churned-up field. I dipped my toes into the river and watched the ripples disturb dozens of pond skaters darting over its murky surface. Bright blue dragonflies hovered and small dark fish were labouring across the flow of water to feed on the abundance of slimy green life. A branch, drooping over the river's edge, was a useful handrail to submerge slowly. It was cold. Bracing. I rubbed my legs and clouds of caked mud and dirt seeped into the gritty water. Rusty parts of agricultural machinery littered the riverbed, like ghostly human traces. Not far from my foot an abandoned old boot unsettled me further, its lonely lace trailing with the current. The pool was no longer my own. After one more plunge, I raced out of the water to get dry.

As I was wrapping my towel around me, a branch snapped with a crack, making me start. Turning around, I was surprised that Philippe was heading my way. The plan had been clear – I was to let him know when I was finished. His arrival felt intrusive. Resolving to be aloof for the rest of the evening, I marched back to our site in my towel and bare feet.

It was another clear, starry night and the field was rustling with life as we turned in early. On edge from the effort of being surly with Philippe, I shuffled about restlessly in my bivvy to find a comfier trench of softer soil. My mind lurched, remembering the moodiness of the river and the sense of invaded privacy. No sooner had I resolved to separate from Philippe in the morning, than my opinion changed again. To have bumped into him like that, only the day before, was nothing short of a gift. He had materialised just when I was most alone, as if to guide me through the opening hours of fear. Watching him adapt to the changing demands of the outdoors was already helping to sharpen my own outdoor sense. The instinct of finding a good spot to sleep or knowing which path to follow was getting stronger all the time. But we were in the relatively populated Basque country, a world removed from the wilder parts of the Pyrenees, where days can be spent walking without seeing another soul. There was a great deal more to learn before then, when I would only have myself to rely upon.

Clearly we were very different. He was happy to trudge along a predictable route and its regular contact with shops and people, relying on a guidebook to break down the daily distances. I was absorbing maps at every opportunity, curious to know where the higher route intersects a track and where it might lead. If I had wanted to follow a path, I wouldn't be on this venture. The growing urge to roam more freely would soon make me restless.

An owl hooted, sounding close. Philippe was already snoring. My mind rested on his simple, direct way of talking, his lack of any pretension. He won't thank unnecessarily or supply small talk unless he wants to, rarely starting a conversation. He lives simply, changing jobs every couple of months as he works round Europe and America, from one seasonal set-up to another, picking fruit or factory work. He talks about the highly educated people he meets who prefer the freedoms of migrant working. It is easy to save money too with the long hours and fewer social distractions. With all the travelling about, the only clue as to what really tethers him is his clear devotion to his mother and protectiveness for his sister. His father is rarely mentioned.

Philippe was still snoring contentedly, unaware of the noises amplified by the darkness: the endless scurrying, scampering, hooting, screeching, and … another sound … splashing – 'Aaaaaaaah!' It could so easily have been someone wading through the river, about to pounce on the two canvas shapes on the other side.

'Aaaaaaaaaaaaah!'

'Er, Mags? Is that you? Are you alright?'

'No – it's so noisy out here! Listen – can you hear that thing in the water?'

'That? Hold on a sec … it's a beaver.'

'But how on earth can you know that? Please … double-check.'

Without hesitation, Philippe unzipped his tent and walked about. He couldn't see a thing but under fire from a volley of questions, he remained 'pretty certain' it had been a beaver. Reassured by the verdict, my bed felt comfortable at last, as my body sank deeper into the soil and my racing mind slowed. The last thing I remember thinking was we should let a few more days pass before going our separate ways.

■   ■   ■

Travelling as two is very different from being on the move alone. The senses dull a little and there is an extra pair of eyes to point things out and share the unfolding picture. Sometimes the familiar red and white markings will have worn away. Often on my own, with a plan to meet Philippe further ahead, the compass or map would steer me to take a fork I may not otherwise have chosen, whereas he was relying on those markings alone. Every time I imagined him outwitted, he would show up, with a radar-like sense of the right way. No matter how many detours I took and frustrating false starts and dead ends, Philippe seldom reported trouble. He was always waiting for me, usually well fed with slices of world-famous Basque gateau, sometimes asleep under the shade of a big plane tree.

The valleys were filled with sheep and the sound of their ringing bells. For every hill walked down, another rose. The sun remained strong and the occasional walker coming from the other way would warn us of the lack of water. The terrain was becoming more rugged each day and the valleys steeper, although the forests remained thick and large. I wasn't used to spending hours at a time under the canopy of trees and as it thinned, I enjoyed the open sky.

After three days on the trail, hot water and warm food seemed distant pleasures. By afternoon, the clouds were darkening and the temperatures cooling in a rising breeze. We were climbing steadily into fog. This had been unimaginable just a couple of days before as we had panted along, grateful for the shelter of trees. The lane wound this way and that, and sheep wandered aimlessly along it with us, unused to cars. The damp air filled with wood smoke and as we dropped down the other side of another hill, a large stone cottage loomed at its bottom.

Its smoking chimney looked so welcoming, as did a chaos of farm animals spilling out of the open gate onto the lane, a charming disarray of hens and pigs, yapping small dogs and strolling cats. A toddler chased a hen flapping its wings across the yard and was then reproached by an irate woman's voice from an open window. All this was serenely observed by horses in their stables.

A sign on the gate told us this was Esteben Farm. Philippe remembered it as a listed *gîte* in his guidebook. We knocked on the door and walked in before anyone had a chance to open it; we were near a kettle and that was what mattered. We headed for one of the tables and a child no older than ten appeared in red wellingtons, asking us what we would like to drink. After hearing a prompt answer of two *chocolats chaud* she raced back through the narrow door to the kitchen. A couple our age, but much smarter and cleaner, were drinking tea and whispering as they held hands across a table. The open fire glowed orange, drawing our tired eyes.

A heavily built woman, presumably the farmer's wife, strode over with two steaming cups of chocolate, her strong forearms showing through rolled-back sleeves. I asked about the evening meal and the tart reply was 'fresh farm food'. I wondered if she meant the pigs and chickens, roaming freely outside. To pitch a tent with hot water would cost six euros. I caught Philippe's eye, who looked away, clearly tempted to break his rules of thrift and resourcefulness. He then nodded at me once, returning my smile. The offer of hot water and home-cooked food can buckle even the strongest of wills.

That night at Esteben Farm is a treasured memory of a uniquely warm atmosphere among strangers, all charmed by the eccentric austerities of their hosts. A happy collision of visitors sharing a meal around a long table with pitchers of rustic red wine are the perfect ingredients for a special sort of social recipe. Perhaps the primitive accommodation in a damp bunkhouse, requiring a brisk walk through the fog to the refuge of a roaring fire was a catalyst, but the rapport among eight strangers was quite simply genuine.

Every so often the angry voice of madame thundered from the kitchen, as she ticked off one of her wild brood, tearing through the house when not under orders to do something. A platter of salty bacon and scrambled eggs, dripping in butter arrived to a stunned table, which was swiftly reduced to giggles as someone quipped what *will* we have for breakfast? A very handsome Spanish Basque man with thick black curls and his new French wife, offered to serve.

As soon as a full plate arrived in front of Philippe he tucked in, while the man was still serving. He then slurped through his meal with an urgency of someone starved, not looking up once until the whole lot was gone. No one tried not to notice. On the contrary, the jokes that started at Philippe's good-natured expense smoothed any awkwardness and he helped himself to more of the tepid food, now congealed in fat, to roars of delight. The rather terse one-liners of my reserved companion could be construed as socially abrupt, but the table regarded them as examples of wit bordering on genius. He was something of a star in this company and all eyes feasted on him, curious as to what the quiet Belgian might offer up next. The pitcher was refilled and I realised how much fun we were having.

This was my first social foray at speaking in French to a group of native speakers. The Spaniard was bilingual. No one stirred for a second, as I would have, with impatience, or spoke over me as I faltered my way along, explaining my plans to walk across these hills, from coast to coast. At one point, slightly emboldened by the wine and the success in making myself understood, I tried something a little more ambitious and got lost. No matter. Someone across the table urged me in flawless English to tell him and he would translate. The evening carried on in this wonderful way and we took it in turns talking as the whole table listened. The connection was never broken by short bursts of chat between smaller groups.

After chopped apples and vanilla ice cream, the unanimous highlight of the meal, it was time for bed. I appreciated all the heartfelt sentiments of 'bon courage' from my new friends who again expressed surprise that I wanted to walk so far on my own.

Outside, the skies had cleared and it was a beautiful night for a stroll. A couple of dinner companions hovered about, looking out across the dark outline of the nearby hills. I was glad not to be heading for a dormitory in a concrete bunker like they were. It really is a much lovelier prospect to sleep under a vast black roof of twinkling stars.

3 STRAINING AT THE LEASH

It is ghostly, sitting above a cloud line lit up intermittently with a firework display going on below. The rumble of explosions and bursts of colour tease us with the cheeriness of valley life. We only just made it here by nightfall. Rain is likely tonight and this will be the first time I experience a downpour inside a Gore-Tex sack. My head is protected by a hoop that supports a canopy, providing just enough cramped space to sit up in, but my legs will feel every single drop of water.

For ages we had debated the wisdom of setting off in the growing heat of late afternoon. There was plenty of cover for illicit camping somewhere in the lush green hills or fields of vines around the snug haven of Bidarret. Its Roman church and medieval bridge, sleepy streets filled with shuttered windows and boxes overflowing with scarlet geraniums, were made lovelier by a conversation I had with a Liverpool football supporter over a *pelota* game. The courts are at the heart of village life, uniting the interest of all generations. Until he was thirteen he had never left these valleys and still speaks to his mother in the Basque dialect.

'To be Basque … is to … belong, you know?'

'You mean to your community? Loyalty to your people?'

'Yes. No. All this … just look!'

He swept his arm, motioning vaguely across the square. The question of identity was in the everyday details. The whitewashed houses resembled so many others in the Basque villages we'd walked through. He pointed out how the shutters, usually red and green, face east towards the rising sun. And the name of the household's founder is carved in stone above the doorway. Even now, he said, a home may have only been owned by one family.

Besides Basque custom, he spoke about the friendliness of people in Merseyside, how he had travelled there as a sales rep, the fitness of their top players and wondered if I was aware Liverpool would take the Premiership this season? The regular 'comme on dit' on both our parts strengthened our rapport, as he searched for a simpler phrase in French, or I struggled to recall words from school. It had been a team effort. Together, we had meandered through the hottest part of the day in idle chatter and when it was time to leave, it was like saying goodbye to someone very familiar.

'Bon courage,' those simple and meaningful words were said again, as I set off to rejoin the path. While Philippe lagged behind to adjust his backpack, the man had given him a scrap of paper with his name and number to ring if ever I was in trouble or in need of a friendly face.

Labouring uphill in the heat, eyes doggedly on the dusty slope in front, we didn't appreciate how dramatically the scenery was changing. Up and up we went, gaining hundreds of metres, until we reached the Crête d'Iparla, a ridge to avoid in bad weather. The path stretched through the steep contour of a U-shaped valley, gouged by glaciers in the last ice age. The granite barrenness was made more austere as we edged along sheer cliffs, with a three-hundred-metre drop in places to the valley floor.

In strange harmony, nature began to reflect the obvious hazards. A weather front was building all the time, the wind whipping up in gusts and the light dimming as clouds smothered the traces of a sunny afternoon. Griffon vultures with their impressive wingspans were soaring at close range. I felt them watching us. To be caught out in lightning strikes or to fall from the mist-shrouded brink are real fears here, and would ensure prime carrion for those stalking birds of prey.

Shafts of light pierced the clouds, turning the rich, green strips between the rocks fluorescent. The weather was as mercurial as the landscape was bewitching. The ruggedness reminded me of Scotland, especially around Torridon. Hunching forwards brought back memories of school in the Highlands, with a keen master never daunted by the hostile conditions, as he strode in front of the single file of shivering, miserable teenagers.

And how different again – this spot by some woods, overlooking a valley we cannot see, the fireworks there like gunfire and the faint glow of orange and pink, smearing the smoky fog.

Philippe is more talkative than he's ever been and I'm happy to listen, tired now all our food is eaten. He tells me that his father is retired and frail, a listless shadow of what he once was; a workaholic, running his haulage business from seven in the morning until ten at night, six days a week. His mother gave the company her best years manning the phones for him and attending his every need. It was a strained, unhappy marriage but she stayed with him.

'So, do you get on with your father?' I ask. He shakes his head.

'Talk to him much?' He shrugs. Best left alone. The clouds are thick and grey. It must rain soon.

'And what about you, Mags? You seem good at talking but I don't know very much about you.' I don't mind answering but tiredness is making me self-conscious, as if I'm not being natural.

'Well, I'm the youngest of four girls. No brothers. My father's announcement in the local paper read, "The Final Daughter!" Went to school in Scotland. My parents live on the southern coast of England.' That about covers it.

'And what do you work as?'

'Between jobs at the moment.'

'As ... ?' He pushes, my reserve making him curious.

'A journalist, working in radio mainly, which I prefer to TV.'

In the silence that follows, it strikes me how Philippe has been a steady feature in the changing landscape, a small speck in a dark windproof jacket, soldiering ahead. However, after four days of his comforting presence following a predictable pathway route, I feel driven to step off it. In the next few days, a famously beautiful stretch of limestone ridges will open up, skimming the border of France and Spain. If I really am to find my own way through the higher mountains ahead, then I need to explore what it's like to be really alone.

For years, I knew a different kind of solitude, living by myself in a flat, in the busy heart of west London. Overlooking Westbourne Grove, I could witness the urban life force careering past, night and day. I liked feeling connected to the changing patterns of a typical day, like the big double-decker buses swerving to avoid the roadworks on their way to the West End, or the mix of accents and languages of the passing throng. But sometimes the poky windows opposite, of countless other solitary urban homes, were like a mirror. My independence was reflected back, which on a bad day could feel like isolation. Were we ever really meant to live this way?

I'm about to ask Philippe about Antwerp but the BANG of distant thunder stops the conversation. Now lightning streaks across the sky. What's that rule? Count the seconds between lightning and thunder, divide by five – the result is the distance of the thunderstorm in miles. There is no time to hang about calculating this. Hurriedly, we say goodnight.

I zip up my bivvy, knowing that to seal off the rain like this will guarantee condensation instead. I have no illusion about the quality of sleep ahead; the ground is hard. The area was the flattest around and I scuffed up leaves to provide some extra padding. Philippe spotted a very basic shelter for animals, probably the house of unwelcome rodents too. Thick cobwebs hung like drapes inside but he wasn't put off. Picturing him in it now makes me envious, knowing that the 'waterproof' bivvy will be tested to the limit.

Much later, the roar of thunder directly above jolts me awake. The shelter of trees is doing little to stop the relentless flow of rainwater from landing rudely on my lower legs. It funnels into streams above my head, that find their way to the soggy earth. For what seems like hours, this drama repeats itself, again and again. It is impossible to sleep, and still the light flashes, the thunder booms and the rain pours. It crosses my mind that sheltering under trees in a storm is the next most dangerous course of action after blithely walking on exposed ridges. What use is that wisdom to me here? It is undoubtedly damp inside, but the sleeping bag remains surprisingly dry. I'm exhausted enough to sleep once more.

The irritating efforts of someone shaking my bivvy and meowing like a cat wake me up. Not good. I roll over, unmoved, unmoving. This happens again. I open the zip and scowl back at the smiling face of a well-rested Philippe. It is clear, bright, and cool. I remember the rain and feel thirsty. There will only be a few mouthfuls of water left. How stupid to have forgotten to catch some rain.

Philippe senses I am in no mood to talk and busies himself with his gear. Every part of me aches as if I've been violently catapulted into old age. I slowly summon some life into creaking, stiff limbs to face the rain-soaked morning. This is the lowest point since starting out five days ago. It is simply awful to be here. There is no fast-forward mechanism to propel me to the valley and into a big hot bath. Philippe whistles now and there is something almost triumphant about his good mood.

'So, you obviously slept well.' My tone is accusing.

'I feel great.'

Silence.

'That hut was the perfect place to sleep last night.'

The effect of this comment is like seeing flashes of colour burst over grey, electrifying me into action. His insensitivity is quite bovine. The bivvy is rigorously shaken free of water and overflowing damp kit punched into my pack. I need to get out of these woods.

He sets off without saying anything. I find two sorry fruit gums sprinkled with dirt at the bottom of a pocket and wonder if I should save them for the three-hour walk ahead. Angry and decisive because of it, I put both of them in my mouth. So what if I regret this later? The rhythm of hauling a weighty sack cranks me into life again as I replay the extraordinary one-liners of the morning, my resolve to make a split hardening with each heavy tread. That's it. From tomorrow I'm on my own – after a night with crisp white cotton sheets and red wine.

Philippe waits for me further along. We have gone off the trail and haven't seen the markings for a while. I pull out the map. He looks away. Maps are alien squiggles to him and he says nothing as I show roughly where we are in relation to where we need to go. We are both thirsty and haven't had a drink for fifteen hours. We can see a way to the bottom of the valley down precipitous, long grassy slopes. It would be the most direct route to food and drink and the village of St Etienne. The path would be safer but we have lost it. I ask

Philippe if he is tired. 'Not at all. ' Ignoring him, I stare at the map – surely only another hour-and-a-half? Perhaps two. Three maximum. 'OK, if we follow the fall line, we should be wolfing lunch by midday'.

We both stare listlessly at the boggy distance, knowing we have to move. Philippe's quietness is making me aware of my rising tension. How much better the situation would be if he spoke just a little!

'I wish we could just get there. I'm so thirsty. What about you?' I goad.

'Yup, thirsty, sure. But generally I am finding this walk pretty unchallenging. It's nothing compared to the Appalachian Trail.'

As I announce the continuous upping and downing to be boring, pointless *and* exhausting, he searches my face, genuinely surprised. He then looks down at his boots, silent again. The atmosphere is delicate now and we have the knee-straining descent ahead, before any reward of water and food. The only way forwards is to shut down. Place one foot in front of the other. Without another word, we trudge on resolutely, thirsty and aching, bent on reaching the restaurants and shops somewhere below; every minute so much longer.

4 DIPPING TOES

The land has flattened underfoot after an hour of steep, steady climbing. The fog is cloaking everywhere in a wispy damp, out of which forms slowly materialise. Stout oak trees and twiggy branches line the track, their distinctive shapes visible only when I am within twenty feet of them. My eyes seem to know where to find the red and white symbols even in such uniform greyness. They are artfully painted on random rocks jutting from the tufted fields full of sheep and cows. When does this trusty network of volunteers venture to these remote places, their hidden role so vital to guiding a walker? Soon, the terrain will be free of markers. There will be no clues to guide me, no human trace. New ground.

I march with a strength I haven't felt before. Unable to see through thicker patches of swirling fog makes my senses more alert. A high-pitched whine starts up, hovers, and then dips altogether. It's impossible to know what it is – although a human voice is the best guess. My imagination livelier for being alone, I am now a mariner, bewitched by the call of sirens wreaking havoc on the foamy seas. Abruptly, the soprano drops a couple of octaves and slows to a gravelly bass drawl; the dwindling battery life of a radio. Out of the gloom a cosy-looking wooden hut appears, its door wide open. I walk a few steps nearer and see a shepherd holding up the source of music, as if looking for better reception. It's a happy, incongruous moment, to spot someone else in this alien place, where only sheep seem really at home. He sees me and waves. I wave back. The radio blares into life again with a hearty choral chant.

He walks purposefully to a stack of wooden crates, as I follow the path skirting another hill. The sun is burning a hole through the fog, fringing it in rainbow colours. It's not far to the top of the slope and there should be a view now the sky is clearing. The map confirms it's less than one hundred metres to Col d'Aharza's peak, so I dump my pack behind a large rock and my longer strides make light work of reaching the top. The sea of green hills below looks like Herriot's Yorkshire country. From the little summit I can now retrace my route and see what I passed, taking in the vista that was obscured on the way, but it's still too overcast to see the thin blue line of the Atlantic. In the coming days, a new landscape of limestone will open up, the gateway to mountains 3,000m high (9,843ft). I've already learnt a great deal and Philippe has helped me adapt to my new life outdoors. I wonder where he is now.

We had parted on good terms. The descent to St Etienne had been relentless, taking twice as long as expected. For nearly three hours we then basked in the relief of moving nowhere and planning nothing, apart from the next menu item. We managed to enliven what had been a shabby day, any lingering tension dissolving over a third plate of food, as Philippe taught me some Spanish and I showed him how to work a compass. Despite the raised morale, I set off determined to find a bed, leaving Philippe to search for somewhere to camp.

The hotel with its purple wisteria and warren of rusting fire escapes looked a little neglected, but not off-putting for that. The lobby inside was musty and dark, with mahogany furniture and tasselled lampshades. I rang the brass bell. A frail madame, with a neat bun of grey hair, peered from behind a curtain, blinked and swiftly disappeared, ringing a little bell for assistance. A middle-aged man took me up two flights of stairs, past stuffed birds and vases of dried flowers; everywhere a confusion of new and old.

A bed plumped up with two mattresses squeezed into an attic room. The bathroom door was ajar, revealing the brass taps and stumpy legs of a cavernous tub. As the man's footsteps receded along the corridor, I tipped the damp contents of my transient life on to the floor and skipped over them to run a bath of piping hot water, before soothing my weightless limbs in the bubbles as the mirror vanished in thick steam.

I remembered how shrunken Philippe had seemed, lost even, as we said goodbye. For the first time, he had admitted to being tired. Even his eyes looked smaller, swallowed by baggy eyelids. I didn't refer to his earlier boast, how 'unchallenging' he'd been finding the walk. He must have wondered where he'd end up next and seeing him clutching his treasured sticks I was overwhelmed by regret, at something left unsaid, as I turned back towards the hotel I'd seen.

Reverie over and bounding down the other side of the hill into a thin patch of fog, I stop in my tracks as I encounter dozens of sheep, standing frozen still, equally spaced apart in neat rows. It's as if they've been arranged this way – stuffed and posed as art installations, surreally urban among these wild boggy fields and peaks. Enchanted, I stare at the mute flock which finds me every bit as interesting. Nothing moves. One of them finally becomes distracted and scampers off, the rest following.

The path drops through fields of corn with orchards far below. The sun is fully out now. Only a few hours from here, the pastoral landscape will be absorbed into the medieval nerve centre of French Basque life. A route shifting through communities and their countryside enhances the best of both. An

American family pant their way towards me in zigzags. After a leisurely comparison of places in the area, they mention a 'fair-haired German' who marched by them, not stopping to say hello. I know at once it was Philippe and that he can only be less than an hour ahead. Wishing each other a 'happy trail', a transatlantic variant of 'bon courage', we head on.

The orchards are a perfect spot for a shady lunch. Reaching them took effort in the midday heat, as thoughts of food had preoccupied me. Through the trees, a lone wooden table with a bench commands a view of the lower valley. Walking over, I spot a sumptuous spread of food, carefully arranged and chopped – tomatoes, cheeses, cucumber, *saucisson* and baguette. A whistle. Spinning round, I see Philippe crouching there, watching. He had been hiding, waiting for me. 'Bon appetit,' he says and gestures me to join him.

Sharing unhurried time under the apple trees makes a pleasure of the final plod along rustic lanes and their winding snapshot of valley life. We reach the medieval fortressed walls of St-Jean-Pied-de-Port and the vitality spilling out of them feels as if we've stepped into another, very different day, at once special. Built in the thirteenth century, the town has withstood attack from Visigoths, Charlemagne's men, the Moors and the Spanish army. Today, a world away from urgent matters, the ramparts and cobbled streets are busy with people drifting about. It dawns on us that it's Sunday, a time for family outings and celebration.

Houses are stacked above the river, with a ramshackle elegance of wooden balconies and shuttered windows. Music is everywhere. Basque bands in traditional costumes trumpet about the streets, as lines of spectators press against stone buildings to make way for them. There are buskers and street vendors and cellars stuffed with local delicacies – cheeses, vinegars, wines and cakes. Pilgrims in sandals and walking boots browse the stands of kitsch religious souvenirs and books. Commerce is thriving in this gateway on the route to the tomb of St James, some eight hundred kilometres or more west, in Santiago de Compostela. Through the *haute ville*, a narrow street coils towards the dilapidated fortress, a spot perfectly removed for bow-and-arrow slaughter. Rolling hills and red-tiled roofs fill the horizon. The river ploughs new spirit through this ancient landscape, as the flow of pilgrims keeps alive the ritual of a two-thousand-year-old faith.

An open-door welcome greets newly arrived strangers. Thresholds with a shell above them honour the tradition of pilgrim hospitality and charge a low board to offset costs. Philippe and I are drawn to one for its bright red shutters and cat peering out dreamily from behind the street window. We settle ourselves in a dormitory, before heading out for the evening.

In the labyrinth of alleys, the smiles of passing strangers travel across boundaries within an instant of meeting their eyes. Costumed ponies clip-clop along led by a dressed-up trumpeter. Philippe wants a pizza. I would prefer something regional. But nothing matters, everything is good. Perhaps because I'm lively, distracted, turning my head at everything, he seems more reserved than ever. This is our last evening together and it is right that we are going our separate ways in the morning. He can't understand why I want the uncertainty of a route requiring navigation and attention to natural hazards like sheer ridges and changeable weather. We wander back to the hostel via the fortress, admiring how the streets are all the more enchanting, lit up at night. A jazz band playing its last tunes pulls us into a bar for some Calvados, until the manager starts to stack away chairs as the town winds down for sleep.

Back at the hostel, I spend longer than I should in the shared bathroom, fascinated by a montage of photos on the wall, capturing the life of our hostess. She was once a beautiful model, with long hair and eyes covered in thick, smudged eyeshadow. There's something a little sad about these snapshots of a life and the ravages of time catching up with it … the toddler holding her teddy bear's floppy hand, the teenager pouting at the lens in open challenge … the wedding … the mother of a child … the mother of a teenage boy … stray holiday snaps with girlfriends, perhaps now divorced. And finally the grand-mother, looking her age, despite the efforts with make-up and tight-fitting clothes to fight it.

The chatter of an Irish woman chirrups about the room as I walk in, perhaps buoyed by the wordless input of her listener. She works in the Probation Service as a counsellor. Her vision of crime rehabilitation and redemption would be fascinating and really might grip me, were it not for my cloudy head and craving for sleep, compounded by a bottle of Basque wine and the two shorts that followed.

5 UNEXPECTED TWISTS

The drama of an unfolding journey was quickly dampened as it became clear that I was walking in circles. The ramparts were built to fox the enemy, not just to fend it off. As I made a second tour of the confines of the citadel, the sense of déjà vu was quickly overcome by irritation. Every time I tried a different possibility in the general direction of where I needed to head, I found myself back where I started. The narrow alleys that had seemed so charming the night before had become oppressive mazes. I wanted distance from this enclosed place, not entrapment. For more than an hour I followed the useless advice of helpful-looking people and commiserated with other hikers, every bit as puzzled over how to escape. At last, a road I wasn't sure was the right one stretched invitingly into the distance, dense with hills. Something I mistook for intuition told me to follow it.

I marched ahead, the rhythm of my sticks helping to work off my restlessness. My goal was to reach the Iraty forest twenty-five kilometres away, from where I would strike out on the higher route, leaving behind the smaller Basque mountains. After the lower Pyrenees, nothing was going to stop me from finding my own way. I was impatient to leave the track and reliance on other people. I would look back on my time with Philippe with gratitude for everything I'd learnt from him. Our time together had been comfortable but unchallenging. Knowing I was bound to bump into him later that day, one final time before heading for the ridgeline, had softened the fear of losing his steady presence. This was what it was going to be like from now on – just me.

The lane was leading me along a river further into farming heartland. I had been too distracted by the lovely morning to stop and check the map, as the route clung to the valley floor, not gaining height as it should have done. The churning water had been hypnotic. Even the ubiquitous green of the pastures was particularly radiant in a growing sun. It was already hot. As I pored over the map, some pilgrims walking the other way towards St-Jean-Pied-de-Port, stopped for directions. I reigned in my annoyance as I realised I should have gained three hundred metres of height by now. A two-hour detour would be necessary to rejoin the track for Iraty. It would be a long day – thirsty work, but achievable.

I took short cuts over stiles and fields, and faithfully headed south-east. A hamlet of houses and barns rose into view during an unremitting traipse uphill in an unforgiving sun. It was late summer, yet the days were showing no sign of cooling down. Tucked away next to a stone chapel and its patch of graves was the reassuring sight of a well, promising limitless drinking water. Filling my bottles with a slow steady rhythm, I didn't notice the arrival of another stranger, ambling along the lonely lane with two donkeys, overloaded with gear. He was strangely dressed, in a straw hat, shorts and a poncho with elaborate patterns in bright woven colours. He spotted the well and started leading his animals towards it, chattering to them all the time. Drawing closer, the man stopped to adjust the ropes that lashed a variety of boxes and a small trunk to their flanks. Camping hardware dangled alongside.

'Do you need a hand?' I asked.

His strong regional accent made it impossible to understand his fast-flowing French, but his shaking head was enough. As he persevered with a tangle of knots, I learnt the trio had walked all the way from Toulouse and were heading for Santiago de Compostela, an odyssey of three months. On balance the donkeys had performed well, he was pleased with them, wonderful workers, but they were creatures that liked regular refuelling and tended not to like sheer heights. As it happened, they were lost. Would I know the way?

The absurdity of the question was delightful as well as surprising, especially after my disorientated performance that day. The annoyances of the morning were now rewarded by an encounter as unusual as this, which could only have happened in this peculiar place, miles off-route. I pointed vaguely over the fields and assured him he couldn't go wrong if he continued that way, eventually coming to a large walled town. He hesitated, searching my face quite anxiously, needing further assurance. What I will never forget was not so much his eccentric ambition and the apparent chaos in executing it, but the way he never once stopped patting and soothing his faithful beasts. His gentle, protective manner was so at odds with his sun-beaten face, creased and worn with hard living.

As I plodded on towards steeper valleys, the rest of the day was unremarkable. It took all sorts of mental tricks to keep going. The heat was unbearable at points, driving me to take long breaks under shady trees. Sweating in the early afternoon heat, desperate for it to cool down but knowing I had to press on, reminded me of similar moments of self-induced misery. Like getting caught out by bad weather in the Trossachs, halfway round my marathon training route, the car park no nearer ahead or behind. Sometimes those hours were torture and I discovered how vital forgetfulness is to our evolution. Walking into New York's subway, wrapped in a silver blanket, shivering and alone, having failed to find my friends, I had believed this really would be my last marathon. Hours later, reunited, more wine ordered, laughter made light of that moment. Feeling very much better, I leaned over and whispered into the ear of my marathon ally, Mairi: 'Chicago, next October?'

Still another five kilometres to Iraty, the biggest beech forest in Western Europe but in this heat and with these gradients, it would take at least another two-and-a-half hours. No sign of Philippe – he was bound to be ahead. The throaty cawing of crows seemed to encourage me to keep going. These remarkably intelligent birds are a typical camp hazard, as they make light work of undoing careless efforts to stash away food from their pecking beaks. I wondered how this overloaded puffing figure must have looked from their lofty perch. The sack, inflicting its usual punishment on my shoulders, would be replaced at the earliest opportunity with the most reinforced design on the market. A state-of-the-art harness would sculpt into the shape of my back, perfect for scrambling over the boulder fields in the more rugged areas ahead.

The denser forest – on the horizon for so long – edged closer, the greens becoming lusher along the river coursing through it. Besides fishing, mushroom picking is another serious pursuit in Iraty. Tents were pitched sporadically with domesticating comforts, like high-performance barbecues and striped foldaway chairs. Mostly the forest was empty and still, a pictur-esque combination of grassy riverbanks and beech-covered hills. The path meandered through the trees with their thick, graceful trunks and birdsong. I walked purposefully into the visitor's centre and ordered a tea and gateau just as it was closing.

Philippe then showed up. It was a joy to see him again after such a frustrating day. Comparing our low points, St-Jean-Pied-de-Port had ensnared him too and it had taken him just as long to find a way out. He was going to set up his tent at a perfect spot he'd found, down the steep banks to the river's edge, surrounded by rocks and large boulders. 'Come and say goodbye. I'm just round the corner, just over there,' adding as he pointed, 'you'll see my tent at the bottom.'

After settling up, I lingered on the café terrace, putting off the final hike of the day. It was always hard to get going again. Balancing my pack against a chair, I looked along the river through the trees to where Philippe would be. There was no tent, which was strange. It was the only place he could have meant. I scanned upstream. Nothing there either. Perhaps he was well hidden or further along than he'd thought. I scrambled down the bank and walked up and down, covering a greater distance than his suggestion of a short walk away. Only river and boulders. I tried the other way again, before searching through an area of pine trees, in case he'd decided to pitch the tent there for greater privacy. I hollered his name, then again, several times. But there was no answer above the roar of rapidly flowing water. I shouted once more, louder now, my throat hoarse with the effort. This surely couldn't happen – a botched rendezvous, within minutes of planning it? We hadn't swapped an address or even surnames. There was no way to track the other down.

The river continued to churn along, indifferent. Indecisive, I stood and stared at it. Even the gentle sway of the pine and routine hopping of the birds among the branches, so perfectly at peace, seemed to highlight my overwhelming sense of defeat. There really was nothing to be done but pick up the pack and carry on.

The green hills of Iraty would soon turn into the wilder territory of higher mountains, a formidable barrier between the Iberian Peninsula and the European mainland. I was looking forward to the contrasts between the lushness of France and the harsher dryness of Spain. The shift starts with Pic D'Orhy and its larger granite sister Pic D'Anie, becoming just visible as I slowly gained another hundred metres. After nine days of forested foothills, it should have been inspiring to be so close to these higher mountains. But the dramatic twist in my unusual alliance with Philippe was subduing my excitement.

More surprised than upset, it began to dawn on me how this might have been the perfect way to end our extraordinary week together. He had quite simply disappeared as suddenly as he had shown up. Fanciful, of course, but it was as if Philippe had been expecting me, to help me prepare for the greater challenges ahead. He had disappeared on the eve of a new stage in my journey: my venture along the ridges and remoter Pyrenees. It was impossible to imagine how he would remember our time together, of the woman undergoing a rigorous initiation into a lifestyle so routine to him. He seemed to accept in his undemanding way all its twists and turns. Strangely, after all we had shared, I really couldn't claim to know him at all.

The web of social connections that spins from the moment we learn to walk and talk is bafflingly intricate. Like fine fibres, they help give shape and bind the whole but their value may only be understood, or even felt, much later. For instance, it was only then, some two years since the unlikely worlds of movie stardom and simple warm-heartedness collided in the Nepali Himalaya, that that colourful episode really came alive. With distance, a very different picture had taken shape. Life is surely all the richer for these mysteries and the many random stories that cannot be neatly explained at once?

PART 2 NEPAL

6 A KINGDOM AND ITS SUBJECTS: 2001

I'm dimly aware that the phone has been ringing for some time before I fully wake up and wonder whether to stagger out of bed to answer it. It's hard to believe the time – who would call me at six-thirty on a Saturday morning? Someone persistent.

'Good morning – can I speak to Miss Margaret MacKean please?'

'Speaking.'

'I'm most sorry to trouble you. Most terribly sorry.' The accent seems strongly Indian. Immediately, the caller's sincerity makes me more curious than short.

'I am contacting you on behalf of the Nepal Embassy. We have had to cancel the Nepal Support Society lunch you were due to attend today ... '

A dim memory starts to form of a conversation I had with a friendly porter while waiting for my passport to be stamped with a tourist visa. Keen to discover more about Nepal before my impending visit, I readily accepted his invitation to attend a community lunch in Putney.

'Oh, really?'

'There has been a great tragedy in our country. They have all died. Our king, queen, most of them have ... been shot.'

'By who? How has this ... '

'We don't know. They say the prince. All we know is this is a real, real tragedy. We feel so far from home. They are like our family. We can't take it in. It would not be right to meet today.'

As the Nepal Embassy in Kensington flies its flag at half mast, the world's press is filled with colourful accounts of a crime of passion. King Birendra, his Queen Aishwarya, and seven other relatives were gunned down by the Crown Prince who, demented with whisky, lashed out over a doomed love affair, before turning the trigger on himself. While Prince Dipendra remained half-alive in a coma, he was officially Nepal's king, succeeding the father he murdered. Queen Aishwarya is understood to have forbidden a marriage 'beneath him', shattering his dream and with it, the illusion of god-like monarchy. In the coming days, attention turns to the woman who won the prince's heart and the scant, dated pictures of her. The high society beauty has since fled to relatives in India.

Initial attempts by the Nepali authorities to explain away the worst mass killing of royalty since the Romanovs as 'an accident', only fan the flames. Birendra's younger brother becomes king, a government long mired in corruption charges limps along and the monsoon rains start to fall. My ticket to Kathmandu remains unchanged. As the day to departure looms, a final decision whether to go hangs in the balance. I approach my editor to check if the six-week career break can be moved if necessary.

'Sure, no probs. Don't see why not. This all gets dealt with by personnel. You'd need to talk to them.'

'I mean, I want to go. I've chosen this time of year, monsoon, especially. And to see Nepal now at this point … '

'So, remind me what you're doing again, Mags.' He leans back in his chair, from which hangs a black leather Armani jacket. His sleek designer possession is not lost on me, after my rather down-market Portobello Road version recently earned his most fulsome feedback to date. He'd been watching my report as it went on air, when suddenly he tore out of his office into the newsroom, enthusing: 'Look everyone! Look at her jacket. That leather look is how I want all my reporters to be – street!'

'I'm climbing a little known peak on the Annapurna circuit. Normally a dome of ice.'

'What, in monsoon?'

'It'll be in the rain shadow so there'll be some protection. Wonderfully remote. Out of season.'

'As part of an organised group?'

'No. I've hired a guide. Otherwise, I'm on my own.'

◼   ◼   ◼

It had turned midnight as a new era dawned in the Himalayan kingdom of Nepal. The worst violence ever suffered by its royal family plunged the country into a chaotic turning-point in its 233-year history. The fall-out was only just beginning. Public faith in the royal fairytale has been shaken in every part of the country, as stories continue to spin of what really happened on that night of 1 June 2001. Conspiracy theories to tidy up the regal intrigue provide the only sense of certainty in a national situation so insecure. Words like *assassin, massacre, thwarted love* are too unbelievable for most loyal subjects. They're more suited to a tragedy by Shakespeare who warned 'uneasy lies the head that wears a crown.'

Nepal, still in its democratic infancy, lurches into an age of profound unrest. The Maoist rebels have killed more than 1,500 people in the last five years and there are fears the insurgency may exploit the power vacuum. As eyes turn towards the palace and army, foreign embassies around the world declare the Himalayan region a prime trouble spot, warning their nationals to stay well clear.

The tragedy is only two weeks old when I arrive and the nation remains orphaned by loss. Young Hindu men carry their grief with shaven heads, as a mark of respect. Armed police have a presence on the streets. For a tourist magnet like Kathmandu, there is a distinct lack of Westerners. Even in districts normally populated with backpackers, I've barely seen more than a dozen.

The capital has changed dramatically since 1991, when I was last here. The charming disarray of cobbled streets and medieval wooden and stone houses has largely been bulldozed by thoroughfares and housing blocks; no doubt more sanitary but less pleasing to a European eye. The worsening pollution from an increase in cars is compounded by the dense monsoon clouds. Yet Nepal remains poor. The per capita income is less than the price of a night in one of the city's top hotels, its king is amongst the richest men in the world.

I'm due to meet my guide later for a drink, to check kit and run through plans. That leaves the best part of a day to wander about and get lost. I am conspicuous and the small groups of men holding hands and chatting stare, as I head towards the Tibetan quarter in the east of the city. Watching generations of refugees walk clockwise round their temple, the largest *stupa* in Nepal, is best done at dawn and dusk. They are the busiest, most colourful times although there is always a great throng of life circulating around the *stupa* during the day too. The old in traditional dress, the young in denim, and monks in maroon and saffron, work their beads and spin wheels in prayer, some chanting, others ambling in contented companionship. All are watched over by the brightly painted eyes of Buddha, ablaze in gold, blues, reds and whites.

The market stalls and shops are a feast of detailed crafts and fabrics. A tea with fresh mint refreshes me enough to head back into town and revisit the famous heart of the old city, Durbar Square and Freak Street, once a prime hangout for those on the 'flower power' trail through Asia. It's not as interesting as it seemed when I was eighteen. The skyline above the city of giant white Himalayan peaks is obscured by a drab monsoon-grey which could burst at any moment with a torrential downpour. I wonder whether to open my map, reluctant to look like a tourist in need of help, preferring generally to discover places by chancing upon them.

'Excuse me? Are you lost?'

I'm about to walk away with a 'no thank you, I'm absolutely fine,' but the friendly smiles of the two clean-cut men, my age, make me change my mind.

'I want somewhere to eat. Where would you suggest?'

'Oh, many, many places. We were watching you across the road. Not usual to see tourists here now and tourist ladies are not usual, not at all.'

The man doing the talking is dressed in Nike trainers and standard Western gear. His friend wears a *topi*, a Nepali hat, a newly ironed shirt and smiles constantly. When they ask if I would like to try some Tibetan dumplings, 'only the deep-fried *momos* – steamed are not so good', I don't hesitate at all in following them.

Kris is a confident conversationalist and quickly refers to his love of world travel and his studies in America. He seems remarkably well connected. His father owns an exclusive travel company that targets wealthy American and Indian clients and he mentions distant royal family relations. He also talks about a cousin of his who is 'the most famous man in Nepal after the king'. At this point, I switch off, saturated by the steady stream of boasts and fantastic claims. Apparently this cousin is the highest paid movie star of 'Kollywood'. I have to admit Nepal's film industry has not made an impact on my tiny corner of the world, eclipsed by the powerful selling power of its more glittering, wealthy rival Bollywood and anyway, is there really such a thing?

His childhood friend, Dipesh, seems to understand everything but only speaks in his hesitant English in relation to politics and how the revered Birendra was a 'God'. Birendra's image is everywhere in Kathmandu. His picture hangs in doorways and businesses, a ghostly snapshot of time stalled in its tracks. In this predominantly Hindu country, religion, culture and politics are closely interwoven. The family is its most venerated institution. It is hard for Nepalis to accept what has happened, he explains. After all, how could a Hindu prince murder his whole family over a simple marriage disagreement? Dipesh, in his gentle way, is firm that there is more to the murders than the official palace accounts.

'Everyone knows they didn't happen,' chimes Kris. 'And what's obvious is Gyanendra was the only member of the royal family absent during that evening. And how come his son, Paras, wasn't hit?'

The story is too detailed to unravel at this point and I want to get back to the hotel to relax before meeting with my guide and organising our dawn departure for the long bus ride to the heart of the Himalaya. Kris insists they'll walk me to the hotel. On the way we have to cross a busy intersection with no apparent system to manage the hurtling traffic. As we hover on the edge, Kris shrieks with delight, pointing towards a billboard across the way.

'Oh my God. God is smiling on us today. That is my cousin! This is a sign you must meet him. Ha ha!'

I glance up and recognise the film promo from the airport. An exotic-looking man on horseback, his open shirt revealing toned pectorals, long hair blowing in the wind, stares into the distance. A beautiful brown-eyed woman in peasant costume looks on from the side; a background of mountainous desert, wild horses grazing; the streaking orange sunset sky above is filled with Nepali typography. As we walk on through the streets, Kris rings a few numbers on his mobile phone, frowning as he can't reach his cousin.

'He is always busy. Hardly around, always off somewhere shooting in the remotes,' he explains. 'What are you doing tonight?'

'After sorting all my stuff, I'm planning an early night.'

'No way. This is your last night in Kathmandu. We will pick you up at your lobby at eight-thirty and we're going out. I will find my cousin. He is busy, a very busy man but I will find him. You will have a night you will never forget. It is our duty!'

■   ■   ■

It is a relief to switch off after all the excitement. I am grateful for a nap but only after dealing with two centipedes nestling in the sheets of my bed, damp from the relentless rain seeping through the rafters of my top-floor room. The steady sound of falling water quickly puts me to sleep and I wake up to quiet, wondering when I will first be caught out in such a deluge.

Late, I rush downstairs and am greeted with the beaming smile of a short, strong-looking man in a T-shirt and baseball cap, leaning against the lobby desk. He immediately springs up and walks towards me, a hand outstretched.

'I am Sonam. And you are Max?'

After a couple of attempts at spelling out 'gs', I settle for 'x' – what does it matter? We head out to get hold of essentials; I'll hire crampons, ice axe, rope, ice screws. Sonam has karabiners and camping hardware. He points to his motorbike and tells me to sit on the back. For a moment I wonder where to put my arms but not having a helmet, I put aside reserve and hang on tight. We weave in and out of streets, busy with sauntering cows and other scooters. Sonam's horn blasts as we encounter life, which is every few seconds in this urban labyrinth.

Business settled, we head for a beer garden that Sonam wants to show me. In the short time we've spent together, my companion, a good two inches shorter than me, has already established his protectiveness. Earlier, as we had made our way back to the bike armed with gear, the dark skies had opened and Sonam steered me into a doorway, where we could wait until the worst was over. It had been mesmerising to watch the deserted thoroughfare quickly turn into channels of floating rubbish, piling up at the clogged drains gurgling with fast-flowing water; the furious rain bouncing off the pot-holed street surface for nearly an hour before relenting to drizzle.

The beer goes straight to my head and I have trouble not staring at a

Russian tourist with a mouthful of gold teeth that glint every time he speaks to a waiter. He picks up his pint and says 'cheers' and we exchange a few words across the empty tables. Sonam has a warm, easygoing manner. His English flows in varying degrees of intelligibility. He tells me about his two sons. One loves science, and longs to be a doctor, but finding a sponsor to pay for medical school is something of a pipe dream. His younger son, just six, is an enthusiastic footballer and 'very, very naughty'. Sonam finds this very funny and his eyes disappear into the creases stretching across his face. It is an infectious, heartfelt laughter.

'And your wife must find it difficult with you going off so much into the mountains.'

'No. She likes me going. More room in house.' Again he laughs. The atmosphere shifts, becoming notably more serious when we move on to climbing. At once, Sonam leans further over the table towards me, our rapport growing all the time. Climbing excites him. He only started six years ago and remembers that first time. His hands sculpt the shapes of the holds as he describes what it was like – the fear, the surprise, the ease of that first attempt that hooked him. He's since been on two commercial expeditions to Everest, living on the mountain for three months at a time. His job was to ferry oxygen between Camp Two and Camp Three. 'Dangerous work. I like it. One day I will climb Sagarmatha. Go to the top.' The Nepali name for the highest point on earth has a number of meanings, including Forehead in the Sky and Face of the Ocean.

The talk of expeditions is making me excited too. I will soon be among the world's highest peaks. It'll take eight days to access our mountain, Pisang, and three days to climb it. At 6,091m (19,983ft) it will be a challenge in altitude. We will begin our climb at around 3,100m (10,171ft), helping us to acclimatise. Sonam assures me he'll teach me everything I need to know to ascend its icy upper flanks. Our two porters will guard Base Camp and Upper Camp while we try to summit. We will then rejoin the Annapurna circuit through villages and valleys empty of tourists, most of its famous teahouses closed for the three months of monsoon. Being there at this unusual time of year will give me a unique social insight into the region, as we will stay with families Sonam knows from his many trips there.

Over a final beer, as time runs out before my evening with Kris and Dipesh, Sonam reveals he is Bhutanese. I'm eager to know how he ended up in Nepal and to learn about the alluringly impenetrable Bhutan. I immediately regret my earlier commitment; how often binding plans stop more interesting prospects from unravelling. But then again, I think, draining away the last drop of Nepali brew, five weeks should be ample time to discover more. After all, it would be a shame to miss the chance of sharing an evening with a film star.

7 A BRUSH WITH CELEBRITY

Perhaps the sulky expression on Kris' face as he sits slumped in my hotel reception is the first indication this will be no ordinary evening. 'You're late. What time do you call this?' Relaxed after my two beers with Sonam, it takes me a couple of seconds to adjust to the abrupt shift in atmosphere. It's only a few minutes past eight-thirty according to my watch. This is quite a leap in familiarity for a new acquaintance.

'Look, what's the problem? Give me ten minutes,' I throw back and head up the stairs for a quick change into some dry clothes. Kris is agitated when I come down, glancing at the clock on the wall. This is becoming very irritating.

'I do not want to keep my cousin waiting. He is a busy man and I told him to meet us for nine at one of his favourite restaurants.'

'We have plenty of time. Kris, for the record I want a relaxed evening.'

'Don't worry,' he says, ushering me onto the street outside towards a waiting horse and trap. I smell traces of rum or whisky on him.

'Dipesh is looking after the table in case Rajesh arrives early.'

As we clip-clop along through the streets of Thamel, my annoyance lifts in the fabulously absurd moment of being transported by a pony draped in multi-coloured plastic flowers. I decide to humour my companion, who I suspect has been drinking to steady his nerves.

'So, when did you last see your cousin … what's his name?'

'Rajesh, Rajesh Hamal. He is a god in Nepal. I see him last, maybe one year ago. He is always so busy – but when I told him a woman from the BBC is here, he called back saying he'd try to join us straight from the set.'

'Isn't it quite late to be filming?'

'Not for Kollywood.'

We are greeted at the door by a friendly waiter in a waistcoat and bow tie, clearly expecting our arrival.

'This way please, Mister Krishnan. Pleasure to meet you ma'am.'

It looks relaxed enough, with mustard yellow walls and beams. When we get to the table, faithfully guarded by a solitary Dipesh, Kris suggests we head to the roof terrace and order some drinks while we wait. The Kathmandu skyline glows in electric light, the night air is close and humid. Dipesh glances at me and smiles as Kris summons a waiter to our table a little too loudly. We finish our drinks and talk through my plans for the next few weeks. I suggest we order some appetisers as it's getting late.

'Oh no. Let us wait. Rajesh will be here any minute.'

'He is more than an hour late, I'm sure he won't mind if we share a little something.' Lunch had been at least eight hours ago and the combination of low blood sugar levels and strong beer is making me confrontational. I haven't forgotten Kris' annoyance back at the hotel. This deference to his cousin is hard to stomach. I try again. 'Why don't you call him and check where he is?'

Kris leaves us with his phone, returning in a lighter mood. 'Rajesh sends his apologies. They have had to re-shoot a dance sequence. He is leaving the studio now.'

After a determined indifference to meeting a 'star' who, from all Kris' adoring accounts, inspires a national following, I am now genuinely curious and excitable as more drinks arrive. As long as I'm back in my hotel for midnight, one at the latest, I'll get four or five hours sleep, plenty for an inactive day on a bus tomorrow.

All of a sudden, there is a discernible shift in atmosphere, as two waiters scurry to our rooftop table with menus and extra glasses. They start to fuss over the cutlery, straightening it, adding extra knives and spoons produced from their shirt pockets, as a third arrives with two bottles of water, announcing: 'Mr Rajesh Hamal has arrived.'

Kris gets up. Dipesh puts down his drink and turns around. The three waiters stand neatly aside, a metre from the table, ready for orders. A vision in black emerges from the stairs and sweeps towards us; a long traditional shirt, loose trousers and flip-flops, the only native attire in the restaurant. At first I am struck how tall he is for a Nepali – at least six feet.

'I am sorry to keep you waiting. It is a pleasure to meet you,' he says, looking only at me, while the others wait motionless. He extends a hand and at that point I rise, to shake it. 'I am Rajesh.'

'And good to meet you too,' I reply, aware how dramatically his entrance has altered the evening's dynamic. If charisma is an invisible quality that fills a room, then Rajesh Hamal exudes enough to fill a street. Immediately he takes over the table, gliding into the seat opposite me. He glances briefly at where the other two will sit, as if to check this fits with his idea of how it should be. I feel a strange pang of recognition; something about him is familiar, though his exotic appearance is anything but everyday.

'So how is my little cousin?' He starts laughing as he produces his phone, pointing to it as he adds, 'your tone was so urgent, I was firm with my director. I clearly couldn't be any later for our arrangement.'

He laughs again and it is quite extraordinary to see how Kris, already slim and neat, looks so much younger now, reduced to the status of kid cousin. Rajesh exchanges a few words in Nepali with Dipesh, giving me a chance to observe his thick, dark shoulder length hair, heavily styled. He clearly works out, as he looks angular and full in his loose shirt, unbuttoned to the chest. I am grateful to the waiters springing into life with the menus after catching my eye. Immediately Rajesh orders a selection of dishes for us to share and asks me what I'd like to add to it. The food takes a while to arrive and it becomes clear Kris is a little the worse for wear; his English harder to understand, his words slurring and sentences trailing off. Rajesh speaks immaculate, flawless English.

'My father was a diplomat. We were educated all around the world in English too. In fact I speak six languages, four fluently, my Russian and German are a little rusty. We've lived all over the world … Frankfurt, St Petersburg, Bangkok, Washington. At one point my father, who is no longer alive, was the ambassador to Pakistan.'

During the meal, Rajesh supplies a stream of details about his high-achieving family. There are three sisters; two are doctors, the other a dentist. He lives with his mother and brother, a recovering alcoholic once tipped for great things as one of Nepal's youngest and most brilliant politicians. Sadly, his dreams of becoming prime minister were shattered in recent years by ailing health. As we tuck into dishes of traffic-light greens, reds, and yellows, the time disappears until we're the only people left in the restaurant. I apologise to one of the waiters as he clears our table, my companions not looking in any rush for the bill. A huge smile and shake of the head reassures me that the management is in no hurry either to see the last of their illustrious client. Kris orders the bill and addresses his cousin in Nepali. Whatever he says must be funny, as Rajesh laughs loudly, throwing his head back theatrically as he does so.

'Krishnan is clearly having too much of a good time with the beer and he is in no mood to stop. He asks, as my car is parked outside, where we should head next?'

My concerns about the time vanished some time ago. I look pointedly at the silent Dipesh, who nods back at me and breaks into a smile.

'Looks like we are heading to one of my favourite places in the whole of Kathmandu for a drink. It is one of our best hotels, close to the palace, very relaxed, good atmosphere.'

The bill arrives and Kris looks at me. Rajesh looks unconcerned and makes no attempt to reach for it. I wonder if I'm expected to pick up the tab for the four of us and I decide to pay half. Kris settles the rest.

Surprisingly, Rajesh's car has seen better days. Prayer beads and feathered charms dangle from the mirror, the cassette player whines into life with Hindi ballads. It seems so odd now to remember us reclining later on two sofas next to a roaring log fire on a sultry night in monsoon, stuffed tiger heads watching over our unlikely company. Kris is asleep, his mouth wide open and eyelids half-closed, creating a sinister streak of white, which makes us glance over once in a while to check he really is breathing. Dipesh remains quiet but happy for that; Coke in hand and *topi* slightly askew. Rajesh and I are enjoying a second Jack Daniels.

'So, we have to ask, what will all this mean for the future of multi-party democracy? It has long been my view, controversial I know, that Nepal isn't ready for such freedom, with its heavy price of responsibility. Every citizen needs to play a part and when illiteracy is what … seventy percent of the population, the system becomes open to abuse.'

'And what about King Gyanendra?' I ask. 'Presumably, he has a tough job convincing Nepalis he has their best interests at heart, when so many remain suspicious about the massacre?'

'Yes. I met the former King Birendra quite a few times. As a child we'd go to the palace for tea – we are distantly related, second cousins or some such on my grandmother's side, but we were invited more in my father's capacity as ambassador. Birendra was quite simply an astonishing man who had huge political nerve. He gives up two centuries' tradition of absolute monarchy but only after ordering the army to suppress street protests and democracy rallies. He then sees his people are serious, so he thinks again and he says, "OK, I agree … you can have your wish" and so he hands over more power to politicians … and … BANG, a whole new can of worms.'

This less attractive stage in Nepal's history is emphasised by a clap of the hands, a dramatic flourish. Rajesh speaks in a measured way, in no hurry to draw any conclusions or round up matters. He is clearly used to the spotlight. I don't mind the lack of opportunity for equal dialogue, as these insights are colourful, delivered in fluent English, as articulate as any political pundit I've interviewed at work. We reach for our drinks at the same time. I sense there's more he wants to say and wait for him to pick up first. Kris continues to sleep and Dipesh stares into the distance, his Coke only half drunk. Rajesh breathes in deeply through his nose.

'Corruption. That's a whole other story. So Birendra is revered as someone representing continuity between past and present. It is too early to know what Gyanendra will do. He needs to clean up the whole national mess. I am not talking just about post-massacre, or the government and the electorate's faith in it, but he has to take on the Maoists, who control large swathes of the country, especially the west.'

'And of course, they want him and the rest of his family gone,' I add.

'It is something of a … big mess, you might say!' He pauses, looks at me and laughs half-heartedly. We toast to Nepal's future, clinking glasses on the words 'however uncertain'.

Kris wakes up and remarks on how well we seem to be getting on. Rajesh feigns shyness, burying his face in his hands: 'I don't always understand what my cousin says, or why he says it for that matter. This is one such time.' We all laugh. A waiter offers to fetch more drinks but it is past three in the morning and we agree it is time to head for home. Kris settles the bill.

As Rajesh drives me back to my hotel – me in the front, the other two in the back – he asks how I stumbled across his cousin and comments on the coincidence of our meeting. This is only the third question he has asked me all evening, after establishing my job title and where I'm travelling to next. As I thank everyone for an 'evening to remember', Rajesh rifles through the glove box, producing a pen and a scrap of paper. He scribbles his number and hands it to me.

'Here. Call me when you are back in Kathmandu. We will catch up. Read it back to me, to check there isn't a mistake.'

He nods approvingly as I do so. After a shake of hands, I wish the carload of weary faces well before turning into my hotel. Passing the reception clock, I note there are just two hours of the night left in which to pack my things and sleep, before meeting Sonam for a dawn breakfast.

8 HIMALAYAN SNAPSHOTS

Showing no sign of let-up, the rain pounded the corrugated iron roof like gravel. Sonam and the teahouse owner sat close to each other to make themselves heard as they caught up with all the excitement of old friends with a history. I tried a few spoons of liquid mashed potato with shavings of buttery cheese, managing to return the toothless smile of the woman who'd served it. The consequence was soon felt, sustained and uncomfortable. My first night in the world's grandest mountains would be remembered as one of relentless indignity. A hole in the ground and a rusting bucket, a rain-soaked walk between the water source and my room, were the unforgettable components that had left me drained and unsteady by morning.

Sitting on the edge of my bed, his hand on my damp brow, Sonam comes into his own. 'You are naughty, very bad. You should have woken me. This is my job. I am here for you and to take care of you in all matters.' After packing my things, he brings me sugary hot tea, smiling throughout.

The pea-green valleys of the Himalaya in monsoon are indescribably lush. It is hard to imagine such rich fluorescent colours can be produced naturally. Walking through them in heavy humidity is hard work and the leech-filled foothills can quickly turn into treacherous muddy swamps. Life is everywhere and the rural communities busily tend their terraced land. Buffalo plough the rice fields, groups of women squat next to big wicker baskets while picking the crops. The lower slopes are filled with butterflies and flowers, especially orchids, easy to mistake for clover.

The high peaks are hauntingly close but kept hidden by dense cloud. My impatience to see Dhaulagiri and the Annapurnas for the first time turns to obsession. They are two of the world's fourteen highest peaks over 8,000m (26,247ft). Flying into Kathmandu, a smothering whiteness had denied me an aerial view of one of the earth's greatest wonders. Conditions will become drier and rainfall will be more contained to early afternoons as we head further north-west. For now, the rivers churn volumes of mud and silt with a force that charges at the rocky banks constraining them.

The communities work hard to sustain themselves. The valleys resound with hammering and sawing as houses are built or renovated. Peasants file along the stony paths in bare feet like ants, as they balance giant bundled loads precariously on their foreheads with a makeshift strap. Donkeys falter up and down the stone paths of ancient trade routes, goaded by owners who treat them with varying degrees of neglect or kindness. Disputes over right of way, hollered out from either end of suspension bridges, determine which party will teeter to the other side first. Their bells can be heard long before they round the bends, forcing us to press into the rocky verges while they overtake.

One day we come upon a particularly savage mule handler, a shrivelled woman no taller than five feet, looking decades older than her probable middle age. She screeches at one of the bonier animals that has stopped in its tracks, overburdened and exhausted. She strikes it with her stick, leaving a clear mark on its thinning coat. Their flanks have been lacerated by the canvas straps attaching their cargo. The woman doesn't notice my stare; her hard face only concerned with watching their lurching progress towards market. The loads they carry will make her only just enough to feed her family. I fight my resentment – it is too easy to judge, without ever having had to struggle each day to survive.

I urge Sonam to walk faster, wanting to get away. As we pass the beasts, their eyes are blank and lifeless, as if they have given up all hope. I stroke one that has stopped at the front of the pack and softly encourage it to move. It does not stir a muscle. Only the beat of a stick will summon its will to labour on up the stony path, so conditioned is it by cruelty. Later, a young man, probably her son, chivvies the same mules into the village where we have stopped to eat. He loosens the canvas straps and the cargo of barrels drops to the ground. Each animal seems to rise a little, free of its load. I watch him make heavy work of picking the barrels up. Giving up, he rolls them along the street to their intended destination instead.

Stopping in the early afternoon to avoid the rain divides the day into two parts. Looking out from under my spotted umbrella is like watching a cultural slideshow. Grubby children tear about the villages with handmade toys, lighting up at any attention offered to them, shouting out the ubiquitous greeting, 'Nameste!' They usually spend the day amusing themselves or helping to sweep floors or collect sticks for kindling. Sonam always stops to play with them. Sometimes he has to gesture downhill to the village we have left, crouching next to a new small friend who is reluctant to let this kind stranger go. It is always fun watching the children's faces fill with amazement, disbelief and then laughter at the idea that a camera can capture their image and store it. Its magnetic pull and the screams of delight that follow attract even more children to rush out from hidden corners and secret doorways. We stock up on chews whenever we can, an easy gift.

The evenings in the higher altitudes are much cooler and are often spent round an open fire while a cook stirs a steaming cauldron of rice and lentils. My lungs rarely get used to the lack of ventilation but the hours before bed slip away with the hypnotic effect of a fire's orange glow casting shadows on the corrugated iron or whitewashed walls. Our hosts become more animated as they sit and chatter around the smoky fire, the centre of family life. Everyone spends more time hard at work in the sun and wind than they do indoors and have the thick creases of life well-worn.

One early evening as the *dhal* bubbled away, Sonam motioned me to follow him outside. We made our way through the village, past the stray dogs howling in the cloudy grey, towards the *stupa*. Religion is an everyday part of life here and Sonam observes the rituals of Buddhism at every opportunity. Strewn in prayer flags, the temple was like so many others we had seen, with dozens of copper wheels embedded in its walls, each one filled with Tibetan scrolls of worship. It's believed that when a prayer wheel is spun, all the words of veneration stored inside are sent heavenward.

'Evening time and early morning time, very strong part of day,' Sonam trailed his hands against the wheels as he walked, setting off a series of bells, striking on every completed revolution. He told me to chant the mantra *Om Mani Padme Hum* and I spun the wheels into life again as they slowed.

We sat down on the bank overlooking the wooden houses, clinging to the edge of the steep slope. The village was beginning to flicker with oil lamps in the dusk. Electricity was a sparse commodity the higher we climbed, as generators abruptly cut off supplies by eight or nine o'clock each evening. Dense wood smoke sat in the thick damp air. Kerosene is promoted as a staple household fuel but still wood fires burn. Over time these have emptied valleys of trees and eroded networks of paths carved into the slopes. We had seen a man topple down one, overbalanced with a sack of piping twice his size. Miraculously, after rolling down for thirty feet or so, he got up unhurt, returned to his load, whereupon he barely drew breath before continuing, ignoring the crowd that had been watching in horror.

'The wind carry the prayer to the sky,' Sonam said, looking at the prayer flags and their fluttering triangles of yellow, green, red, white, and blue, representing the elements of earth, water, fire, cloud and sky. 'Big windy,' he added. I had noticed before that Sonam could suddenly switch from an excitable storyteller to a solemn devotee. He could captivate with an irresistible urgency in rapid-fire Nepali, rising through the octaves, until he collapsed into laughter at the finish. Then he would become thoughtful and quiet.

'Have you always been an active Buddhist?'

'Yes … I was monk once.'

'A monk, a Buddhist monk?'

'Yes. I am from Bhutan. I am not Nepali. My mama and papa want me to be a monk. Big job in Bhutan and I am eldest child and it expects of me. They send me to monastery in Darjeiling when I am nine year old. At first it is fun. Lots of monk look after me. Big mountains like Bhutan. But after three year I want to know what goes on in world. I not want to be monk. Not for me I think. Two year later I escape. My Mama and Papa do not allow me to go. I run away to Kathmandu. I know I have uncle there who will look after me. He big, important man, he rich. I find him. I knock on his door. When he sees me he is angry. Big anger. "You go back to Darjeeling now. You no stay here with me." My uncle have factory, big house, much money, he very, very rich. I have nothing and nowhere to go. He tell me my family shame of me. I never forget this man. Never forget what he do to me.'

'What happened? Did you go back to the monastery for a while?'

'No. I stay in city. I have no money and sleep on streets and find job. I work in kitchen. Bad work but I learn fast. I become cook. I miss mountains in kitchen. I get job in trekking agency as porter. Years I carry big bags. One day I get job as trekking cook. Good job. Tourists like my food.'

'And how did you become a guide then?'

'Lucky. Big lucky. I porter on big trek. Guide is ill. I have to find way. I become guide.'

'And what is your dream? What do you most want to do in the Himalaya?'

'I climb. One day I climb Everest. I love climb.'

■   ■   ■

Every day I feel stronger from working steadily upwards through the thinner air. We have practised setting up belays and tying into a harness. Sonam has demonstrated self-arresting with an ice axe on a grassy slope. 'Much less than Pisang, this hill,' he chuckles, as I rehearse the technique again and again. I try to envisage what the peak will look like, how much of the ascent will be technical. Will avalanches be a hazard and is there likely to be much ice on the older and crusty snow towards the summit? Sonam doesn't have any answers because a snowy mountain can be different every time it is climbed.

Acclimatisation adds to the uncertainty of the enterprise. I have been as high as 5,895m (19,341ft) but altitude can affect you differently every time you venture into it. Pisang is 200m (656ft) higher, a marginal difference, but not one to be underestimated. Speaking in simple English with Sonam strips communication to the basics so even though we are still a few days from our mountain, I am happy to run through as much detail as possible. There is no route map. All we have in the way of paperwork is a permit, allowing us a certain number of days to climb the mountain.

I enjoy the simple banter with my party of four, who like to point to things and get me to chant back their Nepali names. Simple gestures have great weight. An outstretched hand instead of a 'watch out for that', or more attention to eye contact and facial expression all help to strengthen our group rapport. When communication cannot be taken for granted, smiles and laughter make a world of difference.

One of the porters, Sonam's nephew Bitu, is studying archaeology and earning some holiday cash as a porter, his first taste of the backbreaking work. Unlike his uncle, he is lanky and light, not really built to carry heavy loads. He has a striking grace about him. He will inhale any book of mine, transfixed by how the words fit together, although he can only understand little. When he reads aloud in his soft voice, it is with a determined concentration to deliver his best. Bitu has also developed a worrying appreciation for Marmite, a highly unusual flavour for a Nepali palate and my treasured supply is likely to run out.

Indra is a few years older and an experienced porter. Sonam often pinches his arms, laughing as he tells me, 'Indra strong. Very, very strong.' Sometimes they tussle in play fights, which the younger porter would undoubtedly win if they ever got serious. He says very little but holds his own. The other two clearly like his sound, reliable presence.

While I read or write my diary by candlelight, it's comforting to be half aware of the men entertaining each other of an evening. Sonam's laughter is impossible to ignore. Cards get him really excited. That's when he howls, sometimes collapsing over a table, or rolling this way and that as he struggles for breath. His two quieter opponents become quieter still during a game of poker. Both are shrewd and streetwise from childhoods spent in the Kathmandu valley, their straight faces suggesting a lot rests on every hand. Sonam wears his feelings on his sleeve, finding it impossible to look grim and inscrutable when he has picked a promising card. The obvious drop in energy, when his shoulders stoop or he looks more pensive, is a sure sign of a bad one. Yet in spite of this temperament, so unsuited to a game that relies on mystique, he wins every time.

One evening, as Sonam revelled in his resounding lead, I began to feel unwell. I was in bed and asleep within minutes. I lurched between dead rest and uneasy, shallow sleep, full of vivid dreams. The most unsettling woke me up but only after I had watched my disembodied head bounce down a steep slope, after an avalanche of boulders had sliced it clean off. Hot and restless, the fever was driving me into a state of vertigo and even the unfurnished room was beginning to crowd in on me. Frayed curtains and window ledges were now menacing forms. I managed to disentangle myself from the twisted, damp sheets and reach Sonam's room below. The next twenty hours were a blur of fitful rest between sheet changes and a stream of hot, sugary tea. Sonam was the only constant in the turbulence of fever, doggedly nursing me by candle-light, always there; watching, waiting, attentive.

■   ■   ■

There are three days to fully recover my lost strength before we start our way up Pisang. It is unlucky timing to have fallen ill now, yet just as quickly as the fever strikes, it goes. After months of training for this mountain, I am still in with a chance. The landscape is changing dramatically, the lurid greens of the terraced valleys replaced by steeper, rockier faces and gorges. We walk through Bagarchaap where an avalanche tore through the valley on 10 November 1995, killing twenty-five people and destroying most of the village. Despite the rebuilding efforts, it still feels full of ghosts. An eerie emptiness lingers. There is a plaque with a simple commemoration to a 'son, brother and friend, who died achieving'. The British trekker, Nicholas Elleman, happened to be in the wrong place, doing what he loved. These words, an indelible imprint of his death at nature's hands, unsettle me.

As the terrain becomes more remote and rugged, we encounter fewer communities and the clusters of life thriving in inhospitable circumstances are even more welcoming to strangers. We sit round a fire, one of the few with a chimney, while a fourteen-year-old married woman artfully stirs her pot, calm and capable, gliding about her kitchen with its neat shelves of Tupperware and dangling cutlery. I have ordered macaroni with tuna and that is exactly what arrives, a heated up mound of tuna on pasta. At least this is not going to upset my stomach before Pisang – a reason to avoid anything spicy for now.

Two youths bound in, surprisingly urban; one with a baseball cap facing back to front, both in baggy jeans, rock T-shirts over long-sleeved sweatshirts and trainers. 'Where are you going?' the men ask. The excitable conversation which follows and the obvious glee of the boys as they explain the reason for donning their trendiest clothes, inspires them to jump and clap. They're indulged with more questions and suitably animated gasps, before they race out into the dark.

'They go out to watch movie. An hour walk down valley,' Sonam explains. 'Big part of life in mountains. Friday night, everywhere in Nepal, movie night.'

'What do you mean? How can they watch a film out here?'

'Government organise videos to all people in country, every week. It is Friday and whole village watch movie.'

'How amazing – what a brilliant idea! What about electricity?'

'Big problem. Sometimes they cannot have a movie when there is no power. Happens a lot.'

Not for the first time since leaving Kathmandu, I wonder about Rajesh. The mood in the kitchen is light and the men continue to ladle more *dhal* onto their plates until the whole vat is polished off. They are delighted with it and praise the young woman, who looks used to the happy appreciation of her food, though nonetheless pleased for that.

'Have you heard of a Nepali actor? His name is Rajesh – I can't remember his second name. Rajesh … ?'

'Rajesh Hamal. You mean, Rajesh Hamal?' Bitu immediately responds.

'Yes, I think so. Could there be any other Rajeshes?'

'No.' All three reply, looking at me now.

'Rajesh Hamal is a god,' Bitu adds, leaving me in no doubt I had accidentally stumbled across his movie hero.

'How interesting! Is he really so famous?'

'Ask any Nepali, and ninety-five percent will know this man. Rajesh Hamal worshipped in this country,' Sonam concludes.

'He makes great movies. Great actor,' Bitu adds, looking at Indra now, who nods in agreement. 'But he has respect because he not leave Nepal. He says no to Bollywood. He stays in this country and makes movies about life here.'

'Educational films?'

'Yes, like in one, my favourite, he is a peasant. Very, very poor, and becomes a trekking guide. That is good for tourism industry. More men want to be guides now.'

So perhaps Rajesh should be taken a little more seriously, I reflect, in spite of the obvious attention he pays to his looks. He certainly showed a passionate interest in politics that night. And how unusual, for a man who could pick any bride, to be a bachelor at thirty-eight, in a country where most would have a grown-up family by that age.

'Well, it's interesting and funny to hear about all that. I actually met him. By chance. Only for one evening. His cousin, who I met near Durbar Square, introduced me to him. We had supper together.'

The effect this has on my companions is cartoon-like. They take a few moments to to hoist it in. Sonam repeats it in Nepali, for Indra's benefit and to make sure they've all fully understood. 'No. You and Rajesh eat meal together? No way!' Sonam laughs and bangs his hand on the table, looking at me to reveal more.

'Well yes. He seemed nice. Talks a lot. It was a fun evening. You remember how tired I was on the bus that first day? We had had a few beers and whiskies the night before.'

'You see him again?'

'Maybe. I have his phone number. When we get back, I have ten more days to see the valleys and sights before going home. So, we will see.'

The gentle Bitu cannot stop staring at me, smiling and visibly impressed. Sonam then declares we will watch one of Rajesh's films together, on the next Friday night after we have climbed Pisang.

'We ask them to choose Rajesh video. No problem. We make it happen.'

■   ■   ■

The weather is already becoming clearer with vivid blue skies. White peaks begin to tease their way through the thinner cloud. Somehow, little pink, blue and white flowers thrive in the more barren, rocky heights. In the pine forests, woodcutters hack away as farmers in the valley below beat their freshly cut wheat. In sunshine the whole flavour of Himalayan life changes again. The suffocating effect of thick cloud dissolves and the morale of our expedition is raised, as the fresher air breathes new life into us. New *stupas* are being built in new settlements. Industry and life go on, despite climbing further into the remoteness of altitude. Waterfalls plummet in rising volume and the threat of landslides grows. Trees edge towards steep banks, their roots no longer anchored; the next likely casualty of the monsoon's force. We still spin prayer wheels as we pass them, enjoying the whirr of the copper turning on its axis.

We coincide repeatedly with a young Buddhist priest, in his early twenties, hiking in robes and baseball boots, with a man guiding him to Muktinath, a famous site for Hindus and Buddhists. The couple cut an unusual presence in this wild spot; among the few we've met walking in monsoon. Muktinath is mentioned in the classic Indian epic, the *Mahabharata*. Sonam says we'll meet many pilgrims once we clear Thorang La, the world's highest pass at 5,416m (17,769ft), which descends into the valley leading to the temples. At that point, a long ridge of peaks bars the way to Tibet's arid plains to the north. From there, the scenery merges into the infinite brown shades of desert wastes.

The previous night we had shared a meal with this these two men in a windowless hovel, chinks in the roof slates letting out thick coils of smoke. Apart from the moonlight beaming in shafts through the worn roof, we sat in darkness around a fire. It was an atmospheric evening. As Sonam told stories, the guide, with his withered face and big white teeth protruding over his bottom lip, murmured 'oh, oh, oh … ' throughout, almost like a chant, soothing and soporific in its deep-throated way. A sweet little puppy, fluffy and fat, had been trained to lift a paw at the word 'Namaste'. It was extraordinary how it did it every time, delighting the children who urged it on and on. A woman watched sulkily as she slopped the food into life over the fire, dissatisfied with a world of grinding chores.

At some point a couple of men ran in from the rain, sparking energy into the dark evening. They looked smart in their leather jackets, jeans, and trainers and spoke animatedly about the events of their day. The room of people watched and listened. It was impossible not to notice the transformation of the surly woman cook. She had become years younger, smiled continually and softly chuckled at the tales being told. Occasionally, she barked out the odd one-liner, which I imagined to be sarcastic as well as flirtatious. She started to play at being hard when one of the men, clearly her boyfriend, rose to talk to her as she cooked, only to be shooed away, as she needed to concentrate on her creation, to which she was now committed.

We reach a police checkpoint and Sonam searches for the paperwork we need to pass through it. I find my passport and present it to the rather humourless-looking official, with a neat clipped moustache and sturdy, highly polished black boots. He sits behind a desk, in front of a large portrait of the late King Birendra.

'Where are you from, ma'am? Britain? You like Nepali people?'

'Yes. Very much.'

'We Nepali people like British people. Very much,' the official beams, losing some of his earnestness. He starts to copy the passport number into a big leather-bound book, a muscle near his temple twitching as he concentrates.

'Oh. I'm very glad to hear that,' I say smiling back, 'What about other nations, do you like them just as much?' This throws him a little. He looks down at his desk and frowns, as if searching for a tactful way to answer with something inappropriate. A few seconds pass while he continues to look bewildered.

'Are you married?' he then asks.

'Er, no, I'm not. And you?'

'Yes I am,' he replies.

We seem to be running out of things to say. Only sharing details of children and places of birth could follow next. I am also aware it is a Nepali custom to acquire more than one wife.

'Well. It's been a pleasure. *Dhanyabaad* and *namaste*.'

'Thank *you*,' he says, handing back my passport before rising from the desk to shake my hand enthusiastically. 'Namaste.'

■   ■   ■

The ritual *puja* is a solemn event. The Buddhist practice is held on the eve of an expedition's ascent, in which prayers are offered up to the gods to ensure safe passage while trespassing on sacred land. Usually performed by Sherpas, who are originally from eastern Tibet and live throughout the Himalaya, it is a tradition here for most groups about to make their way up a mountain. Sonam is not a Sherpa but says he would never attempt a climb like ours without having a *puja*. He goes off with Bitu and Indra to gather juniper and flowers to burn as an offering, and buy some incense from one of the households in Upper Pisang village. We will hold a *puja* every night we are on Pisang peak, including tonight, to endear ourselves further to whatever force is watching over us.

We are staying in a house built on stilts, reached by a twenty-foot climb up shallow footholds hacked out of a tree trunk. It is a perfect chance to relax on the wooden decking, knowing that the next three days will require all reserves of energy and drive. I am joined by the home owner, the only unmarried woman I have met in Nepal. She lives alone with a cat and looks at least fifty, although her hair is thick and black, and she has a number of striking gold teeth. Every time she walks past me in one of the three rooms of her immaculate home, she enunciates very slowly in her deep voiced way, 'Namaste sister', even when her last greeting was only a few minutes before.

The woman maintained a certain languor while busying about; washing clothes and sheets, collecting frozen cowpats for fire fuel, fetching water from the well, or sweeping with a makeshift broom of bound twigs. So, it was surprising when this motherly woman decided to sit down next to me and share a brew she had made with sprigs of fresh mint. It was even more surprising to hear myself addressed as '*didi*', a term of respect meaning 'older sister'. I asked if you can use *didi* for someone younger? Sometimes, she replied, but not in this case, 'because you are older'.

The voice was even and matter-of-fact; nothing edgy or even playful about it. I looked at the woman I thought was nearly twice my age and couldn't resist asking, 'if life gets better once you are older than thirty?' We then swapped ages and were both amazed; for my part because she was only thirty-four and she couldn't accept the youth of the woman next to her, who she thought was 'forty, maybe a lot more'. We stared at each other, coming to terms with our new understanding. In a wonderful interplay of cultures, the woman had faithfully observed a custom which venerates age; slightly tricky for a Western ear, sensitive to suggestions of premature ageing.

■   ■   ■

None of us feel rested after a night in the smoky room, on beds with hard, wooden boards poking through thin mattresses. The cat was playful, purring quietly as it roamed about the restless bodies, ensuring one victim was fully awake before turning to the next. It is hard not to fret about sleeplessness as energy is the fuel that helps the chances of reaching the summit. We will be lucky to snatch a few hours at Upper Camp on our summit night at 5,400m (17,717ft), forty-eight hours away. Images of the *puja* played about all night as I tossed and turned in the thinner air at 3,185m (10,449ft). Sonam had taken us to another world, as he chanted on the cloudy lower slope of our Himalayan mountain, while Bitu and Indra softly joined in. The smell of burning pine and juniper hung in the damp air and we visualised clear, calm skies for the next three days.

As we leave, our hostess clasps her hands together in prayer as she stands at the door. We are lined up to descend the ladder. Just as I turn, she asks me to wait a moment, returning with a solemn air and a hand heaped with grease. 'Safe time on mountain, sister,' she says, as she smears it in my hair and rubs it into my scalp.

'Yak fat for cooking,' explains Sonam, smiling. 'Good luck for you now.'

I manage to look grateful, aware that within minutes my hair will wreak of rancid butter. As soon as we are safely out of sight, we all collapse into laughter, unable to stop for several minutes. Sonam leads me to the village well and helps to scrape off the worst of it. He then rubs pine into my hair, already beginning to smell.

The path leads up through the village, past the houses hammered into the hillside. '*Poli, poli,*' Sonam says under his breath, a gentle reminder to move slowly. It helps the body acclimatise in the thinner air, as red blood cells start to multiply to carry more oxygen around the body. The woman, undoubtedly unique, has made an impression on me and I think of her as we walk at half the speed of our natural pace. She had offered to give me her coral and turquoise pendant after I'd admired it. I regret mistaking her kindness for politeness; to have accepted it would have been sisterly and binding.

Last night, among hundreds of photos and old newspaper cuttings stuck to one of the walls, I was amazed to see a faded promotional postcard of one of Rajesh's films. He was staring straight at the lens, almost pouting at it, beside a beautiful woman in a sari. Wearing a chunky silver bracelet, his hair was bouffant and long, like a coiffed mane. His worked-out muscles filled a tight white T-shirt. I would have laughed had I not been choking on the thick smoke, forcing me to dive outside for air. The unlikely coincidence of meeting him seems so improbable, especially with these random memory joggers in remote Himalayan situations. Each step upwards should take me ever further from the reminders of my life behind, into a world far removed from status and celebrity.

9 PISANG PEAK

Pink, purple and yellow flowers dot the slopes shrouded in thick grey cloud. Exotic clusters of red and white-leafed plants spring from the earth. My favourite is a beautifully simple, lily-white flower, shaped like an upturned satellite dish. We reach Base Camp in three hours after a steady scramble up the rocky hillside. Sonam is an inspiration of resourcefulness, immediately attuned to the environment. With a focused efficiency, he finds the best sites for the tents, rolls over boulders to secure them for when the late afternoon breeze comes.

He piles up the kit and food and shows Indra and Bitu how best to construct a windshield for the cooking area. His next task, before assembling materials for our second *puja*, is to find water. All the time he sings under his breath and laughs, engrossed in his organisation. Living on a mountain is Sonam's world and we watch his example. One of the tent sheets has a tear; he mends it before attending to the dozens of fresh garlic cloves, which must be finely chopped into a soup, 'best food for altitude'. After a short rest, I wake up refreshed to the sound of the three men chanting. Peering out from my flapping tent door, I watch the smoke of burning pine coiling towards the emptiness below.

Early the next morning, I wake to see the views before they cloud over again. Opposite, the Annapurna massif towers over the jagged skyline above the Manang region. In spite of that, our peak is not too dwarfed. From this aspect it is shaped like a dunce's hat; our line of ascent along the ridge of the south-west face, rocky and exposed, leading to a snowy, domed summit. Suddenly I want the camaraderie of a bigger team, to be fired up for the challenge ahead by group banter and the energy that brings. I have lost weight from the recent fever and still feel a bit weak; not exactly in great condition for the relentless effort ahead. Thinking how to phrase something and simplify it to make sense nearly every time I speak is hard work. Altitude is a strange, inhospitable universe. An avalanche roars in the white vastness of the Annapurnas across the valley. A dense band of cloud sits like a giant white cork one hundred metres below us. It will rise again, smothering us once more in the cold, damp grey.

Sonam piles up pine branches and leaves for our morning *puja*, before we set off for High Camp, 1,000m (3,281ft) above. He chants *Om Mani Padme Hum* and we all join in. I am downwind of the sweet smoke, which the men call '*dubi*'. My stomach feels a little queasy and unsettled, made worse by the continuous smell of maturing yak fat stuck to my hair. My spirits are flagging and I try to remember my reasons for being here. Mountains are such powerful symbols of man's will to act, to change his humble place in the natural world. To climb them involves a sustained feat of strength and fair combat with the unknown. Living at sea level, the image of a white summit awakened in me ideas of what it can mean to be inspired, to change the elements of a life not working. Yet on this barren slope, again in cloud, thousands of miles away from those I love, I am not at all akin to the lofty or romantic.

Later, we reach High Camp in cloud. On a steeper slope than Base Camp, the surface is rockier too. This is the second time Sonam has been up here in a day. He ran off first thing to find a water source, so we could camp as close as possible to it. After beavering about our new base, he set off with the others, returning an hour-and-a-half later, weighed down with big plastic sacks of water from the glacier. We set up ropes for more practice belaying and abseiling and roll down the slope with an ice axe each, turning into it as if to arrest.

The plan is to go to bed as early as possible so we can set off by midnight for the summit attempt. Because the weather looks unsettled, Sonam has instructed Bitu to move the tents back to Base Camp once we have set off. We will rest there after returning from the climb, before continuing with the long descent to Pisang village. Indra is now joining us to help carry the rope loads and gear. I'm feeling stronger generally but not as mentally engaged as I should be.

The most elaborate *puja* yet is assembled. A prayer flag is hung from a bamboo pole, as we are shown how to clasp our hands in prayer and how to pronounce the words to chant. We are given rice seeds to sift from one hand to another, again and again, before they are thrown into the air on cue. The ritual ends with Sonam splashing water at each of us from a cup, ladled by a yellow alpine flower.

We then head to the rocks above our camp for an acclimatisation walk, where the fixed lines are to be set up. Our route takes us along a bleak blend of boulder and scree. Drab browns and lifeless greys blanket the steepening slope. Much higher up, far above this long rocky stretch, the snowline rises into cloud, requiring a tenacious scramble to reach it. From this angle it looks severe, exposing us to whatever the monsoon night carries our way. If the wind is northerly, we will be sheltered but also climbing into extreme coldness. We will certainly have to wear down jackets. Even without the wind chill, in a cloudless sky, temperatures could drop to -20°C or lower nearer the summit. This is hostile territory, unwelcoming to human trespassers.

We move together over the rocks and head for the bigger boulders, where, for the first part we can hop from one to the next. They quickly become smaller and careful foot placement is needed to avoid slipping into the cracks between them. Loose scree of varying ankle-straining sizes melds the larger rocks together. We carry on like this for an hour, perhaps moving more quickly than we should to lessen the strain of altitude. To go much slower would take up most of the afternoon and we need the evening to rest before our midnight departure.

We reach the start of the climbing where Sonam, with Indra helping him, starts to fix the ropes. Initially it does not look too difficult but will need a committed effort of precise footwork and upper-body strength to keep balanced. It is hard to see beyond two hundred metres because of the projecting band of rocks and thickening clouds covering the upper snowfield. The gloomy weather is deadening the shreds of my excitement for what lies ahead. Even the dramatic stature of the Annapurnas across the valley can only be glimpsed through patches of thinner cloud. The uniform grey hiding their glaciated slopes and towering summits is also smothering my will to drive through it.

There are barely eight hours left to get back to camp, eat, drink and rest, to summon some motivation for the seven-hour ascent. Getting off the mountain can take care of itself. For now, the immediate task of climbing it safely is enough to think about. Pisang Peak is going to drain every reserve of energy I have. Overlooked by its larger and more famous sisters, among the fourteen highest in the world, this mountain is not to be underestimated.

At camp, we busy ourselves getting ready for setting off. Plenty of spare food and water are prepared. I'm surprised by my consistent hunger. Losing appetite is more normal at this height. I pack some extra warm gear into a small pack and marvel at Sonam's energy. He has not stopped all day and will have to bear the strain of the climb in the long hours ahead. Whatever he is doing, he will chant a prayer or sing or tell a story at the same time. He laughs when I look serious, as I get him to scan the cloudy skyline and point out what would be there if it was clear. I need this imprinted on my mind's eye to help draw on every possible source of wonder and shake off my growing lethargy. This is a dangerous state of mind to have in the countdown to the climax climb. This is when all the planning and training are meant to come together, when the best hand is to be played against external forces infinitely stronger and more decisive.

We are all in bed by seven-thirty. It is a cold, clear night. Each one of us coughs and stirs during the four hours before we have to get up again. It is hard to ignore the icy temperatures and our wakefulness as the long challenge ahead draws nearer and nearer. I have a bad feeling I can't seem to shake off. The effort of conjuring positive thoughts is not having any impact on my weary state. I can't stop searching for the real reason for being here. How does climbing a mountain enrich a life beyond the peak experience of getting to the top? How is the sense of achievement ever really sustained beyond a fragment of memory, so quickly is it overcome by exhaustion and the fear of getting down again? Every mountain has its own feel, its own chemistry. Turning over again to get comfortable, I wonder if there is some dark secret to Pisang's history – something to explain its unyielding character.

▪   ▪   ▪

The Himalayan sky looks so vast without cloud. The galaxies of stars and silhouette of the Annurpurnas make our camp seem so little and our preparations to climb our smaller mountain so humble. Somehow our efforts seem dwarfed by the mixed mountaineering history of this famous range, its well documented triumphs and tragedies. Bitu sees us off. His last words, 'I wait for you. See you later,' seem so routine for an enterprise so in conflict with the urge to dive back into the warmth of a sleeping bag. Indra, Sonam, and I are saying very little; each of us in our own world as we imagine the hours ahead without sleep. Even to have been oblivious for just half an hour before the climb would have at least broken up the long, fretful waiting.

We set off. Sonam and Indra carry a coil of rope each, all of us using our ice axes to help lever our way up the scree and rock. This goes on for a long time. Occasionally, I glance up at the sky, hoping for that moment when nothing matters except the job in hand, that mysterious connection between mind and body, when the boundaries between oneself and the immediate environment blur. An avalanche thunders across the dark from the icy massif opposite, its power a reminder that nature cannot ever be reduced to a manageable, eye-pleasing snapshot. It rumbles for many seconds, as the falling mass gains volume and speed, triggering smaller ice slides in its wake.

I draw on the memory of the night when I raced up the scree of Kilimanjaro, involved with every aspect of the terrain and my strong movement up it. Clay and I were working perfectly together, determined to break away from the throng snaking its way up the flanks in single file, aware of the effort in their every step.

This is very different. We stop at the fixed ropes and take a break. I am grateful, hunching over my bent legs to get warm, knowing it will be hard to spring into life when Sonam suggests we start again. My companions are silent. Indra's eyes are closed and Sonam looks out over the freezing, windless night sky and remarks how cold it is. The stars above us are so far away and we are insignificant in Nature's grander scheme. Minutes pass but this is not getting us anywhere. One of us has to move. 'Three more minutes and then let's go,' I venture.

Eventually Sonam rises and we tie into the rope, our head torches flashing about as we adjust our harnesses. He will lead and belay me and Indra will follow at the back. This routine goes on for several pitches with long gaps in between, as Sonam searches for the best route up; setting up an anchor from which he will tension the rope as Indra and I climb up to him. Every thirty-foot pitch requires a wait of nearly an hour. The tips of my hands are numb – my gloves really are not up to the rigours of this biting cold. I am warm when active but the waiting with Indra is chilling, stiffening my body into a state of old age.

At one point Indra nods off and slumps into a dead weight, tautening the rope that attaches him to our rocky seat. I am uneasy at Sonam's unusual quietness when we catch up with him. He is clearly tired and his eyes are puffy from the extraordinarily active hours before we turned in. Every time I ask how he is, just to break up the long, tedious silence during our rests, he answers, 'I am OK. It is cold. How are you?' No smiling, or songs or stories now.

We are making very slow progress up this ridge, with its otherworldly feel; seven hundred metres is so much further at altitude. All my muscles are heavy. My mind is disengaged. It is somewhere far below where Bitu has perhaps gone back to sleep before decamping and getting food and tents ready for our return, so many hours from now, such a distance from this inhospitable spot.

Another avalanche; the route goes endlessly on. The rocks are slippery with ice, requiring a forceful swing of the axe to drive it into the unstable surface. Feathers of snow, sculpted by the wind, fringe the edges of the rocks. They would be beautiful if they were formed by something other than this freezing chill.

At no stage does time, or our experience travelling through it, ever speed up. This is perhaps the longest night I have ever spent. Nothing is inspiring me to engage with the drama of this haunting spot, where people are not meant to be. Sheer drops into the blackness either side of the icy spine of rock we scale drive me to try harder. And still the dawn light doesn't streak across the sky. I resolve to ask Sonam about this mountain once we are safely off it. Whenever will that be?

More climbing. More waiting in the cold and bursts of hallucinatory dreams, abruptly ended by Sonam's half-hearted appeal to keep moving. I exclaim out loud that this is hard work. Immediately I regret it. There can be no refuge from the grinding strain and monotony with this admission. Both agree. Suddenly the pressure to commit is critical if we are to press on upwards and complete our objective. Is that not why we're here? I'm not sure of anything anymore except the growing exhaustion weighing down my every move.

Sonam estimates another two hours to the top. Surely not, I cry, we must be closer – look! The white-domed summit is beginning to shine now in the dawn sky, deceptively close. To fall from here would mean to drop thousands of feet to a certain death – it would be impossible to break a fall on the steep slope plunging on and on into the darkness below. Clouds are forming above. Surely that will mean warmth soon? The final ascent will be a race against time to avoid being beaten by cold and cloud. Another two pitches, Sonam promises. We press on. Indra's eyes have narrowed, half-closed with sleepiness. He looks so young now, as if he's lost some of the bulky body weight that makes him a strong porter. I bang my hands together again and again, clapping them into some sort of life they still don't feel.

Time and again we slip down the splintering ice, which looked like soft snow from below. We put on crampons, not easy at this angle. Fixing lines is time-consuming work and the rope is now stiff and heavy from the cold. We take it in turns to wait for each other, cooling quickly after the recent exertion. I am wearing seven layers in all, including a down jacket and have never been so cold.

At last we reach the critical point of the expedition. The summit is ten metres directly above. It is temptingly close and within reach. Only now we have stopped to weigh up our options, we notice how the weather is worsening. Higher, we will be even more exposed to the rising wind. Clouds stream over us, whitening the early morning. The views from the top would be a sea of whites and greys, cloud indistinguishable from snow and ice; a world of no contrast, just varying shades of nullifying dullness. What is the point in all this? Why are we here?

Sonam estimates it will take him an hour to fix the ropes and another hour to climb the remaining ten metres. We are all shivering and quiet as we look above at the way ahead towards an eerie flow of clouds tearing over the top, which, momentarily, we can't see. My hands and head no longer ache with cold – I am close to hypothermia.

'Sonam … in my view, it simply isn't worth it.' A second's pause, then a voice bright with relief asks, 'Are you sure?'

Indra, his firm, strong form hunched against a rock out of the wind, has hardly said a word all night. He remains silent, motionless.

'What you want to do? We can go up. Two hours and we have summit photo.'

I know Sonam means it. I also recognise that two more hours in this bitter cold for a picture in cloud and the words, 'I did it,' are like rolling dice with high stakes. My decision will shape the long way down, from where we will have to descend an even greater distance to reach the valley by nightfall. Only ten metres more.

'Yes, I am sure. Let's get out of here. I don't like this one little bit.'

Resigned, the tension that has kept us going is now swamped by new waves of exhaustion. We shuffle about inefficiently, reorganising the ropes. Nothing is said, each of us perhaps searching for unspent reserves of energy. Somewhere far below this icy spur is the warmth of our camp. To imagine it moment by moment would make every pitch, scramble and step to reach it all the longer. There really is only one way to make it down – to think of nothing but the next foothold to safety.

10 TOUCH OF DRAMA

Bitu waves and shrieks, a tiny form in the thinning cloud. At last our camp is visible. Reaching it, we slump to the ground, unable to return his welcoming smile as he pours us freshly brewed tea. A huge sense of anticlimax closes around our exhausted party. We only share the key points – the cold, the length, the tiredness. Looking up to where we were, it's hard to believe we got so close to the top, now we can appreciate the true scale of this peak.

If the toil there was unrelenting, the descent was even more so. In our weariness, the abseils and scrambling required more concentration. After hours of painstaking foot placement, we could only disengage when the terrain became scree allowing us to slide. My toes ground into the tips of my boots and knees ached with every attempt at balance. As the discomfort became unbearable, adrenaline no longer driving us, the conflict raged: the relief of warmth and safety, tempered by the regret of failing to make the very top.

Hundreds of metres below us, Upper Pisang village is a jumble of specks, shrouded in wood smoke. We devour biscuits and cake with another tea, listening to the cheering sound of bubbling soup. The dilemma over those ten metres, that narrow margin between achievement and retreat, no longer seems so critical. Bitu serves the soup and places three steaming bowls on the grass. Softly, he nudges my arm, gesturing me to take one.

'Sonam. I believe we were right to come down. It was a long way. Especially getting back here.'

'Yes. We make good decision to come down. Long way. Very cold.'

'Tell me – something is not good about Pisang. It was the most difficult climb for me. It wasn't only the altitude. My breathing was OK. There's just something about this mountain. I don't like it.'

Sonam looks up as he dunks a biscuit into his tea. 'Yes, big mountain, Pisang. Difficult mountain.'

'What do you mean?'

'Harder than Everest, this mountain. Harder than the route to Camp Three.'

'But there's a bad atmosphere. Not good. Normally I love being on a mountain.'

'Later I tell you something. Big secret. Only when we are out of here.' His voice sounds slightly playful but he looks serious, shifty even.

'What do you mean, secret? Tell me now – please. We've been through a lot in the last few days. What secret?'

'No. I will be in big trouble with agency if I tell you. Not now. Maybe later.'

'Trekking agency? Why is that? Sonam, I have a right to know now.'

'You promise you keep secret?'

'Yes.'

Bitu and Indra are watching us, curious too.

'You perhaps first tourist on mountain, in maybe two, three years. Pisang closed long time.'

'Why? What do you mean, closed?'

'Big tragedy on mountain. Many die. Big avalanche on this route, whole party killed. Maybe eleven peoples. German expedition.'

'How? How did they all die? Surely with ropes and protection they couldn't all fall?'

'Yes. Bad rope system. I think they all tied together. All climbers on one rope. One falls and they all go down together.'

'Why wasn't I told this? Your boss didn't say anything about this to me.'

'I don't know. Maybe he thinks you not come to Nepal after all.'

After a short rest we dismantle the camp. None of us loiter to delay the moment of moving again. The small flowers dusting the grassy site have managed to thrive on this inhospitable mountain. Pisang seemed to repel us from the moment we stepped onto it. Whether our memories of the climb are more punishing by knowing its history is impossible to know. Perhaps we are driven to descend faster than our aching limbs would otherwise allow by thoughts of a bed and long sleep ahead. Either way, we hurry downhill, bent on leaving these slopes far behind us.

■   ■   ■

From the Manang valley floor, Pisang Peak looked impressive with a new layer of snow. Its elegant shape held its own despite being dwarfed by its grander neighbours walling the region; Annapurna II, III, and IV, Gangapurna, and Glacier Dome to the west. Setting off the following morning for Manang, Pisang's upper snowy flanks glistened in the sun. The last view was important to savour, to mark the summit that had so narrowly eluded me. 'What ifs?' invariably humour the part of oneself left dissatisfied: but refreshed after a night of sound sleep, the decision to quit so close to the top still seemed right.

Later, cups of apple brandy help soothe our burning muscles and blistered feet. It's a staple tipple in Manang where its orchards are rich with the sweet fruit. As we deal another hand and share another unlabelled bottle, our party agrees that this is a perfect place to hole up for an extra day or two to recover.

The walled Buddhist town is a vibrant mix of a thriving community and its ancient cultural jewels. Beneath a large oak tree, looking as old as the street its roots have grown over, I watched clusters of men sitting and chattering at the end of a day's work. The cool evening air was filled with wood smoke. Posters of smiling women looking content with their newly learnt skills advertised courses on the walls of a nearby school. A hotchpotch of cobbled streets and hidden passageways led me past stone houses, their carved windows painted in Buddhist colours and *stupas* with cast iron prayer wheels, engraved in ornate mantra lettering. Some were so old and worn they'd been replaced with Nescafé tins, which spin just as smoothly. Sonam found for me the guardian of a thirteenth-century temple to show us around – a lama peering out from behind thick, square-framed glasses, eccentrically large for his small, chiselled face. Shuffling ahead of us in his Nike trainers, he laboured to open the oak door with a collection of hand-sized keys.

Inside, our eyes had to adjust to the dark, obscuring treasured artefacts. Hanging from the pillars, wooden masks of warrior faces looked menacingly human as well as monstrous. The monk lit a match and held it up to them, revealing tufts of yak wool sprouting from their heads and open hollow mouths, some with sharp teeth. They are worn at rituals during festival time. Hundreds of Tibetan scrolls were piled along the walls, centuries-old. Religious murals in bright paints were like scenes from the remoter valleys we had passed through, of oxen and peasants working the land. As we marvelled at the gold Buddha statues and some faithfully transcribed texts as old as their seven-hundred-year-old home, a gong struck to mark sundown. It was time to celebrate the comforts of the valley, a time for cards and famous local apple brew.

'We are so lucky it is Friday here. Movie night!' Sonam quips. 'We buy tickets at the door. We will go in an hour to get good seats.'

None of my companions have seen the film and their excitement at seeing Nepal's biggest star is increased knowing that I plan to see him when we get back to Kathmandu. Another round of cards and amazement at Sonam's steady luck, before the four of us set off to the town hall.

The makeshift cinema is a windowless room in cardboard, which would burn to the ground within a minute of a fire starting. A man at the door obediently stamps a ticket with a random number before allowing us through. Incense and cigarette smoke fill the space, every inch plastered with posters promoting films and their stars, a cast of princely men and their dark-eyed, voluptuous beauties. We choose the last bench at the back on a raised platform, overlooking the heads of twenty or so male viewers. My conspicuousness is not helped in any way when Sonam stands up and addresses the room in Nepali, after which rows of heads swivel round and gawp at me, breaking into smiles of awe.

'Sonam, what have you told them?'

'I tell them you know Rajesh. They now know you know Rajesh. When we watch movie, we know too that you have met Rajesh Hamal in Kathmandu.'

There's no reason to doubt Sonam's straightforward answer. As we wait for our doorman to spark up the dated video machine and TV set, propped on several stacked chairs, it becomes quite clear he didn't exaggerate. Heads turn, unable to resist another look at the only woman here, who happens to know Nepal's most celebrated actor. My three companions keep watch over me too. There's a growing tension in one of the world's most unusual cinemas, a unique sense of occasion, and one I have every intention of rising to after the recent rigours of Pisang.

After buttons and switches are fussed with, the TV whirs into life, as black and white dots converge into a seamless flow of packets of food and detergents. The Nepali commercials are something of a show in their own right and the audience is hushed and attentive until the movie finally begins. The title sequence reveals the box-office pulling power of the name Rajesh Hamal, as it dominates the screen. Bitu leans across Indra to whisper to me, 'All in Nepali. No problem, we make sure you understand.' I thank him, suspecting rightly that I won't need much help following a costume drama higher in ham than surprise plot twists. The beginning of every dream or fantasy scene ripples for a few seconds to highlight its unreality. Rajesh shows considerable equestrian skill as he rides about the green plains beneath a towering Himalayan skyline, playing a flute at the same time. There are plenty of close-ups of our hero ensuring he's never belittled by the grander natural scenery. Music and singing is a winning film formula in this part of the world and the crowd claps along as the actors skip and twirl.

During a dance sequence, of which there are many, faces search mine across the dark to check I am as gripped as everyone else. During moments of comedy, Sonam elbows me a little forcefully and motions a thumbs up. At one point, the heroine tries to kiss the hero who rebuffs her. The camera zooms on her face, anguished and hurt, her lustrous eyes filled with tears. I am stared at continually throughout her melodic lament.

Several commercial breaks and dances later, they end up together, a surprising finale it seems, judging by the sighs of relief. The credits go up to a round of applause. The movie's closing shots are filled with a radiant Rajesh. He is no longer the heartless villain and cheeky rogue, but a man who has won a beautiful, adoring bride as well as the heartfelt admiration of their entire community.

11 KATHMANDU FAREWELLS

The Monkey Temple, soaring over its three hundred and sixty five flagstone steps, is deserted. Swayambhunath, this most famous Buddhist landmark in Nepal is hauntingly quiet but for the rustling of monkeys and ancient legends which seem to hover about the early Kathmandu morning. Scriptures say the site was once a snake-infested lake. Aeons ago, a perfect, radiant lotus flower appeared on its surface. Manjushri, a man of knowledge, drew his sword and cut a gorge to drain the lake, where the lotus settled, establishing a shrine for worship. He then turned his attention to the snakes, whose powerful spirits, or *nag*, are still at large. It is believed they determine when the monsoon rains will start to fall. The authorities are reluctant to allow excavations in case an upset *nag* brings on an earthquake. Rich in timeless stories, the temple and its well-photographed, all-seeing eyes gaze over the valley's glimmering lights, as toy-sized cars wind along its thoroughfares.

'One legend says when Manjushri cut his hair here, every strand that fell to the ground grew into a tree and the lice turned into monkeys.'

Rajesh leans on a low stone wall near a *mani* stone, with the Tibetan inscription, *Om mani padme hum*. We are both tired and reflective. Tomorrow, I will have to get ready for the flight home.

My memory of our last meeting before Pisang captured the glamour of round-the-clock adulation but not its loneliness. Earlier, when I'd arrived at the bar where we were meeting, it struck me how tired Rajesh looked as he sat there, wearing the same simple black outfit and flip-flops. His eyes were rimmed and baggy, explained by the double shifts he'd been working for the past ten days. There was a tight deadline for a post-production sound mix, and he described the frayed tempers and nervous outbursts behind the scenes. He's starred in eighty-five films in eleven years, often working on two at a time, and is tiring of the formula for healthy box-office sales.

After a drink, for which he eagerly paid this time, he drove me to another ritzy hotel, where he often dines after working out in its gym. The waiters buzzed about their well-known regular but weren't intrusive. We filled our plates repeatedly at the buffet, a sumptuous mix of seafood and exotic curries, fruits and multi-coloured ice creams doused in rich chocolate sauces and nuts. A trolley of French cheeses returned again and again as we relished our unhurried meal, while a pianist trilled some unremarkable background tunes.

'Yes, my father died alone in Pakistan where he was ambassador, at fifty-six. A total shock. My mother used to go out and join him but as a family we were scattered, most of us living in Nepal at that time. Our childhood was colourful, international. He also worked as an attaché in Washington, Saint Petersburg … '

'That's right. You told me all about Russia, Thailand, America and London last time.' I remind him.

'Ah yes. As the oldest son, I was very close to him. I was under big pressure, since a kid, to conform to my father's expectations, his wish for me to be an engineer. I studied in Bombay but then, by accident, fell into movies. He never forgave me. Our relationship was tense.'

'So, how did you become an actor then?'

'I got a holiday job as a student on one of my uncle's sets – he worked in the business – and then it kind of snowballed, you might say.'

'But your father must have been proud of you.'

'Sure, in a way, but disappointed. He never really got over it.'

'So when he died, did you suffer from guilt as well as grief?'

'That was hard. Really hard. Our understanding was mending very slowly over the years. As the eldest I had to open the house and entertain relatives who came to pay respect to my mother and memory of his life. In my country, there's a strict Hindu ritual in grief you must observe. You have to shave your head and fast until sundown for fifteen days, spending the entire time alone, apart from taking the counsel and blessings of visitors. I refused to cut my hair … it just didn't seem right somehow. Hypocritical in some way. There was a lot of public anger at me. Many articles at the time were critical of my decision. But I was not going to be false, you know? I knew that my argument with my father was based on being true to myself, my nature. And I was not going to do anything which suggested I was wrong, that I regretted my choice … ' The dining room has emptied and Rajesh orders the bill.

'Normally there are many more people about at this time, especially at weekends. A lot of card games are played here late into the night, for big money. My brother used to play and gamble here all the time. He's a genius at cards, poker mainly. He won big sums – and lost a bit too. He was a bright star. Bright, bright star. A national talent. It's sad what he has become.'

'He lives with you, doesn't he?'

'Yes. With my mother and fiercely independent grandmother. She's ninety and has more stamina than us all.' He laughs and shakes his head while taking the bill from a silver tray bearing a dish of truffles.

'My brother was once going to be prime minister. At the age of eighteen he was going places.'

'Yes. You told me how he was a precocious talent. Amazingly gifted.'

Glancing up at the lobby clock as we walk past, Rajesh reminds me of the strike called by the Maoists. 'Ah, that'll be why this place is so empty. *Bund* begins in five hours. At six, the city'll grind to a halt. No businesses will dare open. No taxis. Streets will be dead. Have you been here during *bund* before?'

'No.'

'It is quite a thing for you to observe on your last day in Nepal.'

He drove me towards my hotel in Thamel, along streets familiar after a week of being whisked on the back of Sonam's motorbike. We'd explored villages and sites all over the Kathmandu Valley.

'What would you say to visiting Swayambhunath?'

'What – now?'

'Sure. It's beautiful at this time of night. If you haven't seen it when there's no one around, you might as well have never been at all.' A last view of Kathmandu at the dead of night would be infinitely more memorable than my hotel room. 'Why not?' I replied, as he drove the car into an alley and reversed back into the road, to face the other way to Swayambhunath.

■　　　■　　　■

We take our time walking up the worn stone steps, past stray dogs, howling and scrapping behind sacred stone structures. The rain falls gently and the faint waft of pine makes me nostalgic. I wonder how the end of experience defines itself, when is the line that shapes it ever really drawn? Is it during these final hours in Nepal, or at the airport when I thank Sonam for his selflessness, far beyond the role of guide? Or does it happen later, as the future unfolds from what is arising now?

'What do you think of marriage?' Rajesh asks me.

A little out of the blue undoubtedly but I'm feeling more open than usual, resigned to my departure. 'Well Rajesh. That's quite a question to spring on me!' We both laugh as we turn around to gaze at the sprawling electric skyline.

'It's not a priority, I must say. Seems a bit irrelevant to me at this stage in my life. As you know, we marry a lot later at home, if at all.' I steal a glance at Rajesh. There's nothing at all flirtatious in his manner – in fact there hasn't been all evening. He's been very self-absorbed and is again lost in thought as we continue up the steps.

'And what about you?'

'Pretty much my view. I have never wanted to marry.'

'What never – not any of your past girlfriends?'

'No. I've had good relationships, don't get me wrong. I've been close to many, many women. But … it's hard to put into words, actually … marriage is, how do you say this? … a sign you are incomplete; that you lack something in yourself.'

'Really? But what about mutual subserviency or just falling in love and throwing a party for the hell of it? Don't forget social statement either.'

'No. It really isn't for me. A number of relationships, good ones, have stopped because I won't go there. It seems silly. Two people can love each other – but that's the point, they are … two people.'

Mosquitoes start to make themselves felt as we wander about the giant prayer wheels and altars, their candles guttering stumps. We agree it's a good time to call it a night. At the car park Rajesh starts the engine and the same Hindi songs from weeks ago chant up again from the radio as we take to the road once more.

'Do you want a drink, a final end of the night. Beer or whisky?'

Actually I don't. It's been a good evening, the temple a bonus, but I'm not sure I can drum up more conversation.

'Sure. But everywhere looks pretty shut around here.'

'Yup. That's *bund* for you. We can go back to mine. The servants will still be up and can get you any drink or snack you might like. It's not far from your hotel, the other side of the palace, a five-minute drive.'

The roads are empty and businesses are all boarded up. We cruise past the palace and a back road of stately buildings, including the British Consulate. Just opposite lush green trees drooping over high embassy walls, Rajesh pulls up at an electric gate. He presses a buzzer but nothing happens. He then blasts the car horn several times.

'Ramesh should be up,' he says.

'Oh, don't worry. If it's a case of opening it, I can do it,' I offer.

Moments later, a sleepy-eyed teenager runs to the heavy gate and grins as he unlatches it to let us through. I follow Rajesh to the back of the house, sweeping my eyes over balconies facing the spacious garden. Weeks of renovation work are being carried out, Rajesh explains, pointing to the scaffolding and mounds of excavated earth. The household is clearly asleep. He switches on lights as we head to a white studio bleached with spotlights. A widescreen TV fills one wall and shelves of videos line another. Photographs of Rajesh and framed awards are dotted about the remaining space. There is no room for them in the cabinet crammed with trophies and professional memorabilia.

He claps his hands and hollers, 'Ramesh!' Seconds later, the smiling young servant arrives, eager to take orders.

'I want a pot of tea, sugared and a beer. My friend would like … '

'The same please but no sugar in the tea. Thank you.'

I yawn. Somehow we start talking about books and I mention that the great Russian writers brought me great comfort as a troubled teenager. This strikes a personal chord with Rajesh, who shakes his head in disbelief.

'Me too! That is wonderful. I used to read them in the original Russian as a boy. Have you been to St Petersburg?'

I shake my head.

'Well, I've got a film right here, which I think you might like to see.'

He searches the rows of video box spines, his back turned. Ramesh knocks before entering with a tray of drinks.

'Do you want some food? Just ask. He'll make anything you want.'

'Thank you, the tea and beer are perfect. Thanks Ramesh.'

He grins, tiptoeing out, closing the door behind him.

The next two hours are a blur of beautiful chandeliers in palaces that would take weeks to explore, of spiral marble staircases and priceless gold ornaments, of rose gardens requiring an army to prune them, resplendent with their fountains and bridged streams. Rajesh, a special guest of a film festival, is chaperoned throughout the video by a Russian researcher with a clipboard, who blushes as he interviews her. As the footage of the week-long visit goes on, she loses her shyness, apparently a great deal more familiar with Nepal's most famous bachelor.

'Golly is that the time?'

The film ends. Rajesh looks alert, apparently not thinking of sleep. He seems strangely alone sitting next to his library of films and he suggests another video.

'Can you believe it – it's six o'clock! I've really got to get back.'

'My God, is that the time? The strike has started. There'll be no taxis and I cannot drive you back. It will only take you fifteen minutes to walk.'

It crosses my mind that he could have offered to escort me back, but I'm too tired to labour the thought. Outside a chorus of birds welcomes the new morning. We swap contact details. I think how in decades to come I may indulge our unlikely meeting as an elderly aunt might, 'Now dear, I can tell you a thing or two about Kathmandu at the start of the twenty-first century!' Rajesh opens the gate. There's a commotion in the alleyway immediately outside where a small crowd has gathered. Two uniformed army officials with long rifles and khaki caps are pointing towards the main road outside the exclusive enclave. Someone walks by, shaking his head and says, 'There's a bomb over there. The Maoists have planted it.'

'What? A bomb?' I reply.

'What are the police doing?' Rajesh asks.

'They are telling us to walk past the device, slowly and without alarm. They have summoned their bomb disposal unit. They are on the way.'

It's hard to respond to this surprising explanation and to the deadpan faces of the public and grim seriousness of the officials, summoning them into a line. The stranger is unmoved as he tells us he's just walked past it and 'look, it didn't blow up!' Rajesh asks how long before it'll be made safe and the man shrugs. Aware of the time, I announce I can't be bothered to wait – if this was really serious, wouldn't a cordon have been set up? The men agree. Rajesh extends his hand, 'It has been a pleasure meeting you. Have a good life.'

Resolving to mull over these words later, I march purposefully towards the military men. Three people are in a queue waiting for the instruction to run past. The square gadget has wires trailing out, resembling a kindergarten creation, not the maiming device of feared political rebels. An officer waves an arm on the barking cue of his more senior colleague and a man breaks into a sprint. It's impossible to take this charade at security seriously. Defiantly, I saunter past, with all the time in the world. The bomb continues to sit outside the heavily fortified walls of the embassies like an abandoned toy.

Once clear, I turn around to see if Rajesh is there to wave me off, having witnessed my close encounter with a potentially violent end. The gate is closed and there is no one leaning against it. I set off, my eyes ahead, and walk and walk, never wondering for a moment if I will ever see him again.

PART 3 APPROACH TO HAUTES-PYRENEES

OCCIDENTALES/
HAUTES - PYRENEES

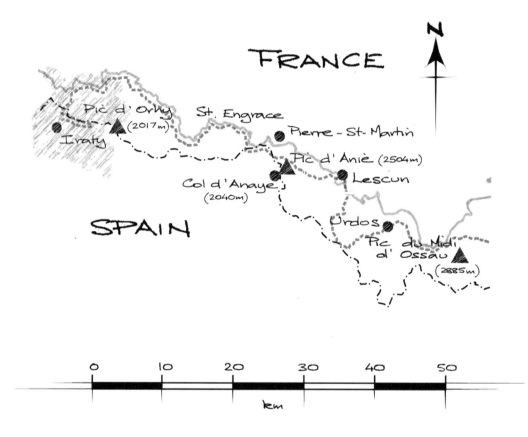

FRANCE

N

Pic d'Orhy
(2017m)

St. Engrace

Pierre - St- Martin

Iraty

Pic d'Anie (2504m)

Col d'Anaye
(2040m)

Lescun

SPAIN

Urdos

Pic du Midi
d' Ossau
(2885m)

```
0        10        20        30        40        50
|---|===|---|===|---|===|---|===|---|===|---|
              km
```

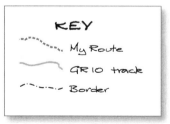

KEY

.... My Route

~~~~~ GR 10 track

·—·—·— Border

12 FLIGHT OF THE GRIFFON: 2003

The light grew golden in the dusk, making the pastoral colours of Iraty all the more welcoming. A hostel notice board had a weather forecast for the area neighbouring the Hautes Pyrenees, that warned of strong winds and rain for the next two days. It was all the excuse I needed to rest up and prepare for the adventure ahead – bad visibility and gusty conditions could be a lethal combination for ridge walking, especially on my own.

In the kitchen, a chatty, middle-aged British couple were going to some length to create a stir-fry feast over a bottle of red wine, upstaging my humble mix of packet soup with pasta, garlic, and cheese. As they sliced a generous pile of oriental mushrooms, I overheard them talk about their 'luck' in making it off the ridge before the weather changed.

'Excuse me, I'm heading towards Lescun, via the ridge from Pic D'Orhy. Is that where you've just been?'

'Don't do it!' the man said and winked at me through his glasses before gulping back some wine. Grinning, he turned back to the chopping board, apparently with nothing more to add. His wife giggled and threw him a glance of mock disapproval. 'It's quite a route, that, certainly. The forecast isn't ideal either. Lots of fog builds up there, so you've got to be pretty sure of a clear run.'

'You've also got to be quite clear about route-finding,' he rejoined as he chopped. 'It's not easy because the limestone's a bit like a hunk of well-eaten cheese and it's damned hard to see through it. Would you like some wine?'

The hours passed in a jolly blur, eventful on several counts. Peter and Jenny entertained with their tales of mishap and adventure. Their children now grown-up, they were having the time of their lives blowing their savings on intrepid trips. They were rambling through the highlights of the Hautes Pyrenees, relying on lifts between the duller parts. Peter had soloed the High Level Route when he was twenty-three. He had known 'nothing, nothing at all' about mountains or weather or navigation. 'Miracle I made it – it helped being completely ignorant – I had no idea at all what I was letting myself in for.'

After a catalogue of terrifying stories, of getting lost or caught out in bad weather, he held my eyes, suddenly serious. 'Storms are a real hazard here on in. Dangerous. Really. Make sure you get off the ridges fast when that happens.'

As we compared maps and routes, I recounted my colourful tales of 'l'homme bizarre' and 'the-man-who-rescued-me-then-vanished'. We scarcely noticed the bearded newcomer, clutching a rather sorry-looking bowl of soup. He asked whether we'd mind if he joined us, blurting as he sat down, 'I'm English, as you've probably gathered, and to be absolutely frank I'm seriously lonely. Never been so lonely in all my life. I can't speak a bloody word of French!'

We were drawn immediately to this curious man with his Trotsky beard and army fatigues. Attractively self-assured, his inbuilt confidence could make light of an opening line about loneliness. He was studying for a doctorate in conservation and believed the natural world was 'the biggest classroom for the few humans who listen.' Passionate about griffon vultures, he was living in a corrugated-iron hut in Iraty with a community of volunteers who'd also given up their summers to count the migrating birds flying overhead. He loved salsa dancing, was tired of the predominantly male group he'd been mixing with for two months (few of whom spoke English), was craving a change of food and believed it would be 'suicidal' for me to press on along the ridge until the weather cleared.

'Why don't you join me tomorrow for a lesson of the untold, uncut story of the griffon, king of the birds?'

Peter and Jenny had made up their minds on this. 'She'd love to. Excellent idea. We'd stay if we could, except we're running out of time to get to Pau for our flight home.'

■   ■   ■

The *meteo* proved accurate, as thick banks of grey cloud rolled over the skyline. This was a day to drive most indoors. A team of vulture counters were charging about an exposed plateau, not at all put off by the impenetrable band of low pressure obscuring anything higher than a few hundred metres. I was fully layered up and armed with snacks. Watching birds would be a chilly business in a blustering wind. Chris, the self-appointed griffon instructor was nowhere to be seen among the enthusiastic throng. Binoculars were being passed around and someone was patiently waiting next to a telescope for the views to clear, clapping their mittened hands to keep warm. A laminated folder and pen dangled from it, to ensure a faithful record of every griffon spotted.

In the hilly distance a fluorescent orange jacket marched into view. It was Chris, who must have been looking out for better viewing spots. Spotting me, he headed over with some binoculars.

'Here. Your own set. Not much going on today – we've been here for a couple of hours already. Only seen four.'

'What happens when the weather's like this? Do you call it an early day?'

'Oh no. There'll always be a few people here while there's daylight, and we take it in turns keeping watch.'

As we talked, there were murmurs of excitement, and a couple of arms began to point to the sky, as a huddle of woollen hats and hoods scanned the horizon from left to right.

'There's one. Just adjust the lens to focus and enjoy!'

I learned the griffon, or *Gyps Fulvus*, is easily recognised by its tail, which is proportionally shorter than the width of its wing. It has a distinctive white collar around the base of its neck, which is dark brown when the bird is young. They nest on rocky ledges up to 1200m high (3,937ft).

'They look really graceful as they hover. Look – there! Watch his slow, soaring flight. It's always amazing to watch that control, that power.'

Most of the volunteers lived here for weeks at a time, some the whole season from spring to late summer. Throughout the day, a stream of hot drinks and bowls of pasta materialised from a rudimentary shack, as a catering-sized vat simmered over a large gas canister. Flasks and biscuits were passed around the lines of shivering people. I remembered my lightweight kitchen and lamented how rarely I used it – eating tinned or cold food is immediate, as well as cheerless. Having it is a luxury, adding to the weight to be hauled over distances.

'The griffon is like the dustman of the mountains – hoovering them for carrion. Rotting sheep and cattle carcasses mainly. They nearly became extinct. I think knowing this makes them all the more beautiful.'

This passion was rather infectious. I wanted to see more of these birds that have a bigger presence in Ariège further to the east and in the wilder, higher areas on the Spanish side of the Pyrenees. It's certainly a well-travelled bird, drawn to hot and cold parts of Europe, Asia, and Africa.

'I'm going to test you. Length of wingspan?'

'Easy. Eight feet. Fire some more!' I reply.

Laughing, hands in pocket, he bounded off towards some day-trippers who'd parked up to see what was going on. Leaflets, with facts and numbers to ring with sightings were given to them. I liked Chris' energy and watched him endeavour to speak French, his hands flying wildly as he tried to answer questions and share information.

The expectant crowd was craned at the grey above. A father had fixed his binoculars on a black form gliding across the skies, his mouth open in awe. To my untrained eye, it might have been a common jackdaw, or a type of crow. But for the man, there was nothing at all unremarkable about the bird. He glanced down to make sure his young son had seen it too. The boy grabbed his father's hand and they both looked up again, in silent wonder. The clouds were lowering and Chris reckoned another griffon sighting would be unlikely. He suggested we meet up later in the afternoon for a walk. In the meantime he'd stay to take care of any curious passers-by.

Later, we went through my route plan again. Chris had traversed the ridge a couple of times since living in Iraty. I was nervous at Georges Veron's warning in the definitive HLR guidebook, to 'avoid the French side' and only to attempt the ridge in 'settled weather'. Of course that was sensible counsel but it was so hard to know whether a settled spell of overcast weather was still too hazardous for setting out.

'You'll be fine. You know what it involves. If you're in any doubt, just turn around. Either spend another day watching the birds and try again, or you can always join up with the GR10, which is a much safer bet.'

We were perched on domed rocks, perfectly comfortable. The somnolent flow of a nearby stream and the sheltering presence of large pine trees made it easy to idle time away talking. Chris described his student lifestyle and talked of his dream of earning money without giving up the freedoms to which he'd grown accustomed. I admitted that I'd been too comfortable in a familiar working pattern to be thinking freshly or originally. We wondered if routine dulls performance. It struck us how we'd outgrown the urge to strive for pension-saving security. Working towards a safe future was an empty certainty anyway. Surprisingly, getting older had made us challenge those very values for which we'd settled and had used to define our adult lives so far.

It was getting dark and I needed to get back to the hostel to prepare for a dawn departure. As we hovered over our goodbye, I asked if he fancied a day off from bird watching, to share a jaunt along a limestone ridge with 'wonderful views in clear skies'. We both knew the forecast hadn't allowed for any such optimism and the weather wouldn't improve dramatically overnight. It had been a throwaway line – but if Chris decided to take a break from his routine and come along, so much the better. An answer came from him, so surprising that it stunned me of any ability to respond.

'Look, I'm heading off for a shower. It's been really very lonely the last couple of months. You're nice and … it would be really wonderful if you would choose to join me.'

The ground, an unremarkable array of stones and pot-holed tarmac, gripped my attention. There really was plenty to notice, with such a rare opportunity for examination.

'Oh dear, that's blown it,' he continued. I really hope you're not shocked. It's just life is so short and you're heading off tomorrow. I think we get on so well. We could have a really great time.'

I'm not sure what was more amazing – his lack of self-consciousness or the wish to dress this offer up as anything it wasn't, or that during all the hours we'd spent together, this earnest admirer of wild birds and champion of conservation had his heart set on other natural pursuits. Yet I had to admit, it was not unattractive to risk looking foolish at his expense.

'Look Chris. I am really flattered.' We both smiled a little unconvincingly. Neither of us knew where this was going.

'I just think ... I guess it would be wrong of me to take advantage of you when you're ... not desperate exactly ... but a bit lonely. I've enjoyed your company, had a great day and want to remember it as that.'

It was so strange how my reply, indulging a rare moment of superiority in the tricky area of sexual relations, seemed to satisfy him. We kissed on both cheeks, scribbled e-mail addresses, even mobile phone numbers, and promised to look each other up should we pass the other's part of the world. Another smile, another goodbye and good luck for what tomorrow would bring, and we headed off in separate directions, as if we had just shared a very regular twenty-four hours in Iraty.

13 CHANGING FORTUNES

A dog barks from inside one of the holiday chalets, as twigs on the pine forest floor snap under my boots. It is overcast and barely light. Birdsong is the only other sign of life to have woken up. My heavy breathing and heart rate jar with the stillness. I persevere upwards, my compass dangling from my neck, and route committed to memory. The path should level off and start to bend before steepening up the northern flanks of Pic D'Orhy.

The path opens up above the tree line and a thin blanket of fog is blown towards me by a steady breeze. Sheep droppings and cowpat decorate the slope. Tinkling bells can be heard in the smoky distance long before sheep come into view. I check my altimeter and compass. Another two hundred metres before the ridge bears left, south-east. My senses are fully alert from the poor visibility and being alone. There's enough of a drop here to sprain my ankle should I stumble; not a serious injury perhaps, but it would put an end to my adventure. I must pay attention to my feet and where I place them, at all times.

I run into a herd of goats every bit as surprised as I am. Some bolt into the gloom but the rest of the flock stares at me suspiciously, as if to consider their unlikely visitor. I wonder whether it's right to be here – in a murky universe all the more alien as the valley below sleeps on. It would be easy to get lost in the limestone, maybe even disappear for days before being found. After all, no one, apart from Chris, knows I'm here. Would someone more experienced carry on or regard this as stupid? A denser cloud of fog swirling across the slope answers for me. To continue would be reckless. No matter – this is only my first foray off the beaten track and it's been instructive. To rely on myself alone for the first time was always going to be uncomfortable – but it would be foolhardy to ignore my misgivings about the weather. Next time, the conditions will be right.

Being on tarmac feels like a setback. At least there can be no doubt that it leads to Larrau, where I can pick up another track and rejoin the ridge further along should the weather clear. Immediately I'm cheered by having options. A car speeds past and I wonder if it'll stop at the boards promoting the griffon lookout. Not much to see today either. I wonder how Chris will remember the surprising twist of our goodbye. Hundreds of sheep are crossing the road ahead towards an open gate, tapped along by a farmer with a stick who's making strange throaty sounds. As I draw nearer, I answer his 'bonjour' with a hearty 'bonjour – salut!' These are my first words of the day. He asks me where I'm heading and I ask how far it is to Larrau. Another hour, he says. As we wait for the flock to settle, I mention the fog and how it turned me back from the ridge.

The man is slightly shorter than me and with his ruddy cheeks and windswept hair looks as much a part of the landscape as his sheep. We gaze silently at the sheep dawdling across. He then motions me to follow him towards his tractor to give me a lift. The offer is abrupt and seems out of place. Instinctively I decline, deciding in an instant to press on. He is immediately agitated; my refusal is a rebuff to him. His face now pinched, he points emphatically at the tractor. I thank him again, point down the road and start to walk. He is angry now and hurries alongside me shouting. I stop to express my surprise and his eyes narrow. This makes me uncomfortable, enough to shout 'Non!' as, to my horror, his hand moves abruptly towards his flies. Surely I can't be flashed at again?

'Non!' I'm surprised by the force of my voice, loud with anger.

I storm off and only turn around a minute later to check he's not following me. The man's been shrivelled by the distance but I can hear him shouting still as he prods the last sheep through the gate. He clenches his fist at me, confirming my suspicion he was excited, overwrought even, by the rare early morning vision of a lone woman walker.

I plod alongside hedgerow consoling myself with thoughts of a café breakfast ahead when I remember the Oscar Wilde line, so easily paraphrased for this unlikely encounter few would believe: ' … once may be regarded as a misfortune; twice looks like carelessness.'

■   ■   ■

The top of Pic d'Arlas overlooks a lunarscape of limestone karst, marking the end of Basque country and the border with Spain. Its porous whiteness has an otherworld quality, with its harsh, churned-up mass of irregular, perforated, milky-white sculptures. This is bewitching landscape, beautiful as well as deadly. Water will be hard to find. Even at 2,000m (6,562ft) the distinctive profiles of the higher mountains dominate the horizon. The hurdle is to navigate towards them through a maze of rat runs and infinite choice of passages. Day-trippers appear as if from nowhere, rounding a corner between two boulders resembling giant grey honeycombs. Stubbly pines somehow grow from the desiccated ground. There is a new sound to the ear – Spanish. Even the style of passing hikers looks a little different; the odd glimpse of Latin glamour like a fur-lined glove dangling from a daypack, darker eyes, and olive skin.

Pic d'Anie looks impressive as the towering landmark at the boundary where the Occidental Pyrenees end and the Haute Pyrenees begin. It crosses my mind to climb it next. The sun is hot, rather too uncomfortable for quick scrambling. I open a can of olives and try to get comfortable on some limestone while deciding whether to make a dash for it. A network of passageways runs underneath me, one of Europe's biggest cave systems. I have never been attracted to being inside the musty earth, preferring instinctively the freedom of the open air.

Right now the air is close and dry, as if it's worn itself out. Only a storm will clear it. A breeze stirs through the stone channels and I notice the fluffy patterns of new cumulus clouds. The few hikers who walk by are relaxed, in shorts mostly. There is a sense of late-summer leisure, as you'd expect for an August Saturday. I check my waterproof gear is at the top of my pack, knowing how early afternoon storms can strike at this time of year in the higher mountains. It's startling how quickly mountain environments can change. Within minutes, the skies turn from bright blue to grey, from light to shadow. I press on.

By nightfall my plan is to be as close as possible to Lescun, where I can stock up on provisions. The wind is picking up all the time and passing walkers are moving more purposefully now, sensing the urgency of darkening skies. This already barren place seems all the more desolate as it empties of people. The grey is more like an angry front now. The clouds are thicker and blacker and pushing up against the nearby peaks. A faint groan of distant thunder makes me stop to put on the waterproof layers, before heading further into the limestone mass. Like a tap turning, the skies start to pour rain. I huddle against an overhang and watch the spectacle. Amazingly thirsty, I gulp a whole litre of water. Lightning forks across the sky but doesn't last long; the thunder becomes more dramatic and louder as the storm gets closer.

The worst of the storm passes and as the rain thins, I set off into the heart of the limestone mass. There is no one else about. In winter La Pierre St Martin is a ski resort; in summer, it is hauntingly deserted. Large concrete hotels look abandoned, after the life in them in them stopped on the last day of thaw. The slopes bulldozed into the mountain are like scars. The rain stops and I take off my kit, the sky already clearing. There is no trace of the initial deluge, except scattered damp patches of darkened soil. My excitement to be making progress is tempered by the ghostliness of the environment. A ski lift creaks above, stirred by the breeze, the only movement apart from mine. I pass a simple wooden hut that might be for seasonal workers and peer through its window. A family is sitting around a table, with a candle burning in its middle and an open bottle of wine. No one notices me. The dryness and rapidly growing heat remind me of my own thirst and make me crave water. Just over a litre left. I follow cairns through the limestone, reassured by them. Time passes as I head east, set on the forest before Lescun, still four hours away.

It is dramatic scenery: wild, dry and remote. I have never seen anywhere like it. Out of the scree and sheer white faces, bright blue and purple flowers have managed to live. Lone pine trees also break up the vast area of rock and stone. My lightweight backpack offers no support and grinds me down so that I have to work harder. All this movement in the dry heat is making me fixate on water – I only have half a litre left and could easily down the lot in four greedy gulps. This needs to be rationed. Looking at the map there are water sources but they might be two, maybe three hours ahead, where the terrain becomes a mix of pasture and forest. There are also two huts marked that are bound to be near water, but it's hard to gauge distance and I am inching my way across the map more slowly than my conservative forecasts.

Already an age seems to have past since last night in St Engrace, nestled in its cosy valley beneath the Spanish border. The rural enclave is the Eastern point of Basque country, and its lush greens and eleventh-century Romanesque church are so hard to recall now, like the remote comforts of a fading dream. For nearly a thousand years, those heavily buttressed walls have withstood rigorous weathering. I'm already jaded after a few hours of it.

For no reason at all I look up, distracted from my growing self-pity. For the first time it dawns on me how the rocky landscape is softening. I notice a big granite boulder balanced on the edge of the sheep track. It's unusually shaped with a depressed middle, like a cake that couldn't quite rise. Something makes me walk over to it – an instinct to investigate its concave dip. I am greeted by a basin of fresh rainfall, gouged by numberless storms and containing just enough to quench my thirst. Chance is an extraordinary thing when loaded with luck, promising help. The land seems to have otherwise absorbed every drop of moisture. I could easily have walked past unaware, lost in chattering thought. I am able to fill my mug twice and the taste is fresh and perfect. The lichen lining the rock's hole is an inspiring statement on the stubbornness of life to thrive in challenging circumstances. I celebrate providence with a rest, to bask in the delightful relief of nature's cure.

Emboldened, I press on east. There should be a river soon, well before the forest above Lescun. The land is wild and rocky still but is blending with the more hospitable shades of green. Lower down, a small wooden hut enclosed in a sheep's pen seems to beckon to me, and I step up my pace. A scrap of slate is propped against its entrance. 'Fromage à vendre. 6 euros' is written in chalk. I wonder how much trade there can be in this valley, accessible from Lescun but so isolated in principle. The door is ajar. I shout a 'bonjour' but there is no answer. Instead, I hear shuffling and the thud of feet on wood. A young man with a rosy, rugged face, steps out into the light, looking a little surprised. I point to the sign and ask if there really is cheese to buy.

'Oui. Five hundred grams – six euros.'

A supper of tinned lentils, bread, and tomatoes would be greatly enhanced by a fresh chunk of cheese and so I ask for some. He disappears through the wide-open door into a chaos of rusting tins and tools, clothes strewn about and a plate of half-eaten food. He comes back with an old set of scales and collection of weights. I find out he's been on his own for the summer. There was another man who left a few weeks ago. No, he doesn't mind being here by himself at all and did I get caught in the storm? No sooner do I answer than he hurries off, returning with a large triangle of cheese and some wire to cut it.

'That is a little over. Six euros and … let's call it fifty.'

His self-assurance and feel for straight dealing is impressive. There's no suggestion that fifty cents worth of extra cheese will be thrown in, as a kind gesture to a lone passer-by, the first in several days, he tells me. I rifle about for some money, only a twenty-euro note and a few coins, and look up at him apologetically. He is not fazed in any way and could I 'just wait a moment please?' He reappears with a wad of notes and then sifts through a handful of coppery coins as he counts the change. Not quite fifty – forty-three? In faltering French, I tell him the cheese is easily worth the extra seven cents. His sunny smile reveals that he is equally happy with our arrangement. Unable to resist, I break a piece and assure him it is delicious. With that, I wish him well in his 'little hut' and he urges me to take great care in the storms – there is nearly one a day at this time of year. Apparently the woods are no more than half an hour away – 'just follow the stream'.

I head deep into the woods and look about for somewhere suitable to camp. An overgrown trail leads past a giant boulder covered in chalk handprints and onto a flat grassy clearing either side of a meandering river. Its jutting rocks amplify the whooshing melody of flowing water. It wouldn't be possible to imagine such a perfect setting, one blanketed in daisies and pink clover. A simple wooden bridge delivers an easy passage to the other side, bordered by drooping trees and their beards. There'll be no visitors trampling through here now as the sun starts to sink. The bivvy pitched, I assemble my food next to the river, eager to polish off the cheese. A milky silhouette of the limestone mountains overlooks this treasure of a scene. My first outing through the higher mountains has been rewarded with surprise gifts. The cheese tastes even tangier with slices of apple.

I yawn and stretch as I think of bed. As the light fades, zipped up in the bivvy's mosquito net, I am no longer bothered by the sounds of the night that Philippe had taught me not to fear. I think back to the many moments that have made this day so memorable, as one of changing fortunes.

14 THE GOSSIP OF LESCUN

'Oui, oui, oui. Absolument là. Dans les bois en-haut. C'est absolument vrai!' At the other end of the village hall, a grey-haired man and middle-aged couple look enthralled by what they've heard. After a moment's silence, the animated voice of a woman, whose back is turned, starts up again. The old man stares in disbelief, frowns, and says something. The little group is too involved with the conversation to notice me watching them. The narrator, confident of their whole attention, and unaware she has won mine, adds another 'Oui!' for emphasis. Pause. A shake of the old man's head, then the retort: 'Non, C'est pas vrai, non!' The other two look at the woman, to see what she will have to say next.

I turn towards the framed exhibits, the photographic legacy of Lescun's mountaineering past. The climbing pioneers of this valley stare into the lens, as if to meet the gaze of those who will one day behold them. The heavy wooden ice axes and stiff coiled ropes are captured in a time when danger and discomfort were necessary sacrifices for exploration and discovery. The pre-Gore-Tex age is filled with figures in tweed and cravats, warming whiskers of facial hair and improbable ankle-length skirts worn by the women. Yet there seems an interchangeable chemistry between then and now. It is easy to recognise the courage it must have taken to roam and scramble about unchartered heights with their popular associations of dragons and the supernatural.

I feel a rush of excitement at our shared experience. Those rugged faces chiselled with purpose were also drawn to the limestone world above Lescun. These mountaineers couldn't draw on the experience of history and so played a defining role in an evolving sport. They branded their knowledge of the Pyrenees – this often overlooked mountain range – dwarfed in reputation by the grander scale of the older Alps. To think that these men and women on top of their snowy summits defied danger as they pursued their calling to be up high, setting off into the unknown landscape. What spirit to act on the drive to be the first to see, the first to tread!

The perfectly preserved medieval village with its cobbled streets is towered over by its famous limestone buttress, the Lescun Cirque. I had staggered in exhausted, hungry, and unwashed. My arrival had felt like a homecoming. It had taken far longer to descend from the top of the wooded valley than it had seemed on the map. I had slept restlessly, waking up to lively nocturnal noises and struggling with childhood associations of woods and witches. Reading distracted me briefly until I imagined how visible my head torch must be to curious eyes peering out from the dark. My fear seems so indulgent and stupid now in the warmth of electric light and other people.

The woman's voice starts to rise and fall again, making me aware that I'd been staring vacantly at the exhibit in front.

'Toute seule? Une femme vous-dites? *Une*?' The old man asks, as if he can't accept the information being relayed to him.

'Oui, *une* femme, oui.'

'Et où sont les bois exactement?'

The raconteuse has shifted position, enabling me to observe she's middle-aged with a badge pinned to her white shirt that reads 'Assistante'. I notice her glasses attached to the chain around her neck and suddenly recognise her. I had met her a few hours before while waiting, bedraggled, for a *gîte* to open, yearning for hot water, a filling meal and a bed. Elegant and fragrant beside me, the woman was waiting to pick up keys from the *gîte's* owner to open the exhibition for the afternoon. We whiled away an hour in simple, slow French, sheltering from the noon heat under a chestnut tree. The murmur of courteous conversation among a queue of villagers at a mobile grocery carried over to our spot. Weekly supplies of plump, ripe produce were loaded into an array of bags, overflowing with groceries. I had been grateful for the conversation and indulged the woman's curiosity about my walk across these mountains from end to end. I enjoyed her exaggerated responses as she paid close attention to my story, as if she herself was experiencing the horrifying sounds that had kept me from sleeping. She had been an excellent listener.

The woman continues to command the obedient attention of her audience. Straining to overhear, only key words stand out in the stream of monologue, but the pointing helps me to fill in the gaps. Woods, bridge, river, path, two-hour ascent from Lescun. What a coincidence – I have also encountered these very things – in the last twenty-four hours. And then it dawns that she can only be talking about me, recounting almost word for word what I must have told her. Her wide open eyes and singsong voice, now reduced to a whisper, are vividly reproducing the fear I must have conveyed to her – only with infinitely more drama and immediacy it seems, than my earlier account.

I glance back at the photographs – this time less absorbed. If she spots me, I might be summoned over to convince the sceptical man shaking his head and I'm too tired for that. I head for the door, thinking about burrowing down in the *gîte*, another anonymous guest. The woman smiles as any stranger might and bids me a good day. Amazingly, I haven't been recognised. My washed appearance and change of clothes have transformed me from an unusual solitary walker into someone ordinary. As I open the door, I hear an 'incroyable!'. Crossing the street, I repeat the 'incroyable' in the same startled way as the doubter, amused at how a chance meeting had made me, however fleetingly, the *cause célèbre* of Lescun.

15 FOLLY AND DANGER

It is a prime moment to sit and marvel. The Pyrenees National Park opens up like an amphitheatre, an expanse of jagged peaks and their valleys, a confusion of greys and greens To the right, the softer undulations of the Basque hills; in front, flashes of desert starkness. The allure of Spain's more savage landscape is in its contrasting bleakness. To my left, the impressive M-shaped form of Pic du Midi D'Ossau and beyond it a clear run of the direction to explore in the weeks ahead – around three hundred and fifty kilometres as the crow flies. It'll be a lot further underfoot, as the route traverses the relief of the valley contours; a continual pattern of up and down, day after day.

I head southwards on a grassy ridge skimming the Spanish border. Maintaining 2,000 metres, there is a boundless feeling of height and uninter-rupted space. The views have been inspiring all morning, and the winding climb out of Lescun was eventful. A couple of marmots emerged from their rocky hideaway for some fresh air and tussled playfully, for a moment unfazed by the heavy tread of their uninvited visitor. I follow the natural curve of the ridge, looking out for the easiest descent south-east into a rugged cirque of rocks, zigzagging a way through cliffs and then a glade before reaching a tiny valley to camp.

A darkening belt of clouds is getting closer, promising rain. But I'm more concerned by bursts of lightning flashing towards me. I check the map and take a bearing. This is no place to get caught out. Birds start to dart about, agitated, sensing a brewing storm. I follow the gentle curve and notice a couple of vultures soaring overhead. Their presence, just as the light takes on a yellowy green hue, feels hostile. I'm close to a jog, wanting to get well away from the ridge, expecting to encounter the band of rock, my exit route to shelter and safety. Just ahead the grassy slope stops abruptly. I edge up to it gingerly and peer over a forty-foot-high cliff, a fall which could probably kill me. Is this the Banasse Cirque? Veron might have warned of how suddenly it appears – this is dangerous territory. I want to take stock and look at the map, thoroughly go over it, but the thick black skies and forked lightning, getting closer every minute, are making me impatient to find a way down.

The prospects immediately to the right are hazardous. The rock looks impregnable, needing a rope for a safe scramble down it. To the left, more of the same, although less steep, dropping to a slope of stunted, gnarled pines, bent by their exposure to the wind; perhaps the most possible of all the unappealing options. Drops of rain fall, warning of downpour. I'm in my waterproof gear and press against a wall of overhanging rock for some shelter, to look at the map. I feel cornered here – unable to envisage how to continue to the valley floor. It crosses my mind to dash back the way I've come and find another way. But the thought of being on the ridge as lightning strikes keeps me put. I've heard that a dozen die every year in the Pyrenees from lightning strikes but have no idea whether that surprisingly high figure is reliable. Nonetheless, electric storms have been a nagging concern – what a foolish way to die; so unlucky and so final.

It's a calming distraction to plot Veron's instructions against the map and try to recall exactly how I got here. Follow the track from the hut as it bends around a spur. Yes. Did I miss a turning to the south-east? Not sure. The compass steered me around the spur and I then followed the natural fall of the slope to arrive at this point. So far so good. OK, look around. Relate the features to the map. Valley with a river running through it. Yes. A band of rock that could be called a cirque? Yes. The map is Spanish and doesn't have the same detail as the French IGN maps I've relied on until now but it fits the general picture. My eyes fall on a narrow sheep track running through the bracken and rocks, on the least severe slope.

The rain's stopped. Only the tail of the storm skimmed by and it's already moved further west. I lever myself over a nine-foot-high cliff and slowly trust my grip on its small jutting rocks. Balanced on a grassy ledge, I assess the safest line of descent; a scramble down a funnel of rocks that look unnervingly loose, probably a dried-out waterfall. I should really turn back, but I am committed. The air is a lot cooler and overcast – the risk from lightning long since past. I devote myself completely to the next rock down, checking it is truly secure before risking all my weight on it.

Progress is slow. It requires an unusual exertion of strength to balance every step. I never find a rhythm and labour on, trying not to think about the greater distance ahead. The sound of clapping stones breaks my concentration and I look up. A rock is bouncing down the chute towards me, like a missile gaining speed, chipping away a trail of small fragments. Louder and louder, it looms larger and larger. Instinctively I press against the boulder and cower into it. The rock plummets past my head and smashes into the next bulge lower down, splintering on impact. The High Level Route guide mentions nothing about the only descent down being a steep, dried waterfall, to be attempted only in climbing shoes with a lightweight pack. Here I am, in sturdy boots with a twenty-kilo backpack, lurching with every move, my balance dislodged with every tentative attempt at safe lowering.

Far below a hopeful shade of green with grazing sheep teases me towards it. The river ploughing through the valley would be the surest and quickest way down. But I will have to reach it first. I leave the waterfall and fight my way along a tangle of tightly bunched trees whose bristly branches scratch right through my trousers. Their roots are wispy and shallow but no less menacing for that. My backpack has to be wrestled free every time it becomes ensnared. This is bushwhacking of the most demanding order and my ankles continually give way as I edge along the steep ground. Only when it levels a little and the trees thin, do I allow myself to see what I've done. From here, the waterfall is impossibly steep, the rocks too sheer to climb down. Higher up, the thick buttress of rock shines, slippery smooth. To attempt it with a heavy pack and without rope would be suicide. It's pointless to look at the map again. My eyes won't spot the point at which I went so disastrously off route.

A dog scurries about far below, rounding up sheep. Its owner is a tiny speck that disappears into a hut, from which billows a cheerful cloud of wood smoke. I move faster. The dog barks as it spots me getting closer. It bounds up to me a little too energetically. It is only now I realise my nerves are shattered. I can't see anything through the hut's misty windows and I remember I'm here on my own, on someone else's ground. Worry spreads through me, an overwhelming panic. What am I doing here – how have I gone so far wrong?

Hesitantly, I rap on the door and a man in a tattered tweed jacket steps out, sucking on a rolled-up cigarette. I hold up my map and ask if he could confirm where we are. He nods willingly and beckons me in, motioning how cold it's become outside. I shake my head and say I am in a hurry. I'd be grateful if he could show me right here. A woman's voice calls out from behind the door in a dialect I don't recognise. Reassured, knowing there's nothing to fear now, I step into the warmth.

Through the dense cigarette smoke, the three of us scan the map. The woman disagrees with her companion's faltering assessment of where we are and moves his dirty finger from the mass of brown and green squiggles as he tries to settle on a location. The ash of her cigarette falls on the map, which she ignores. I wonder whether to blow it off but don't want to seem uptight.

'Non, non. Pas là … ici, oui. Je crois nous sommes … là. Oui, juste là.' Her declaration is hard to accept. She must be wrong.

'Non, c'est pas possible, madame.'

This bats to and fro a couple of times but she stands her ground. We stand in stubborn silence, while the man's eyes rest on the map. Finally, he settles the matter, nodding as he does so. 'Oui, là! C'est vrai.'

I am in the wrong valley, north-east of where I should be. How did I manage that? I must have overshot the turn to descend and by continuing for a lethal few minutes, I veered off course by more than ninety degrees. Inevitably, the relief of the land and its curving fall line compounded the deviation. The severity of this mistake is hard to grasp. How can I trust myself now? When will I be certain of any decision again? This is a major setback, the consequences of which will have to be worked through.

The couple see how unsettled I am and suggest a hot drink before I find somewhere around here to camp. We all smile at this – there are certainly acres of wild space to choose from. I turn down their kind offer, needing to walk off my tension. The man can accompany me out of the valley, as he's heading that way with his mule to shop for supplies. Thanks, but I will press on. They advise climbing over the pass and dropping into the valley I should now be in – only three hours of work, no more. I can't bear the thought of trying to correct a broken journey. Instead I will see where this surprise new turning leads.

Humbled, I wave back at them a final time as I follow the river in the remaining light of a blustery evening. It weaves between steep hills of bracken and boulders. Not for the first time, I'm reminded of Scotland and the bleak drama of the Highlands. The path drops through trees and into fog. Somewhere below, a dog barks; another joins in, restless. Eventually I hit a lane that bends its way down the valley past the occasional house. Wood smoke sits heavily in the thick damp.

The assurance of repeated 'S' turns enables me to switch off. The border village of Urdos is at the bottom and being on autopilot will get me there just as quickly. Round and round again. Somehow, an ankle gives and I trip, rolling down the hill until I stop abruptly, sticks in hand. Too stunned to move, I watch the blood seeping out of my right knee. The palm of my right hand is scuffed, dirt and loose chips of stones hanging from shredded skin. Nothing is broken, only stinging. One of the aluminium sticks is bent but still functional. I don't have the energy to cry. I just want to reach Urdos. Only a warm meal and cosy bed will dictate how I look back on the day, as one of luck or misfortune.

A railway appears through the clearing fog far below – my new target. Once there, I cross over the track to a deserted platform. A cheerless Victorian building with gothic turrets of heavy red brick has a cement placard that reads 'Station Master', reminiscent of more prosperous days when the windows weren't broken. Old warehouses and mounds of gravel sprawl along the tracks. The station is on the edge of town. The main road leads me for another mile past an uninviting campsite, with its poor roadside location, lorded over by mist-shrouded mountains. To stay here would be miserable. Ten minutes further on, I am in the heart of Urdos, with a ribbon of unmemorable houses and closed businesses either side of its one road.

I head for the first hotel I can see, full of the transient trade shuttling between France and Spain. After a bath, I order a *vin chaud* and a bowl of soup and gaze vacantly at a beige wall. Memories of projectile rock, vultures and stormy skies project across my frozen vision. A second glass of wine arrives. Tomorrow is a new start, alert to the hazards of changeable weather and hurried, sloppy route finding, where the ridges will lead me further east on the long trudge home.

PART 4 LONDON AMERICA

16 GATEWAY TO CHANGE: SPRING 2005

Fired up by the feel-good tunes blasting from the loudspeakers and buoyed by another bear hug from a warm-hearted stranger, anything seemed possible, nothing off limits. The giant screens filling the east London arena zoomed in on the radiant smiles of the energised crowd. Some were tearful, everyone undoubtedly moved. This was the second day in the Docklands, immersed in positive thinking. Thousands here had demonstrated that temperatures of 1,000°F couldn't scorch their bare feet if they chanted 'cool moss' over and over. Nearly everyone had wrestled with the instinct not to take part in an eight-second fire walk. In the end, they'd chosen to believe their charismatic guru, roaring from the spotlit stage in his Californian accent, that they 'really could do it'.

Showmanship is a powerful force when combined with conviction. So what might happen next? Most in the stadium were buzzing with thoughts of change – breaking ties and making new ones. As the weekend slipped by, the drive to reinvigorate dull lives and tired relationships became almost bellicose – futures are going to get brighter, damn it, starting now! The rallying cry of mass resolve would help others make more subtle tweaks to their life's direction, which, over time, could shape a very different path. For me, after months of dreaming, a future of boundless horizons and snowy peaks was emerging.

Scouring an atlas of the world's wilderness areas, I was drawn to spend a summer in Alaska, a month in the Pacific North-West at mountaineering school, then a winter in New Zealand to develop snow and ice skills, followed by consolidation in the Himalayas of north India. The more I planned, the more I discovered how a vision of the world barraged since childhood, by the media, upbringing and education, had begun to stale. Why was pension-saving certainty a good thing and what if one of life's random elements blew the whole effort off course? As the housing boom continued to promote mortgages and notional ladders, the idea of four walls defining lifestyle parameters seemed increasingly confining. And it wasn't just me. People everywhere were achieving their rigorously defined goals, only to be disappointed at the finishing line. There were plenty of others who wanted to challenge the benchmark for a contented existence. Perhaps I could share my experiences at a later date, combine my passions for high places and working with stories, to help and inspire others rewrite their own scripts. There was only one way to find out.

■   ■   ■

Queuing at a transit counter at Chicago's O'Hare Airport, nothing was going to ruffle me, despite only having half an hour in which to make my connection to Alaska. Rigorous immigration screening for passengers heading to somewhere else were part of the post 9:11 world and travel through America was bound to be time-consuming. It had already taken two hours to have my passport looked at by a glum customs official, after being escorted by armed officers to the back of a long line of 'aliens'. Queue jumping to make a tight connection wasn't tolerated. It simply didn't matter to me, though. My eye was only on the world's mountain ranges and a flexible timescale to visit them. I was no longer on the BBC payroll with an obligation to fulfil anyone's expectations. Eighteen months after returning from the Pyrenees, I had been working towards a freer future. Now the landscape of my world was really changing.

'Excuse me, ma'am. Ma'am?'

A grey uniform with a cap was ushering me to the next available desk, dominated by the ample form of 'Mary'. Crowned by a pageboy haircut, her tidy brown eyes blinked sympathetically through John Lennon glasses. Mary was one of the countless personnel in an anthill structure operating America's vast service machinery. Between terminals I'd already been overwhelmed by market researchers, dodged industrial cleaning devices bent on mowing me down, porters and food sellers, all programmed to bark 'you're welcome' on the cue of being thanked.

'Hello. And where are you heading next please?'

Her singsong voice ended in an apologetic laugh. After frowning at her computer screen and 'aha-ing' every so often, Mary informed me there was no way I would make it to Anchorage that day. 'Aha … oh dear, oh dear. Nope. It's not going to happen. Is it, Melvin?'

Her neighbour Melvin, looking unflustered and capable in a shiny well-cut suit, was going places Mary wasn't and he knew it. 'Give me a moment, Mary. I'll be right there.' Melvin handed over some newly issued tickets and grinned as he bid his customers, 'have a nice day'.

'Please just hold tight,' she asked of me and laughed again apologetically.

'OK. Let's see what we have here. And where are you going, please ma'am?'

'Anchorage via Seattle.'

Melvin was leaning over Mary's shoulder and pressed a couple of keys as they both stared at the screen in front.

'Mmm. Yes, you've certainly missed your flight. It's boarding now and the gate's closing. But I'm confident we can get you there by tonight. Try Denver, Mary. See if you can fit this lady on the plane leaving in an hour but check the transit time onto Anchorage.'

'Nice one Melvin, will do. And thank you.' As Mary laughed, relieved at her colleague's reassurance, I resolved to be her most compliant customer to date. Minutes passed as frowns and sighs, shakes of the head, and nervous glances at Melvin resulted in handing over my passport for Mary to check once again.

'Melvin? So sorry Melvin … would you mind … '

'What can I do for you, Mary?'

'Can you just check this works … sorry ma'am, your patience is appreciated.'

'Let's see … no. That doesn't work. See that symbol there? That shows the flight is full. Try the next, leaving at seventeen hundred hours.'

The process repeated itself.

'OK. We're making progress here,' she said unconvincingly, her voice filled with doubt.

Weary after hours of standing without food or drink, I decided to speak to Mary in a language she would understand. 'It's been at least five, six hours since I last ate. Do you have compensation snacks for people in my position?'

Now this was something Mary knew about. Taking off her specs, she grabbed my passport to identify this underfed passenger. 'My, Margaret. You must be starving! I can give you fifteen bucks-worth but please make sure you spend every last cent. There will be no change or refund.' She then proceeded to give me the catering layout of the airport and its highlights, while the clock ticked on, and I got no closer to a new ticket.

'Now, this really is wonderful. You are lucky, Margaret. Oh yes. I can see there is a cancellation and I'll be able to put you on the next flight to Denver. You then proceed straight to the gate for Anchorage. You will be there … now, let me check Alaskan time … two-thirty – just two hours after you would have arrived.'

Melvin glanced up and asked if we needed any final help before he clocked off.

'No sir,' beamed Mary. 'We're in business here!'

We waited for my new tickets to print, while Mary told me I had the 'patience of Job' and was 'worthy of a medal.' Walking off, I felt moved having spent so long in the incompetent hands of Mary – who had tried her hardest to help me. My tedious wait had been a highlight in her day, where long hours are counted and endured until its end, when I imagine the solace of a large comforting meal can finally be enjoyed.

I never did make it to Alaska that day. The turnaround time to connect from Denver to Anchorage was impossible – as the plane would have left thirty minutes before the Chicago flight arrived. After hauling my heavy bag of mountaineering hardware along terminal corridors all over again, I queued once more to be told all Alaska-bound options had been squarely missed for the day. But, newly armed with three meal vouchers, I planned to drink a toast to Mary in my hotel room at the earliest opportunity. Nothing was going to stop me enjoying my first twenty-four hours in North America. Even if it was to be spent in an airport compound.

■   ■   ■

Alaska, America's forty-ninth state, seemed even more alluring and separate from the 'lower forty-eight', after a battering journey to reach its sub-Arctic boundaries. Being frogmarched off a plane on the Denver runway by mechanics dealing with a sudden 'navigational systems breakdown' only added to its snow-white magnetism. Alaska was the vista of Jack London adventure stories, of lawlessness and refuge. The absence of federal tax and a state dividend for every resident from the oil boom profits of the 1980s enhanced its maverick appeal. The struggle to reach the rolling tundra and icy wastes, the glaciated barriers to a universe of altitude and danger, made the eventual arrival all the sweeter. This was hallowed ground where resourcefulness, not money, was necessary for quality of life. Alaskans understand how to work their world and the values needed to thrive in it. I expected to encounter people who would hole themselves up for months at a time, miles from the nearest home or road head, who knew the secrets of survival. The forty-ninth state is famed for its ratio of one woman to three men, as home to one of the world's densest populations of bachelors. More than once I was told, 'Oh Alaska? The odds are good for you. Boy, but the goods are odd!'

Its spirit could not have been better introduced than by Andy, the owner of a guesthouse I'd found on the Internet, and his network of offbeat associates. He met me at the airport around midnight, his hair a bush of unkempt curls. Police officers had been eyeing up his suspiciously unroadworthy-looking vehicle parked in front of the exit as I walked out, not imagining for a moment this was waiting for me. The beaten-up, rusting yellow Volkswagen, still with its winter chains, stalled every time he braked. Andy, a blues musician, tours during the long winter months and escapes to the sunny beaches of California, while his closed Alaskan business remains shrouded in dark. Much of his energy is diverted into fighting an oil multinational, set on buying up Inuit land for development in the north Arctic. The hunting ground of caribou and the traditions of the close-knit community of Kaktovik would be destroyed if the sale goes ahead.

The iron will of Shirley, Andy's housekeeper, manages his chaotic bachelor life. Looking far younger than her seventy-three years, with her neat perm a subtle shade of bottle brown, she has a penchant for pink slippers and a matching dressing gown rarely removed before noon. It was easy to warm to this fiercely independent woman, her bright eyes enlarged by oversized glasses, as she rattled off with a disarming forwardness her views about most matters, including her real opinions about certain guests. Her active mind generated a stream of new insights, always busy beneath her no-nonsense, capable persona. Her vivid memories of the blitz during her wartime childhood in east London still torment her. She can recall every detail of the day her parents didn't return home from a raid. After unhappy early teenage years in strict boarding schools, she emigrated to America, joining relatives who'd long since settled across the water. Over a second pot of tea, the highs and lows of her life discussed, she concluded that, two husbands on, heaven 'is a condo with a cat'.

Then there was George. He was my chaperone around downtown's more disreputable haunts. Tall, thin, and completely bald, he was on course to make the apparently giant leap from a successful oilfield engineer to a street performer. He hadn't worn a suit 'in years', despite his corporate employment, and on social outings opted for a bizarre combination of sleeveless T-shirts, waistcoats, and shorts. I met him through Andy in a dimly lit bar and marvelled that he could still see through his bright pink shades. He told me, while showing off his newly acquired balloon-contorting tricks that 'it's taken me fifty-four years to accept I'm kind of weird'.

Open and receptive, Anchorage and its colourful cast of characters felt like a homecoming, the perfect first stop for my unfolding odyssey. Late April is pre-season and so I was made particularly welcome as an early visitor before the invasion of high summer tourism. With the help of handmade maps of their 'must-see' places, I hired a car and took to the road. Heading south-west to the Kenai Peninsula, I sought out the turquoise world of the sea and its open horizon. In two weeks, I would be based in land-locked black rock, and frozen oceans of blinding white snow. The road trip passed through untouched land, with a raw sense of timeless age. The snow-capped mountains rising from pure water were like vast creases recently pushed out of the constricting earth. Such is the unscarred beauty that seems so pristine and new, time becomes impossible to really grasp. Looking at these landscapes is to behold the workings of the earth and its secrets, whose origins lie somewhere unreachable, far beyond man's grasp of how it all began.

Time and again I encountered memorable people in random places:

pavements and cafés, boats or pontoons. A whole host of free spirits demonstrated to me the infinitely varied ways to reinvention, as I began the long process of de-institutionalising myself. Mossy, a grandmother who in her late fifties or early sixties, had aged impressively, was one such influence. Staying in her state-famous seaside farm hostel in Homer, I met her as she piloted her giant tractor through pools of thick mud, sporting a red felt hat with drooping velvet flowers and a gapped-tooth grin. She bred wild birds and over the chugging motor hollered an invitation to join her the next day for a dawn breakfast and to meet her menagerie. She seemed to have an open house for anyone who cared to stay. A number of stray travellers would end up there, helping out for months on end and, in some cases, years. This alternative family of workers were part of the lively, shambolic fabric of the farm, with its roaming chickens and the thunder of crashing waves along the nearby shoreline.

Inside, where everyone lived, the building was a charming chaos of chipped objets d'art, alternative reading material on eco-science, and lampshades with charred holes. Time quickly ran out during my stay and I had to get back to Anchorage to meet up with the expedition party I would be climbing with for the next few weeks. There was a casual system of posting money through a letter box to settle the modest accommodation bill. I didn't have change and so set off to find Mossy to pay her direct. I hunted high and low, eventually finding one of her workers, a fit-looking man, not much older than thirty, hard at work digging. He had some smaller notes and agreed to pass on the money I owed to Mossy later. Just as I was about to say goodbye, I asked if he was going to stay at the farm the whole season?

'I guess so,' he replied, eyeing me up and down. 'After all I am Mossy's husband.'

17 ALASKAN HEIGHTS

The Otter weaves through a mass of snow-covered peaks and their icy faces. The whiteness glares through the Perspex windows, its beauty all the more alluring for its menace. Never before have I seen such brilliant scenery, as the perfect light of a freezing, sunny May day creates the unnerving illusion that these mountains are closer than they are. Behind us is the green contrast of the flat swampland around Talkeetna, a hub of life in otherwise untouched wilderness. Ahead, the infinite distance is crammed with jagged shapes, ensuring our isolation. It is this very isolation and exposure to climatic extremes that makes the Alaskan Range one of the most challenging mountaineering destinations on earth.

We soon get our first perfect view of Mount McKinley or Denali, its more commonly used native Athabascan name, meaning 'High One'. North America's highest peak towers above vast fields of icy, rocky tundra. Its granite and slate core is overlain with ice hundreds of feet thick. Even in summer, temperatures at its 20,320-ft summit (6,194m) are severe. We've equipped ourselves with every advantage of science for the alien challenge of climbing it. It can be stormy from early June, so we hope setting off at the colder start of the season, a month earlier, will mean more settled weather. Recent sunshine has triggered potentially deadly changes in the ice forms and there's evidence everywhere of snowmelt and avalanche, adding to objective dangers. We are told there has only been nine feet of fresh snow on the mountain since last year.

The pilot of the Otter, the workhorse of glacial air travel, cuts quite a presence in his cockpit. Despite his unkempt beard, jeans and trainers, Captain Doug Hayman commands authority over his rapt passengers. As we dip suddenly in an air pocket as white forms flash past, he warns us over the tannoy, 'Watch out, these things drop like rocks.' At sixty-five, Captain Hayman's CV is impressive. He climbed the ranks of the California Highway Patrol where he was regularly called out to the scenes of natural disasters. His speciality was earthquake responses, landing on the churned-up debris of suspension bridges and urban infrastructure. He still lives half the year in California, escaping the long dark winter. Ferrying mountaineers to and from Base Camp at Denali during the three-month season is his 'retirement job, like driving a taxi'. None of us are swallowing this effort at being casual, knowing it takes enormous skill to master the potentially deadly navigation through polar terrain and its weather systems.

One of us coughs into an open microphone attached to our headsets so we can communicate during the thirty-minute flight to the Kahiltna Glacier. The captain barks, 'Turn the darn mike off if you're gonna have a spasm like that. How come you've got one of those flying into Denali? Everyone comes down with one.' I want to know what altitude we're cruising at. Captain Hayman notices I'm adjusting my mike, about to say something. 'Just shout into the darn thing, like ordering your husband to take out the trash.'

At 10,000ft (3,048m), I notice other planes heading home, like red mosquitoes against the vast whiteness. They are so well maintained, accidents rarely happen through mechanical failure. During the summer, it's a round-the-clock job maintaining the fleets of Beavers and Otters. Talkeetna Airport is a blur of mechanics running in and out of the worn hangers and storage rooms, unchanged since they were built decades ago. Rusty scales are on hand to weigh the piles of expedition hardware. Calculating cargo limit is an exact science and the job of scribbling an item's weight on stickers seems staggeringly unsophisticated for such a serious enterprise. The air is a dense mix of diesel, oil and grease. The planes, burdened with climbing cargo, labour across the sky as parties are shuttled to and from Denali National Park.

It had taken hours of organising to clear the airport forecourt of mountains of food, kit, and every shade of backpack and bulging canvas sack. A couple of natural leaders were already emerging, knowing instinctively how to get things done, clambering over gear as they quickly saw the best ways to load everything into the waiting crafts. It was easy to spot the expedition extrovert, the loner, the joke-cracker with a ready smiling face, the thinker, the team players, the possible moaners. Like everyone else I had weighed up my companions in their expensive kit, wondering who would summit, who looked the most experienced.

Our focused efforts made light work of the morning, despite our having indulged the night before on an Anchorage diner's 'best homemade beer in the State'. Our party of nine men and two women had not taken this boast for granted, becoming increasingly vocal as the night wore on. The shift in spirits seemed quite a contrast from the polite laughter and awkward small talk of the strangers we had been. This was, after all, the social icebreaker, the chance for some group bonding, before familiarity would accelerate with each plodding step up Denali. Our three guides started the circle of introductions. Dylan, in charge, had already singled me out, having spotted my now dated BBC e-mail on the expedition form and was eager for details of war zones and celebrity. His eyes lit up as he looked at me to go next. Americans are so much more at ease with social forwardness and I admire them for that.

'Hi, I'm Mags, from the UK as you can probably tell from my accent. I've been in Alaska a couple of weeks and I just love this place.'

Everyone smiled supportively and I resolved to work on this gauche personal resumé. Next up were two Mormons, mid-quest to summit the highest peak in every American state. A helicopter pilot, on leave from Afghanistan and with a strong Southern accent, wanted some time 'to relax'. His reserved manner made it difficult to know whether he was joking. Earlier, I'd seen him hugging a stray dog – interestingly sentimental for someone hired for a cool head and impersonal reactions in times of pressure. The other woman in the group, a female firefighter from Seattle seemed sound, not saying a word more than she needed to. Her bobbed brown hair suited her unfussy, practical appearance. She surprised me by choosing a Martini cocktail, while the rest of us drank beer. Sitting next to her was a lawyer who'd once represented a group of Texan cattle farmers in a failed high-profile libel suit against a leading chat show host, and had a stream of self-deprecating stories that he told wittily. There was a Belgian pilot, in his late fifties, who regarded our expedition as a possible pre-Everest warm-up, and a rather wispy man with a flamboyant, handlebar moustache about to give up his thirty-a-day habit after the evening ended. As the night got hazier, it became clearer that in the tougher times ahead, there would be plenty of relief in this colourful mix.

The high spirits spilled into the sunny start of the next day. Well fed with waffles, synthetic cream, maple syrup, and bacon pancakes, we knew the 'carb-loading' comforts of the ample American breakfast would soon be remembered as even tastier, during a daily ritual of energy bars, gels, and freeze-dried alternatives. Photo-taking opportunities broke up the remaining journey to Talkeetna. This was the last civilised outpost on the fringes of thousands of square miles of unfolding wilderness, only accessible a hundred years before by river boats, mules and dog sleds.

We pulled up at a big retail park for a last chance to stock up on essentials like luxury snacks, batteries, and strong coffee. I was intent on buying a cotton bandanna. My guides had initiated me during a pre-departure talk into the intricacies of lavatorial hygiene. It seemed, as well as a funnel with a plastic tube and a requisite durable bottle designed for women, a cloth would also come in handy for the delicate procedure. To imagine having to leave the snug layers of down and armour myself against the icy night to go to the loo was too awful to contemplate – surely the extraordinary contraption had to be given a go?

The giant store was overrun with aisles and best-deal promotions dangling from the ceiling everywhere. Not sure where to start, I had walked up to a man in an orange shirt, who looked like he was about to stack shelves. As it happened, he didn't know where the bandannas were and so together we started to search. We scoured aisle after aisle, walking up and down and doubling back on ourselves. At last he spotted them tucked away behind domestic hardware. 'Thanks so much' I enthused, aware of his selfless effort in helping me. Just as he was about to walk off I asked where to find some freshly-squeezed orange juice. 'Just point the general direction,' I added. 'Er, I'm not sure lady,' the man replied. 'Let's ask someone who actually works here.'

■   ■   ■

Captain Hayman asks us to prepare for landing. He tells us to look down, where an improbable runway of snow carves into Kahiltna Gacier. A canvas village is neatly set up on the edge nearby. As the plane glides into the snow on skis, churning up a spray of whiteness, we look round at each other in mock disbelief. There has been nothing ordinary about our expedition so far. The engines are cut and for a few seconds there is silence. This icy wilderness and its raw, overpowering sense of isolation is hard to take in. One by one we jump off the craft into the soft, slushy snow and reach for the extended hand of Captain Doug Hayman. I look at the neighbouring mountain giants of Hunter and Foraker and try to scan possible routes to the top. I see a couple of perfectly formed 'S' tracks made by skis in the lower flanks of Foraker. Now I begin to accept we really are at Base Camp.

Planes purr through the skies to drop off supplies or take parties back to Talkeetna as we set up camp. On a clear afternoon like this, the glacier runway is busy. A minute after taking off, the small craft are swallowed up by the towering white forms past which they cruise. Mountaineers can be stranded here for days at a time in bad weather and most stash food, in case their return home is delayed. After a few weeks living on the snow, waiting in a fast-growing queue for the skies to clear would be a test of patience. There are only so many planes and weather windows.

We watch our three guides make light work of stamping a compact area for the tents. The exertion of adapting to life and movement on an unstable, changeable surface is immediately felt. Building a temporary home is demanding and will become a lot harder in the thinner air at altitude, especially after a long day of hauling sleds of gear and supplies up ever-steeper slopes. Every team member circulates the four shovels and does a spell digging. Constructing walls for wind shields and trenches to anchor the guy ropes will be crucial disciplines for the higher, more exposed camps. Expert demonstrations are given with snow saws and shovels on how to make perfectly formed ice bricks and the best way to clear tonnes of snow for ambitious kitchens and mess areas. It is extraordinary how creative you can be with such a versatile resource as snow. It is bound to be a false economy to conserve energy by a half-hearted effort at making camp. A well-organised space for cooking and eating inevitably keeps morale raised and makes the downtime outside a small, icy tent more comfortable. The kitchen is also the most important priority for a group, to get snow melting for hot drinks. Over the days we would design more elaborate layouts for benches and work surfaces and more fortified walls of snow bricks.

'Going to the bathroom', as my American companions insist on calling it, is one of the most unavoidably challenging aspects of being on a mountain. It's a wonderfully incongruous term for what amounts to a hole of ice, requiring the hit-and-miss effort of balancing on one's haunches in thick, doubled, plastic boots. Creating some sense of seclusion and dignity for such an inelegant event requires imagination. The higher up, the less slope space there is to share with the other parties in need of the same relief.

Initially, we're instructed to use a biodegradable bag for the more solid aspects and at 'all costs' pee somewhere else first. Those inexperienced in such intricacies will have to accept that this is far easier said than done. The bags are then thrown into the nearest crevasse. In the higher camps, all expeditions are issued with an exact number of CMCs or Clean Mountain Cans – plastic barrels just wide enough to crouch over but not big enough to conceal what has been before. The National Park Service instructs every team before heading off, 'what goes out up there must come down'. Hefty fines are levied at those who do not return with the amount of waste and rubbish expected to amass over a trip.

Negotiating with a CMC or biodegradable bag pales in comparison to the ruder challenge of the plastic funnel, which manufacturers claim is 'lightweight and discreet, designed to give women the freedom we deserve!' It is an operation that requires a receptacle that can then be emptied the next morning into a designated snow hole. Sharing a tent for the first time with Nancy, the Seattle firefighter, experimenting with the device is fraught with awkwardness. I wake up during the night, snug but uncomfortable, knowing sleep won't be possible without relieving myself first. It occurs to me this is not the best environment to risk an untried procedure like this and I look over at her restless form to check whether she's awake or just sleeping lightly. I whisper her name. No answer. Reaching for the components, I use the head torch to find a suitable area and clear anything vulnerably close in the event of mishap.

Rather like trying to give a sample at the doctor's, I struggle to relax and the freezing minutes tick by as the bottle remains empty and the crouching gets more uncomfortable. Just as I'm close, Nancy stirs. Another long wait and it finally happens. Relief is quickly tempered by the realisation the bottle is dangerously full. Without any practice it's hard to assess such matters. I soon learn the science of fluid capacity in a thoroughly time-consuming and disagreeable way.

18 DIGGING IN

We set off later than planned, under cobalt blue skies and an unforgiving sun. The reflecting whiteness would soon make punishing work of carrying loads to the next camp. After a first night on the snow, lessons have already been learnt – dismantling a camp needs to be as efficiently tackled as building it. Packing up gear in a cramped tent and chipping away at guy ropes and tent pegs frozen into the ice takes time. Establishing rope teams and a well-spaced system is not yet routine. The sleds have to be attached to the ropes at a comfortable distance from the hauler, to avoid knocking them out in the event of falling into a crevasse. Prusik knots, a mountaineer's lifeline to climb out of an icy chasm, need to be standardised as a team and tying them on an expedition's first morning is fiddly work.

These first hours are long, adapting to a heavy pack, at least twenty kilos, while hauling a sled which bangs into the back of one's boots on flatter stretches, rarely easing into a comfortable rhythm. Weight needs to be distributed so that most is carried on the back, supported by a tight hip belt. Hauling a sled is like pulling a dead load, so only the lightest gear should be strapped to it. Rope discipline is another consideration and will require daily attention – avoiding slack, without letting it tighten or pull at the person in front.

Perfect weather of bright light and piercingly clear visibility can never be taken for granted. We are sitting on the snow, as three adjacent rope teams, throwing salami sausage and cheese up the lines of hungry people. Snow geese flying across the horizon, displaying their powerful wingspans, are mesmerising and graceful against the backdrop of the white and black razor edges beckoning to be climbed. All of us chomp quietly, immersed in a quality of silence unique to icy terrain. A small, plump-breasted bird, that has been carried along on the back of a sled for the last hour, flies off but soon settles back again. It is one of hundreds we encounter on our way up the mountain, disorientated and hungry after their long winter flight. We barely notice imperceptible clouds thickening as the light flattens. The horizon of vast, jumbled ice blocks, known as seracs and the route to our next camp are soon obscured. Those more experienced who had the foresight to put storm gear at the top of their pack make light work of adding weatherproof layers. Others have to unpack, twisted in rope. These are useful moments, the necessary tweaks that make an expedition more comfortable. Applying more sun block, the rays just as much a hazard in overcast conditions, we set off again.

A wind starts to gust, stirring up wisps of snow from the slope, and flurries bear down on us as we resume our slow, steady plod. Barely twenty minutes pass and there is trouble. An expedition soon to be beset with unforeseen dramas begins to unwrap. Rick, craving tobacco after abruptly giving up his heavy habit, already needs to stop. At first he seems breathless, as most of us are, unused to dragging heavy loads uphill, and walking in weighty boots which sink into the snow with every tread. After a break, he tells us to carry on. Not long after he needs to stop again. One by one we shout the request up the rope to the guide at the front. This exhaustion is worrying for a day that will later be regarded as the easiest. The repeated stopping and starting makes slow, cold work of the way to camp.

We settle into the work of shovelling and stamping, wall building and tent erecting. Nancy quickly establishes herself as a tireless worker, as if each moment depends on her total commitment. She is surprisingly strong for her average build and is only a little taller than me, seeming thoroughly at home with rigorous, heavy labour. Generally, she impresses me with her straight, plain-talking style, lightened with plenty of dry wit. Together we establish a strenuous relay routine, which becomes harder to maintain in the weeks ahead. As soon as Rick's tent is up, he disappears and we don't see him until after supper. One of the guides takes a bowl of soup to him and returns with it barely touched. Dylan, Matt, and Dave, our three guides, talk quietly among themselves, in contrast to the banter and storytelling over the group meal.

Rick appears much later, pale and thoughtful, huddled in his duvet jacket, while the rest of us are warm enough in lighter kit. He stares quietly at the beautiful circle of mountains enclosing our camp in the fading light. He is going to see how he fares tomorrow before deciding whether to continue. Such a sudden development is surprising for a virgin group, still establishing itself and its personalities. Yesterday we shared a funny conversation about our choice of reading material for the trip and I mentioned the pocket-sized musings of Marcus Aurelius, who was Emperor of Rome at the height of its power. Perfectly partitioned into lists and chapters, his social insights and record of civic wheeling and dealing are entertainingly relevant, as well as readable, after a tiring trudge through snow. Rick couldn't stop laughing at my carefully considered choice, shedding his reserve in an instant. 'I think I'm going to like you, Mags. Marcus ... Aure ... ha ... ha ... ha ... lius. You're funny – very funny!'

His sincerity couldn't be doubted, as he howled and doubled over until he couldn't breathe, wheezing and coughing as more laughter tried to escape. I found myself joining in. Laughter can be so infectious, especially when sparked by something mundane. I walk over to him now, unsure whether his absorption is a sign he needs support or silence. Aware of unwittingly striking the right note the last time, I mention the Roman again, his questioning of why the mountains or sea are seen as the best means of escape. 'I think he might have a point, don't you Rick? He basically tells you that instead of investing all that energy and effort, use it more wisely by daydreaming instead!' A sombre response from the listener this time, who stares listlessly into the distance.

'Yup, you could say that … '

It's as if he wants to say something more and stops himself. The atmosphere has become charged and very serious. To walk off now, to respect his space, would not seem right. To say anything would be inappropriate. So we stand in silence for several minutes, scanning the mountains which glow a faint rose pink.

'You know, I've dreamt about this mountain for so many years. So many years I thought about this very moment. It's … it's like the end of a dream for me. I'm so tired.'

He can't be older than his mid-fifties. His hunched form looks so frail in this cold, unforgiving space. 'Just see how you go tomorrow. Life is too short to push yourself unless you think it's worth it.'

He blinks as he stares at the vast icy protrusion opposite us and nods slightly. Someone else walks over and it's a good moment to break away.

Tomorrow will be the first of the pyramid-style load carrying, where we leave camp intact and stash gear and food at a higher altitude before descending for a second night. The holes piled with gear are marked with colourful wands so they can be found again. This stages the loads and helps with acclimatisation. The atmosphere before retiring to our sleeping bags for the night is reflective. We are all aware of Rick as he heads for his tent, only saying 'goodnight' if it's been said to him.

I join Nancy, Steve, and his older friend Dennis, the two Mormons from Utah. They are hugely warm and likeable and rarely apart, except when on different rope teams. After the years they've spent in each other's company on fishing or mountaineering trips they are like a married unit, despite the fifteen-year age gap. They finish each other's sentences and wear their affection for each other so openly, that it's impossible not to treat them with a similar familiarity. Steve, solidly built and cuddly, has five children, four of them daughters, and a very handsome wife, his teenage sweetheart – he shows us a picture, which we pass around and admire. He tells us about his lumberyard which he's built up over the years.

Dennis, who resembles an older David Bowie, immensely handsome for his sixty-four years, does a fantastic impersonation of his wife, who welcomes his trips with Steve, relieved to be left behind to shop without reproach. 'I have no idea why or how we have remained together all these years. I am fond of her – don't get me wrong. Talk, talk, talk, she does and I like my silence.' As if to make the point he pauses before adding, 'But boy. No one can say marriage is easy.' He jokes he can't afford to retire from his family construction business with his wife's love of finer things. His passion is for the rivers of Wyoming and fly-fishing. She prefers the garish neon of Las Vegas casinos. 'It works,' he tells us by way of conclusion. 'Don't ask me how, but it works.'

■   ■   ■

Another perfect day and Denali is coaxing us to settle into our life here. When the sun shines, it's easy to forget its reputation for prolonged storms. Our guides tell us stories of hunkering down for days in a white-out, with Arctic blizzards raging. The summit is 18,000ft (5,486m) above the rolling tundra at its foot, whereas the base of Everest sits at a higher level, giving it a smaller vertical rise of 12,000ft (3,658m). None of us underestimates the challenge ahead, but for now the scenery absorbs our attention. The glaciated granite mountains look closer than they are and their ridges razor-thin because of the tricks of light refraction. The fine furrows of snow rolling into the distance are like folds on white fabric, the crevasses its tears. In the heat the ice towers are unstable and can collapse spectacularly, as thousands of tonnes of loose ice blocks tumble and roar down the mountain. It is an astonishing transformation, beauty becoming deadly.

I've been entertained sharing a rope with Mike. He left the army to become a lawyer and hides his obvious brilliance, only mentioning some of his most memorable cases at my insistence. As we chatter during lunch, it emerges his wife is heavily pregnant and this is the 'best window of a bad bunch' to pursue his long-standing wish to climb Denali. Perhaps because of his understatement, Mike becomes the target for our most earnest guide's anxiety. This is Matt's first commercial expedition on a serious mountain. He is young, keen, and is feeling the weight of responsibility leading others in crevassed terrain. At surprise moments he'll turn to check the rope's tension. He is right to do so, but every time Mike's technique is singled out for reproach. 'Not again, Mike! This is a lifeline, not a death leash'. There are times when, from my position, the rope in front of Mike looks exactly as it should, not too tight or slack. He'll still face another dressing down by the man half his age, 'You're letting down the team, Mike – this is serious'. I can only admire the cool Californian's handling of his hotheaded scolder, never once deploying the defensive wit which could pulp an opponent in court. Sometimes catching my eye, as I struggle not to laugh, he'll shrug and say, 'I'm so naughty. I can't help myself. I'm in trouble again.'

Not for the first time I'm struck by how Americans are first-class team companions, with their refreshingly unstuffy ways and general social ease. Time and again this quality has kept the atmosphere light, so unlike my experience some five months before, as the only woman on an all British-Irish trip to Argentina to climb Aconcagua, the highest mountain in South America. At the time I hadn't realised just how strained the trip dynamics were and how isolated I was among a group that only felt comfortable enough to joke or tell funny stories. There was no light and shade or discussion to get stuck into. The clearest sign the chemistry wasn't working came to light before a big day of climbing, after long days acclimatising at base camp. I had asked the all-male table how they felt about the day ahead – not expecting a rush of in-depth responses but perhaps some shared relief that finally we were moving. There was a silence too sudden to be meaningless. No one said a word. All twelve men froze until someone cracked a joke about something unrelated. Later, the oldest member of the party, who I liked the most, quipped, 'Mags, you've got to realise, guys don't like that kind of talk. Take my advice, just don't go there.'

We get to the stash point and it's hard work digging a hole deep enough to bury our supplies, even though we know we'll be grateful later for the lighter, repeat journey. Rick is withdrawn all day. After racing down the slope back to camp, it surprises no one when he admits to being under-prepared and not strong enough to continue. He will be escorted down the glacier by Matt and Dave, setting off at two in the morning, in time to make the first flight off the mountain back to Talkeetna. Before collapsing for an early night, he hands me a big catering-sized bag of M&Ms, 'I guess I won't be needing this for energy.'

None of us hear another word from this enigmatic man, after his sudden and unexplained departure. After living together in such confinement, no matter how short a time, traces of someone's presence linger long after they have gone. Perhaps this early loss to the group ensures a tightening of ties – we are looking out for each other, the focus as much on the spirit of our group as the prospect of personal struggle in the rigours ahead.

19 SUMMIT SETBACKS

At 11,000ft (3,353m) Camp 11, as it's called, is a milestone. It is just over halfway and is important for acclimatising and staging more supplies to the next significant destination, Camp 14 (13,999ft/4,267m), where the real assault and discomfort begins. We will be here a few days, so we take time planning the best way to build the camp. It's been a tiring day hauling the loads up a steep section to reach our new base, so we are slow to reach decisions or take initiative.

Luc, from Belgium, who shared a tent with Rick, has been quiet since making a fairly vocal impression on our first evening in Anchorage – but what he does say tends to carry some punch. He'll sometimes assert himself in a leadership role, like now, as he instructs those shovelling on how best to clear the snow. 'Not that way. The platform is not level. Trust me I have a feel for these things.' Luc has the 'seven summit' banner in his sights and has mentioned he'd like a go at Everest depending on his experience on Denali. He sports the most cutting-edge altitude boots on the market, whose expense reflects their quality. Rather loudly, he'd confided to me once that, in spite of my inferior brand, European mountaineers would only consider boots like his for an expedition like ours.

It's Mike's turn with the shovel. Luc points out to him that he is making holes rather than levelling the snow. 'Here, Luc … ' I surprise myself by saying, ' … take this and show us how it is done,' thrusting my shovel into his hands. Later, Mike thanks me and we laugh, not unkindly, at the Belgian's brusqueness and the way I had copied his style so convincingly.

In our tent, Nancy and I struggle to get comfy. It's a bitterly cold evening. My altimeter reads -12°C, despite the combined warmth of our bodies cocooned in all our layers and sleeping bags. A thin coating of ice covers the tent from the meagre warmth we manage to generate. Sudden contact with the canvas can trigger fine ice to shower over our huddled forms. Marcus Aurelius opines the benefits of wakefulness over sleeping, as to 'lie-in' is to miss the chance of giving to the wider world. I plan to test this theory when 'breakfast' is called in the morning. Nancy's in a talkative mood. We haven't exchanged anything very personal so far with each other, knowing there would be plenty of time for that ahead.

She tells me of how she met her husband, a cop. She heard his voice before she saw him and recognised it straight away, although they'd never met. This was on a hospital ward. Nancy was checking up on someone she'd rescued from a house fire, which he was investigating for arson. Despite their paths coinciding during strange shift patterns all over the city, it took two years before he asked her on a date. They share a passion for the sea, for relics from maritime wars and boats, with Nancy at the helm and her husband in his role as 'a good deck hand.'

'So how does he feel about you climbing this, being away for so long?'

'Oh, he gets it. He wouldn't like this at all. We hike together but not this sort of stuff.'

'Sounds ideal to share some things and be able to go off on your own too.'

'Being here isn't just about the mountain. I'm here for my brother. For Jonathan.'

The orange tent radiates a soothing glow over our curled bodies as the snow outside reflects the fading light. Nancy tells me that her younger brother died eighteen months before in an avalanche. It's clearly a relief for her to talk. Story after story, many very funny, is told without pause, of how close they'd always been and how much they'd shared. The sailing and hiking trips, their love of dogs.

'Look! Here's Jonathan.' She shows me a picture of her darker-haired brother. 'I'm taking him all the way to the summit. I don't care how tough it's going to be. I will get there, carrying Jonathan with me.'

A bond has been formed between us. I now know the true extent of Nancy's motivation and how personal this climb is for her. Being here is a quest; the act of reaching the top a key to unlock the weight of her loss. Turning back without reaching her milestone, the top of America's highest mountain, is never going to happen without a gritty fight.

The next two days unfold surprisingly. On the first, we descend to retrieve the stash of gear. Dennis becomes aware of a twinge in his groin as he climbs steadily uphill, pulling a sled loaded with more kit. When he stops moving and cools down, it doesn't bother him, but as soon as he warms up the ache starts up again. He monitors it back at camp. In the mess tent again, every variety of cookie and snack bar, bagel, and waffle is devoured, as we psyche ourselves up for the big acclimatisation tomorrow. We will be pulling heavy loads up two steep sections to stash at Windy Corner. As its name suggests, this exposed stretch is one of the last places you'd want to be in bad weather. Luc is very quiet and doesn't have an appetite. He struggles to eat, knowing he will need the energy tomorrow.

It is a gruelling trip up and the route is icier than Dylan, our most experienced guide, can remember. The lack of snow this season has turned steeper stretches into headwalls of sheer blue ice. The melting effect of the sun is triggering dangerous rock falls too. We should be wearing helmets, a precaution which wouldn't have been necessary in other years. Bottlenecks of other expedition parties pile up as ice screws and ropes are fixed. The views of the North-West Buttress are extraordinary in the clear, cold skies. Our attention is on careful crampon placement and maintaining pace; to stop would be dangerous. The technical considerations take time and the guides are quiet and focussed. Ice crystals glint like cut glass. The cloudless skies match the shades of blue inside the gaping crevasses.

Returning to camp, the snow is sludgy and we pass over thinning snow bridges. I'm grateful for the rope and keep it tighter than usual, at the risk of pulling at the person in front, making harder work for them. The mountains glisten in the sun's glare, which is breathtaking, but its more sinister impact is visible too. The mountain faces are scarred with rocks peeping everywhere, as the pounding rays shrink glaciers and melt snowfields. This environment is changing all the time, the snow becoming sparser. At this rate, it will look very different a century from now.

Back at camp, Dylan bakes a cheesecake. Tall and willowy, he's immensely capable and fun with it. As we gain height he shares his impressive knowledge of rocks, enlivening the changing landscape. He's getting increasingly fed up with the frugal climbing lifestyle and has spent most of the last ten years scaling some of the hardest routes in America. He effortlessly recounts tales of hardship and high-altitude terror climbing in wild parts of the world. He's just come back from a trip to Pakistan, where he was stranded on a rock wall for days in a fierce storm.

As we listen to Dylan, it becomes clear that our third guide, Dave, who's naturally reserved, is even quieter than usual. He tripped on the descent and thinks he's slipped a disc. He's in great pain and goes to bed, knocked out with the strongest painkillers in the first aid kit. There is no doubt that he will be unable to continue. Dennis' groin strain is hurting more now and as we try to assure him it'll get better, he says repeatedly, 'I don't want to let the team down. What happens if it gets worse higher up?' Steve tells 'Danny' to sleep on it but looks quietly resigned to losing his buddy, who may have to descend with Dave in the morning.

Meanwhile, Luc has noticeably lost his bullishness and has only pecked at his food in the last few days. He returns to the kitchen where we are all huddled, having called his wife on the satellite telephone. He clears his throat as if to make an announcement and then tells us he's been struggling to summon energy. Every day has been difficult for him and his 'heart is no longer in it'. He will also go down with Dave. It is so difficult to take this in – Luc is tough, with sound expedition experience, yet he now admits it's too much for him. Touchingly, he asks aloud if he is 'simply too old for all this?' We will miss his gruff company. Suddenly, our bright party teeters, as we try to come to terms with losing part of this happy band of people. We all turn in early, aware that the imminent farewells will change the whole course of the following two weeks.

■   ■   ■

The depleted group has to re-establish itself again. Steve is going to feel the loss the most. Hugging his friend goodbye marked the end of their dream to climb the highest peaks in America's forty-nine states together. Voices cracked as goodbyes and good lucks were exchanged. Dennis muttered time and again, as if to convince himself, 'I can't let you guys down,' and Luc wiped his eyes hidden behind black shades. Dave would also have his own demons to work through leading them safely off the mountain. He wanted to be on this trip and was in his stride, gaining great expedition experience. We wave them off and watch them drop height, before clearing all traces of our camp.

Silent, our two rope teams set off for the long, hard slog to Camp 14. Every uncomfortable sign of effort, each snag and strain becoming more significant now among our shrunken group. Vulnerability strikes in unforeseen ways on a mountain, especially when the refuge of civilisation is a spell of settled weather and plane ride away. Matt has not been higher than 14,000ft (4,267m) and cannot be sure how he'll fare with the unknown demands of high altitude. Dylan must be reassessing his outlook for the trip. As the leader guide, he will have to work twice as hard even though the group has nearly halved. Losing Dave as an experienced hand will add to the anxiety and judgement he will shoulder. Nancy's been afflicted in the last few days at Camp 11 by pounding headaches and hardly says a word, looking uncomfortable and pinched. Mike is steady and quiet. Jason, on leave from the army, is bound to open up more in the coming days. He hasn't said a great deal generally but is unfailingly considerate, offering to help whenever he can. He is at his liveliest and least reserved around Mike, with whom he shares a tent.

After a long effort to Windy Corner and even greater energy spent recouping fuel from our buried cache, Dylan falls into a crevasse, shoulder high. Immediately he struggles to climb out, panting and swinging to lever himself up, as we stretch out to tighten the rope. Covered in snow, he is shocked after dangling over the shaft of blue ice, its floor a hundred feet below. Gingerly, we walk round the gaping chasm, vigilant for menacing cracks and the signs of snow bridges thinned by the sun. Groups passing us on their way down report how unstable weather stopped them from climbing higher than

Camp 14. From here upwards, we cannot plan beyond a day or two at a time. We all know and don't need telling that if one of us becomes ill or injured, a guide will have to descend. Ideally there should be a maximum of four to a rope. Unless we team up with another expedition, we would not have the guide-to-client ratio to continue.

The weather is fickle, mirroring the many uncertainties – one minute we shed storm layers, unbearably hot and thirsty, the next we layer up, shivering. Even the gaping crevasses, their wind-whipped edges like conches, seem to enlarge in the glare. Ice crystals sparkle everywhere and fine snow flurries catch the light as they shower us like fairy dust. A biting wind starts to gust down the slope, a strong resistance against every plodding step. We hunch down, eyes trained on the rope in front. Small curls of snow whirl ahead, reminding me of sand churned up by a breeze. This goes on for hours. It is eight in the evening and we are still not in camp. Nancy is very pale. She only nods when asked about the state of her headache. Jason says he's been in a feverish sweat. The rest of us are exhausted and the light is dimming. The telltale sign of imminent weather deterioration, a lenticular cloud, has formed above Denali's summit. A rope team racing past us towards Windy Corner for a last dash for supplies tells us we are nearly there – twenty minutes from Camp 14 at most.

We arrive disorientated and cold. The sudden sight of canvas civilisation on a vast snowy plateau is hard to come to terms with. A thriving international community of down-clad people, in various stages of acclimatisation, are preparing to go up or down. We stagger through the carefully constructed igloos and wind shields of snow bricks, barely noting the different flags from around the world planted proudly at icy thresholds. The last thing anyone wants to face is the backbreaking effort of clearing tonnes of snow before the building can begin. There's no communication between us or sense of cohesion. Anyone watching our weary efforts would see an ineffective disarray of bodies shovelling, doubling up tasks with a lacklustre lethargy, as an unstable wall takes shape. As soon as the tents are up, Jason and Nancy have to take to their beds. Mike also needs to rest. Steve and I struggle on with Matt, who looks wasted but keeps going. The thinner air has taken its toll on him. Dylan has gone in search of the extra manpower of a ranger.

Much later, I finish eating Nancy's supper as well as my own, as, after a cocktail of painkillers, she finally sleeps through her 'sledgehammer' headache. It's close to 2am as I fall into a black void of exhausted sleep.

The experience of Camp 14 is meant to be one of rest and preparation for the sleepless rigours of the tougher, higher days ahead. Although the summit is little more than 6,000ft (1,829m) higher, the hardest part is yet to come. So close to the rarefied air of the Arctic, the physiological impact of climbing Denali can be as demanding as a mountain several thousand feet higher. Mountaineers use spells of bad weather to lie and wait or spend a minimum of two days acclimatising, in a cycle of sleeping and eating whatever they can force down. Our time at Camp 14 was one of exhausting drama and uncertainty.

The morning after we'd arrived, Jason woke up shivering and sweating in the turbulence of fever. Like a hibernating mammal, he burrowed deep into his thick downy layers, emerging every twelve hours to rehydrate. His tent mates, Steve and Mike, would empty his 'pee bottle' for him whenever necessary. Once his temperature had dropped a few degrees to 100°, he made a series of satellite calls to his girlfriend and family all over Georgia. I overheard his best Southern accent, valiantly telling his 'auntie', that 'everything is fine up here. Just fine.' He never once admitted, as he later told us, that at the fever's height he really thought he was going to die. Dylan and Matt melted snow for round-the-clock hot drinks, holding regular consultations with each other. At one point they checked with guides in descending parties if Jason might join them, as he was begging to do from his horizontal position.

While his temperature raged, the conditions of my other team mates were beginning to look bad. Nancy had never experienced pain like her headache. Only the strongest steroids could relieve it and then only a little for short periods. An acute headache can also be a symptom of the fatal swelling of the brain, known as cerebral oedema, caused by reduced oxygen. The only way to treat it is by an immediate descent or a pure oxygen supply. Nancy was escorted to an impressively well-supplied medical tent, set up for the summer. Doctors monitor carbon monoxide poisoning from camp stoves as well as emergencies, of which there are usually several during the climbing season.

Steve joined her in the tent. He had developed a nasty, hacking chest cough that was causing breathing difficulties, stopping him from sleeping and he was losing energy fast. Nancy's oxygen count was looking promisingly good and although doctors wanted to monitor her, they didn't regard her severe headache as unduly worrying. Instead, alarm bells were ringing over Steve's low count of seventy-one. It should be at least eighty-five, ideally ninety. His higher than average heart rate was not making doctors at all upbeat about his chances of continuing either. They were both issued with a high dose of diamox, a powerful blood-thinning, high-altitude drug. Steve was told to come back for another check-up to decide whether he was strong enough to go higher.

The deterioration of Steve and Nancy was a constant concern. We hadn't noticed at first that Mike was spending long periods lying down and wasn't eating very much. We were all taking it easy in our tents, resting up after the battering journey to get up here. His natural strength of character always downplayed how he was feeling and so we accepted that he didn't want to eat or get up, overcome by the typically common symptoms of acute mountain sickness. He remained noticeably withdrawn. After two days of this, Matt, Dylan, and I agreed that the team prospects of a safe or sensible ascent were very slim. While the others remained stable although uncomfortable, Mike was getting worse. They took him to the tent for a blood test. Hours later they returned without him.

Within minutes they had seen that he was seriously ill. Urged by doctors to walk in a straight line, Mike zigzagged like a drunk. As a back-up test, they told him to tie his laces, which he couldn't. Lack of coordination is a brain malfunction from starved oxygen. His lungs were gurgling with fluid. He was diagnosed with pulmonary and cerebral oedema, a combination so rare that calls were being made to America's leading altitude medics. Cerebral oedema can kill more quickly than swelling of the lungs but is usually associated with much higher altitude. To have both at the same time was highly unusual. Duty doctors later discovered that there have been barely more than a handful of cases ever recorded in America.

Mike was immediately put on oxygen and wore a mask throughout continual assessments. Meanwhile, rangers were working out how to carry out an emergency evacuation. The oxygen supply had bought them time – but Mike could suffer irreparable brain damage unless he got to sea level quickly. A weather forecast was warning of a low front and high winds. The only helicopter pilot who could risk a journey to this altitude had time off and was not answering calls. It was clear Mike could not be walked off the mountain. Was descending with a stretcher possible in such icy conditions? We visited Mike in relays, peering through the medical tent door, as he lay unaware of us. For the most part, while his body drank in fresh oxygen, he slept. The doctors took it in turns to sit by his bed, monitoring him all the time. There was nothing we could do but brood and make every effort to eat and rest during this endless lull of waiting.

20 RESCUE

A queue of volunteers, mainly male, line up outside the medical tent to give blood samples. Inside, a trainee doctor sits with a clipboard, on which she records the amount of carbon monoxide she finds. Inhaling stove fumes that build up inside tents from cooking is a common expedition hazard. This high altitude hospital is like a greenhouse, its propane-fuelled warmth driving each visitor to shed layers. The glow from its yellow canvas walls adds to the surreal scene, so different from the ice-cold whiteness immediately outside. Mike has a plastic tube running from his nose to a primitive-looking oxygen tank, resembling a fire extinguisher. He is in surprisingly good spirits and is used to entertaining the flow of people who check up on him.

'Don't be taken in by their jokes and smiles,' the doctor urges us, referring to her next volunteer. She tells him to bare an arm as she starts getting her needle and cotton wool ready. 'It's all an act. Men hate the sight of their own blood,' she continues, her voice showing no sign of mercy, only sport. As if to corroborate, the man tries to grin but gives up. He looks away, a side view of his profile braced for pain, as the doctor warns, 'it's only a prick and a sting. Quickly over.' A few seconds pass as he shakes his arm and pulls down his top, clearly relieved.

'You have an above average rating of forty-eight – this means you're adapting well. Your haemoglobin count is above average. Healthy kidneys.'

Happy with that, he walks out. Nancy is the next volunteer whose results will be recorded for the research. She is promptly informed, 'you're a great case for acute mountain sickness.' Jason takes her place. After two days of feeling wretched, he has made a Lazarus-like recovery, revelling in jokes at his own expense. Perhaps from the relief of feeling better after such an intense illness, he emerges as more outgoing than before. As an army helicopter pilot he has been to war zones and seen any manner of gruesome injuries and treatments in the front line, yet his closed eyes and clenched left fist as he allows his right arm to be sterilised before being punctured betray a sensitivity to the sight of blood.

Mike and I watch the gripping entertainment. If all goes according to plan, in the morning he'll be flown off the mountain to a hospital in Anchorage. The head ranger continues to monitor weather updates radioed from Talkeetna. Nancy's headache still hurts but has been helped by the increased dose of diamox and plenty of rest. Steve's cough persists but there is nothing about his quiet and steely manner that suggests he'll give up unless doctors order him to. We will press on as a party and acclimatise by gaining height, leaving another cache of supplies before descending to spend one or two more nights at Camp 14. It will then be a relentless push to the top, stopping at the notoriously exposed Camp 17 with all its discomforts.

A senior doctor walks in sporting enormous rubber boots from his time serving in the Korean War, 'perfect for a mountain like Denali,' he tells us. 'They don't make anything like these now.' He's here to check on his patient, Mike, by whom he's clearly charmed. As he checks Mike's pulse, he tells us how much he enjoys escaping a summer in Anchorage to volunteer on Denali, where he can ski as well as carry out interesting work. His bushy eyebrows rise every time he fixes his smile on his affable patient. I notice he's lost part of a finger and wonder if it was to frostbite.

Outside the busy canvas hospital, Camp 14 buzzes with new sled-pulling arrivals, searching for a recently vacated site. Games of volleyball are played in most weather and the roar of cheers or claps echo through the camp. In a mix of languages, pleasantries are exchanged and notes swapped about summit hopes or experiences. These exchanges happen in mess tents or in a queue for 'the bathroom'. The camp's two pit toilets are shielded on three sides by crude wooden boards, exposing the front view of a half-clothed squatter. Perched above a thirty-foot-deep hole, one quickly adapts to the absence of awkwardness of those who stomp past this usually private moment. Some even loiter a few feet away to admire the wonderful panoramas. Invariably, socialising takes place clutching a Perspex bottle of varying shades of orange and yellow, waiting to be emptied. At 14,200ft (4,267m), this familiarity is unremarkable.

A large part of these rest days is spent eating or waiting for the next meal. Matt has come into his own in all catering matters, after arriving at Camp 14 in such a worn-out state. His fate had been hanging in the balance over whether to go down with Jason, Nancy or Steve unless they got better. His great cooking helps with morale, especially his deft hand at deep-fried bagels with melted jack cheese, lashings of peanut butter and turkey jerky. Jason hovers about the chopping and frying operations and can't get enough of Matt's creations. Refreshingly unsentimental for someone who often calls his family twice a day, Jason doesn't romanticise the outdoors or its rigours. Heaping more hot chocolate into the watery mix he announces, 'Frankly, this mountain will do me for three to four years. Won't need to step foot on another till then.'

Dylan could not be more different. He thrives on reliving his death-defying adventures, like when he gave up all hope of rescue after being stranded for two weeks in Patagonia in merciless storms without food. A local man got worried when the party failed to reappear and set off in his boat to find them, with only the vaguest idea of where they might be in the labyrinthine waterways.

A couple of Matt's friends have returned from their longer, harder route up the West Rib and drop by our kitchen. Cold weather drove them back two hundred feet from the top. One has been treated for frostbite on the tip of a finger but his circulation is returning. They've been living in an igloo that is beginning to melt, forcing them to descend a day earlier than they want. They're impressively resourceful and modest. One is a fisherman in the halibut-rich waters of south-west Alaska and the other a carpenter whose stories about his solitary experiences in the Alaskan bush at the age of twenty-two fascinate us all. He lived alone for an entire year in a log cabin he had built. He chose the most isolated spot possible that would still enable him to reach supplies every few months. He decided on four hundred miles north of Fairbanks, the last main settlement before the Arctic wilderness. As part of his preparation for this 'social experiment', he had to learn how to handle huskies and a sled. In between the trips to civilisation, he hunted with a rifle. His resourcefulness and quest for solitude is all the more surprising as he grew up in New York. Later, Jason, who'd made no secret of his love of domestic comforts, dismissed such ideals, perhaps exaggerating his Southern twang, 'I can't see why anyone would want to go alone in the wilds for a year. Frankly that's weird!'

During these gatherings, Steve and I play rounds of Yahtzee. When he wins he dismisses his luck with a Mormon modesty and is genuinely delighted when it's my turn to have a high roll. Sometimes he disappears into the tent he shares with Jason to read extracts of his bible. His wife has pencilled passages that might inspire him in grittier moments. He tells me very gently, 'Mormonism gives answers, certainty.' Nancy has also been opening up round the camp as her headaches lose their severity. At the start of the expedition, she seemed more at ease around the men, perhaps used to the banter from working in a predominantly male profession. Now, I look forward to the time we spend chatting in our tent.

One afternoon, worn out from labouring with a heavy load of supplies up fixed lines to our next camp, we retreat to the warmth of our sleeping bags back at Camp 14. It was the hardest day yet. The stretch to Camp 17 is too steep for sleds and climbing with a heavier pack at such an uncomfortable angle was exhausting. Queues of people piled up between the end of one fixed line and the start of the next, drawing out the day's hardships. Using a breaking device with teeth, called an 'ascender', that grips the rope when under load, we shuffled on up the face. Gravity pulled at the heavy packs, as if to make ungainly turtles of us in our foolish efforts to civilise the higher mountain. The stopping and starting, the unclipping and re-clipping around anchor points that fix the line to the slope, were the most irksome trial of the expedition yet. After burying our supplies for the summit assault, it was a relief to get down to the relative comforts of Camp 14. Now, on my back at last, I moan to Nancy that the heat, the weight and the co-dependency were a lethal combination that will have to be endured all over again.

News reached us earlier that fifty-five-year-old twin brothers had fallen, unroped, to their deaths on the upper mountain. They were descending when one of them fell, perhaps knocking into the other. One had a son who was soloing lower down. He had now been helicoptered off the mountain with the bodies of his father and uncle, the first climbers to have died this season. They must have been like us, beginning each day only with thoughts of reaching the summit, never about whether they'd return home. Nancy senses how miserable I'm feeling, lost in my own moody world. Judging the moment perfectly, she lifts my jaded spirits, 'Look around. Look how beautiful it is out there. Every day is different. All this space. I've been hoping for a miracle being here on Denali – and I think it's this … being here, all of us together, sharing all this.'

The next morning, dense pink smoke seeps into the sky from somewhere beyond the medical tent. Word's been spreading throughout Camp 14 that the Park Service has organised a rare helicopter rescue to take Mike, still seriously ill but stable, to hospital in oxygen-rich Anchorage. Curious onlookers gather as a number of staff charge about the landing space, making the area identifiable in the whiteness. A distant beating drone increases as the helicopter transforms itself from a black speck to recognisable life-saving transport. Mike, still wearing an oxygen mask, is helped along by two sturdy figures either side of him. He is stronger than he was and smiles broadly throughout, but he's noticeably thinner, his cheeks drawn. He had asked Matt and Dylan not to radio word back to their office base about his condition in case it reached his wife before he'd had a chance to speak to her. Somehow she had found out and so he'd reassured her that morning over a satellite connection that he would be back home in California in a few days.

It's an emotional occasion. The medical team take it in turns to shake his hand. Last-minute group photos are taken of our depleted team. He hugs each one of us while clasping a hand. Before turning to the crude steps up to his escape to safety, he says to us all, 'Climb her for me. Make sure you climb her and be safe.'

21 RESOLUTION

For hours, the three of us have been lying on our backs as the canvas walls flap violently in the unremitting storm. Twice my face has been whipped in the struggle to turn over, fed up with the feeling of cramped enclosure. Steve is like a radiator nestled between Nancy and me. There is no novelty in being cosy like this or in our efforts to make ourselves heard above the screeching whistle of the wind. Outside, tethered objects are lashing about: nothing can be secure for long on this icy plateau, in this force of wind. Dylan has fought repeatedly to recruit help in building up our wall, facing lethargy and sometimes outright reluctance.

All our energy seems spent. This is our eighth night above 14,000ft (4,267m). Our time is running out, the window to summit narrowing with every rumour of worsening weather passing between the few tents up here. Our bodies will only get more tired, not just because it's difficult to sleep at 17,200ft (5,243m) but recovery is impossible with all this noise and turbulence. Our routine is to lie in until it becomes too uncomfortable to ignore the need for the toilet. It takes time putting on all the layers necessary to face the whirling whiteness outside. Even collecting three bags of hot freeze-dried food with a gloved hand through a chink in the zipped door of our neighbouring tent needs cast-iron resolve. An oxygen-starved body rarely feels driven by hunger.

Nancy collapsed on reaching Camp 17 and needed a special breathing device to force the stale air out of her lungs. Her headache was piercing. More diamox and painkillers were immediately administered. Unable to eat anything and barely able to talk, she went straight to bed once the tent was pitched. Steve too was feeling extremely weak, needing sleep. Jason seemed remarkably cheerful and put my brick-carving efforts to shame. Matt focused on melting snow – we would need drinks and food soon. Dylan set a pace of building and strengthening the wall that was difficult to keep up with. To lose a tent here would be a serious setback and he was not taking any chances.

More food is passed between our adjacent tents. I have a surprising hunger at altitude and eat anything Nancy and Steve can't manage. Both of them are better but still weak. I feel bloated from the pure carbohydrate diet of sugary snack bars, bagels and rehydrated bagged meals I have been living on solidly since fresh food ran out ten days before. The squawk, scrunch, and squeak of plastic boots on compressed snow can be heard in the storm's lull. The world experienced at snow level challenges perception; it is impossible to tell where the footsteps are heading. We debate again the chances of the weather clearing. In calmer moments, Steve is the most optimistic. I have never felt grimier and miss cleaning my teeth. The three of us fantasise about our first meal in Talkeetna and how long we will spend in our first shower in three weeks. We even find the energy to laugh at how we can have invested so much time and effort, money notwithstanding, to be here, in varying states of hardship. A discussion follows on the nature of 'value' and how you measure it.

As the tent tries to free itself from its icy anchors, its flapping sides almost taking off like kites in the stronger gusts, the summit chances seem even more elusive than they did at the height of uncertainty at Camp 14. All we can do is wait and hope.

■   ■   ■

It takes some minutes to adjust to the evidence that the storm has blown itself out. It really is hard to believe the view from our unzipped tent, after hearing Dylan shout to us, 'Hey team – what do you reckon? I think we say yes, don't you?' Where there had been blizzard, there is now an assembly of ridges and peaks, already reflecting a sun in a windless sky. This change was not forecast to happen. Nancy is still pale and afflicted by headaches, but her spirits are up. Steve is feeling slow but positive. I have to summon the will to get out of the ice-filled tent and soggy sleeping bag, with its incubating effect. It takes a lot of energy to track down the appropriate summit kit jumbled inside it and wrestle with stiff, frozen boots. Getting ready always takes so much longer than it should and a lack of adrenaline from lying for so long in a comatose state slows mental functions. By 11am we are finally ready for our big day.

As two rope teams, we edge carefully along the exposed icy route to the Denali Pass. An ice axe would not arrest a fall here. All along this slippery stretch, it is hard to ignore the spot where the twin brothers had fallen to their deaths. Being early in the season, we have more of a sense of intimacy with the ten or so other climbing teams. There are still cold and lengthy waits at the many anchor junctions, as the unclipping and clipping of the rope to these fixed lifelines stops and starts. I think for the umpteenth time that this will be my last guided experience and Denali my last popular mountain. I had learnt a great deal about expedition practicalities. At some point this knowledge was going to be tested. Thinking independently is an altogether different experience from being thought for and protected.

The higher we get, the more Nancy seems to shut down – responding only to instructions to move and stop. Her headache is miserable but no amount of pain will stop her now. Her photo of Jonathan would be exposed to the summit light of day, no matter what. Jason seems cheerful and focussed. His two days of being knocked out at Camp 14 had made him spring him back, keener for whatever lay ahead. Steve is moving slowly and deliberately. Perhaps thinking of his friend Dennis, his mind made up on reaching the top for them both. Although weak, he is resolute.

The day is remarkably warm for this height in early May. Dylan, comparing notes with other guides, has never experienced such a benign summit day as this. All of us draw on hidden reserves of energy as we slowly make our way along the blue ice and snowfields towards the summit ridge. A thin veil of cloud shrouds the upper mountain and its varied terrain in a strange light, smothering our jaded spirits as we struggle to place one foot in front of the other. The blacker rocks of these higher slopes are like charred spiky walls. They draw me to stare and slow down as I pass them. Occasionally I prise myself out of my introverted state and look at my friends; their eyes only on the endless snow and rock in front.

The summit ridge is a knife edge. To fall down the sheerer side would mean death. All of us are aware of this as we tread carefully, every step counting. The last half an hour could have been six times longer – time is meaningless in prolonged encounters with exhaustion and frayed nerves. Finally, at about eight-thirty, more than nine hours since leaving camp, the summit mound is immediately before us. All that separate us from it is a thirty-second trudge.

The moment we have all imagined and worked towards during many days and weeks happens so suddenly. Here we are, at the very top. Yet standing on it and surveying the summit's prize is like watching a drama in blurred vision. The climax and relief are not as intensely felt as the grinding effort to get here. Automatically, we remove mittens and gloves to get cameras for the trophy shots – the frozen moment of weather-beaten smiles that suggest the hardships endured really have been worth it. The highest points in the Alaskan Range encircling a sea of clouds are captured in five or six takes. Different combinations of our two rope teams, trying to avoid tangling up, are posed hurriedly for posterity. There is still a good two hours of daylight left but all of us know we face a long way down. It is bitterly cold after a few minutes of standing still. Down-clad forms sharing this confined space stamp feet and rub hands together to stir up some life in them, while aspiring summiteers wait below.

Nancy looks confused, almost hypothermic, her headache disabling any ability to speak. Dylan and I agree to go down without delay, knowing it will take longer to move safely. All my instincts want to flee from this exposed top, this highest point, which has inspired thousands of people to risk their lives since it was first climbed in 1912. The way down is broken up with occasional rest stops, ended abruptly as we fight the urge to lie down and sleep. During them, Nancy hunches over her legs in obvious pain. To have toiled up most of Denali in such extreme discomfort cannot be measured or understood. This lonely and dispiriting ordeal could only be tolerated as a gesture of selfless devotion to her brother, whom she had loved most and lost.

We are back in High Camp by midnight. I wait up to meet Matt and his party, to check they will find us in this plateau of whiteness, where a multitude of similar tents are shielded behind the ice-wall shelters. Few words are said. We had carried out what we set out to do, now our thoughts are only of sleep and getting off the mountain.

■   ■   ■

Life on the slopes from a descending perspective, with showers and food in our sights, was very different. The crowded lines of mountaineers looked like one seamless rope team at times. After sleeping, we descended the long way down to Camp II, reaching it just as a settled, low front came in to settle. The postcard panorama we had enjoyed for days transformed into featurelessness. The plodding parties we passed on their way up were being followed by cloud, now blanketing the landscape and its magic from their fresh eyes. The brightly coloured multitude of edges, shapes and contours were now indistinguishable greys and whites.

A restlessness settled on our group – all of us were ready for our return. Raised morale and energy from the thicker air coincided with a growing despondency that until the low pressure cleared, we would have to wait for a plane. But to live on a mountain is to accept its terms; we would simply cook all our recovered supplies buried on the edge of Kahiltna glacier airport and relish every sedentary moment eating them over unhurried talk. After nights of broken sleep and waking up to frost-filled tents, the slumber ahead would be all the sweeter.

22 SKAGIT MAGIC

The criteria were fairly specific: a challenge that was remote as well as attainable. That the mountain was guarded by wilderness was essential, but not so impenetrable that it would take days of bushwhacking to be reached. The search had been narrowed to an area covering more than five hundred glaciers and almost one hundred square miles of ice. We'd need to scale it down further. In an age of dwindling wilderness and vanishing forests, the Cascades in America's Pacific North-West offer a treasure house of natural features and diversity. In this remarkably untouched backcountry, it's easy to forget its proximity to the dense population swathes around Seattle, less than two hours drive away.

After spending a month in different parts of the National Park sampling its varied terrain, the mountains of the north felt the most magnetic. For days, Mount Shuksan had seemed striking with its perfectly pointed peak among the cratered summits of this volcanic territory rising on a fault-line vulnerable to tremors. Matterhorn-like, it's one of the most beautiful mountains in the Cascades and, like its Swiss sister, one of the most photographed images to identify the range. In the end, its rugged beauty of granite and glacier, overlooking our recent ascent of Mount Baker, nailed our choice.

My friend Walter and I took two days to assemble everything we needed. We spent hours weighing up and bagging the exact quantity of food, as we had been taught to do. NOLS, the celebrated National Outdoor Leadership School, had brought home how creative and resourceful life can be in the 'woods'. All it takes is planning and imagination. For a calendar month we had learnt such nifty skills as baking pizza and bread, using nature's oven or 'twiggy fire'. In a country where consumers have a brand for every taste, there was something thoroughly wholesome about our time adapting to the rich simple fruits of nature. Everything we needed was provided by our environment. With a 'food-repair kit' of all the herbs and spices of an ambitious kitchen and raw ingredients, including baking essentials of flour and yeast, it is possible to feast like royalty. The backdrop of trees, lakes and peaks, the mouth-watering smells as pans boil and bubble, enjoyed from a rocky or leafy seat, is an event. To share this with others, every bit as charmed, is a simple formula for fulfilment. Forgetting the threads of a faster-paced life brings us closer to a time when man didn't question happiness as if there was a choice. His experience surviving in nature was accepted, never thought about.

The Pacific North-West gets seven feet of rainfall every year. Its rich green luxuriance is a consequence of dense precipitation. It once had some of the most extensive forests in North America, with some of the world's largest trees. The temperate rainforest that remains close to the coast is known in local slang as 'cold jungle'. Leaving the highway, our route to the trailhead wound through its thick heart, where dirt tracks regularly crossed the unsurfaced road, becoming quickly engulfed by the wild foliage. We had detoured to pick up our permit from a ranger base to cover our four-day trip and after shuttling back to the nearest gas station, worried by an ominously low petrol gauge, the day had slipped into evening. By the time we pulled into a clearing where we would leave Walter's car, we had two hours left of daylight.

'Again, I'm sorry. It's annoying but I don't regret this. To run out of gas round here when we come back all tired would not be good.'

Walter's an organised operator. He didn't like discovering that even with his meticulous planning he had forgotten something as simple as filling a car with fuel. I was grateful for this oversight. Two weeks on Hawaii, enraptured by its mix of live volcanoes and ocean, had made me more relaxed. After the non-stop movement since arriving in the States nearly three months before, the rigours of Denali and a month of mountaineering school, I now welcomed setbacks and hold-ups. They gave time for pausing and catching breath. So what if we started later than planned? As we had both experienced the 'NOLS way', we had everything we could possibly need or want for comfort and adventure.

We took our time sorting kit into two piles to share the carrying. We were strict followers of the 'leave no trace' principle, so that our trip would have minimal environmental impact. There was no toilet paper, or packaging surplus to necessity, no food that was not part of a meal plan and only a chemical-free soap, still unacceptable to use near a water source. We had all the equipment for glacier travel and to spend several nights on a creaking tongue of moving ice was exciting. Looking at the map again, it was unlikely we would get to the glacier by nightfall. The walk-in took us through increasingly steep forest and it would take three or four hours to get to the mountain's edge. The most likely spot to find somewhere to camp would be on a flatter stretch nearly halfway, by a stream, about an hour-and-a-half's steady effort uphill. After a few adjustments with our straps and buckles to make our sizable loads more comfortable, we set off on a narrow winding track into the bush.

Birds and wildlife unused to human traffic were still busy in the remaining daylight. At first, we snaked along a river, the path overrun with fern and large

waxy leaves like giant lily pads. Thorny tendrils draped the muddy route and
sodden tree stumps coated in moss drew me to sit for a while. We had only
been walking half an hour and the forest's luxuriant charm was firing up my
already excited mind. Orange fungi and large white flaps of mushroom resembling elephant ears clung to the thick tall trees. We were walking purposefully,
taking it in turns to overtake each other as the path meandered upwards.
Walter seemed absorbed too. I'd been looking forward to this time together. He
was eight years younger than me and had an unusual level of drive, pursuing
his varied interests and dreams. We also shared a love of Alaska. He had fished
for months at a time on commercial trawlers, risking the unpredictable Arctic
waters and weather. The fisherman's nomadic nature suited his restlessness and
need to spread his wings far beyond the inward-looking Deep South of his
childhood.

The light was beginning to fade and we were making slow progress
through the trees. I wondered how our two instructors would see us now, faithfully carrying out their alternative textbook tips. A route plan with a flexible
schedule would meet their approval. Although disciplined in technical ways,
both Ravi and Michel had a healthy irreverence for anything too formulaic or
rigidly applied. We had spent weeks with them and their different cultural
outlooks, miles from the nearest 'road head'. Ravi was Indian and infused every
group goal with an Eastern elegance. Even on days of military-style exertion,
travelling two miles in ten hours through trackless forest, with packs close to
half our body weight, he might meditate during a well-earned rest. He wore a
pendant given to him by his spiritual mentor who he'd met in a Himalayan
cave. As we huddled en masse during a deluge under a giant spruce, Ravi would
sit crossed-legged under his black umbrella, never touched by a drop.
Sometimes he chanted to the 'rain gods' to thank them for their efforts. For
him, living outdoors was to be 'in the woods'. Never afraid to ask a direct
question, he had all the time in the world to wait for the faltering answer.

Michel, from Chile, also threw himself into every unfolding moment. For
him, the ritual of brewing 'maté', a bitter tea of stewed holly leaves with
caffeine properties, to share over a story, was a savoured part of his day. Passing
around his thermos flask with its silver pipe and soggy brew, which none of us
liked but always accepted, marked playtime. On the summit of Mount Baker,
he planted the Chilean flag and proudly beamed in the kneeling position for
the queue of admiring photographers.

Usually over a camp fire, our group would listen to Ravi reading from our
extensive library (which added to our hiking burden) or one of the many
photocopied extracts from his favourite writers. Storytelling was an important
rite in all its forms. Michel told one tale with such unshielded honesty that it

still haunts me. He recalled stumbling across the original expedition camp of legendary British explorer Eric Shipton in the wilds of weather-battered Patagonia. His voice trembled as he relived it, not in awe, but outrage. The site was a ghostly record of how it had been abandoned more than half a century before; its legacy a chaos of rusting and decomposed debris. The land, a jewel to be preserved against the forces degrading it, had been abused by a man who had championed this wilderness and made his reputation by it.

What we had taken from that time in nature's classroom could only truly be understood now. We would put together everything we had learnt as a group to become 'educators', responsible for taking groups into the backcountry. Yet, on our own and unaccountable to any system or its protection, Walter and I wanted to test these ideas, open to their outcome. Is that not the essence of adventure, never really knowing what will happen?

It's getting late and we take it in turns to leave the path and search for clearings to put up the tent. Forests and woods at dusk have a certain electricity. It is a time of expectation, when the natural world is shifting to the change of rhythm. The light fading, we stop still and watch an enormous moon rising one end of the forest floor, just as the last of the sun disappears into the other. It's an extraordinary sight, this pendulum swing of day and night. The trees glow, lit up by the band of orange and the unusual yellow of the largest moon we had ever seen.

We pass a snug space between bush and tree right beside the trail. It's a bit too exposed for comfort, so we carry on and make a note of it in case there's nothing better ahead. As it gets darker and the path steeper, we turn back to the clearing. It is perfectly sized as if made to order, just big enough for the tent and backpacks and little else. Walter is keen to pitch his tent without help and so I assemble everything needed for supper on a log with rotten grooves that serve as shelves. He stops his work and searches for something in his rucksack.

'What are you looking for?'

'My penknife. Just need to tighten a couple of guy lines. They're new and a bit long. I could use the spare cord. Here she is.'

'Water's already boiling. Fifteen minutes, supper will be ready.'

'Great.'

We've barely said a word to each other since the drive. Both of us are adapting to our surroundings and finding our place in them. It always takes a day at least to shed the clock-conscious sense of hurry or the clumsiness and inefficiency that's nurtured by the ease of urban life. Walter splices the cord with the same intensity he shows whenever he's concentrating. I pour a packet soup of tomatoes with beans into the mix and turn off the heat so it can sit. Pasta cooks just as well in a hot pan.

'Damn. Where did I put it? Have you seen it?'

'What?'

'The knife. The penknife. I put it down.'

'Where, roughly?'

'I'm sure I chucked it right here by the log.'

We both look. I move the pan and food bags off the log and roll it, in case it had slipped down behind.

'That's weird, it's bright silver. You'd expect to see it in all this brown. It could only be near me, here where I was crouching just now, or somewhere round the tent.' He pats his trousers and empties his pockets. He circles the tent twice and looks inside before checking the compartments of his rucksack. He then starts to throw things out, all the time muttering how 'odd' to have lost it.

'So you were using it to cut the cord … '

' … yes and then I put it down. I'm sure right there,' he says pointing to the log. I get up again, wanting to help. We both search everywhere again.

'Look, just forget it Mags. Alright?'

'It's got to be here somewhere. Bet you, in the morning … '

'I said forget it. I don't want to talk about it, OK? I've never lost anything in my god-damned life!'

The force of this outburst surprises me. There is nothing to distract my awkwardness or the delicate atmosphere between us. Walter becomes preoccupied again. The uneasy quiet that follows makes his anger seem all the more abrupt and wounding. I stir the food. It's ready. We heap it into our bowls. We are hungry and it does taste good.

'Look, I'm sorry. It's not the knife I'm bothered about … It's just how thoughtless to have lost it. That's what's shocked me. Not only do we need it – it's just I never, ever lose things. I don't think I've ever lost one thing, not even as a kid. What else might go wrong if I can do something like this?'

'Don't worry. It doesn't matter. We're tired and have an early start.'

'What time do you want to get up?'

I feel cornered and haven't quite shaken off my crumpled feeling. There is still an edge in the air.

'Well, it's well past eleven. Six, six-thirty?'

'The earlier the better. I want to set the alarm for five-thirty. As soon as it gets light.'

We go to bed. It is a relief to shut off. An imaginary dialogue in which I lecture a class of students how well run expeditions should be 'fun and light' soothes me. By the time daylight stirs at around five-thirty, it is an altogether different day and Walter and I both wake up in fresh spirits.

Before setting off we take a last look for the knife. Leaves are scuffed and branches prised back as we thoroughly scour the confined dark-brown surface for a glimmer of silver. Nothing but soil, twigs and leaves. Resigned, we head off. The penknife is not mentioned again during our absorbing three days on the mountain.

■   ■   ■

Bad weather turned us back from our route to the summit, just five hours from the top. It didn't matter. We had learnt a great deal. Heavily crevassed glaciers are not places to run risks in poor visibility. We practised our crevasse rescue skills, and shovelled and patted snow to reinforce the melting anchors keeping our tent in place. Walter was a great companion. Our tricky first evening had brought us closer together. We soon learnt that under stress he said less and I more. In a dilemma requiring a decision based on reasoning, I like to debate the options, whereas Walter likes to think about them. During those hours spent together, we built a cast-iron understanding in which we could refer comfortably to our differences and how we handled them. Walter talked about his disciplined upbringing, his military father who liked order and timekeeping. He had a similar need for control, tempered by his need to roam, unfettered by structure. By contrast, so accustomed to being on my own, I was used to changing plans at the last minute and adapting to a shift of pace or outcome, not having to think about the impact on someone else. My preference for unpredictability could jar with Walter's more considered efforts to plan and organise.

Back at the tent, satisfied and tired, we decided not to spend a third night on the glacier but make a dash for the car and camp by Baker Lake. It would give us a different perspective of Shuksan and the National Park itself, where we'd spent so much time in recent weeks. Not having seen anyone else for days, our first encounter with some friendly hikers panting their way up to Sulphide Glacier was strange. We felt a little territorial, so used now to the uninterrupted space and our own company. It was Friday afternoon and there was bound to be more weekend traffic.

We had been up since before five to set off for the summit. It had been strenuous descending under load and so we took regular breaks to admire the different views of Mount Baker before the forest obscured it. The route down seemed much longer than the way up and passing the clearing where we'd camped before, we stopped again. Taking off our packs made us feel giddy with lightness. We flopped down and listened to the hum and buzz of the forest. After the world of snow and ice, we were both more sensitive to nature's variety and pace, the sheer force of its vitality. The undergrowth and trees around us rustled continually and changed in the shifting light. Time no longer mattered. Tiredness had relaxed us and slowed our thinking, so that we were aware of little else but our environment, as we watched and listened.

I was leaning against a tree and Walter sat facing the depths of the forest when we first heard something unusual. It was like the blades of a helicopter. The sound seemed to orbit about us, as it got louder and louder. There was a mechanical rhythm to its alternating volume, as it rose and fell.

'What on earth's that, Walter? Sounds like a low-flying aircraft … maybe more like a chopper?'

'No idea. Whatever it is, it's getting closer.'

I imagined a moment of impact. It was now so loud that it was bound to crash any moment soon. It was strange how there was still nothing to see. We waited in silence, listening. The sound started to labour, as if running out of power but it was still forceful enough to be threatening. Whatever it was, it seemed more mechanical than natural. Minutes passed and nothing appeared through the trees. A breeze then stirred, scuffing up leaves as it strengthened.

'How weird, it's a storm.' Walter didn't sound convinced, although this was the only conclusion to draw.

'Can't be. The afternoon's been so clear – it's been getting better all the time, not worse.'

The light shifted quite suddenly, the sun clouded over. So it was a storm after all. The forest looked as it had three nights before during dusk.

'Walter, I think it's going to rain. Is that the sound of hail?'

It was like hearing the soft patter of pellets fall to the floor. The mechanical whirring sound was almost whispering now.

'Could be rain. Or is that wind?'

As if his question was being answered directly, the leaves around us gently rustled before rising in small piles. The whole forest was in motion, nothing still. Something was playing strange tricks with our perception. Everywhere was then bathed in a strangely dramatic light – an orangey yellow and fluorescent green, both colours identifiable at the same time. I don't remember being aware of anything other than what was happening, except that I half-noticed Walter amble off.

I sat, propped against a tree. My mind blurred with images, unfolding without order or meaning, similar to the state just before sleep. Something was urging me to quieten my mind, where an answer would be waiting in its stillness. I 'knew', without any rational basis, that Walter had not misplaced his knife, and that it would appear as suddenly as it had vanished. I was certain we should not try to understand this strange spot but accept it as it was. That was its challenge, all that was required of us. Maybe it was a meteorological quirk, or if a helicopter with a faulty engine had hovered close by, it had gone. In either event, a presence had been stirred indescribably out of time and place.

Craving sugar, I reached for an energy bar in my pocket and tore off the wrapper. I sat in a trance, munching. Twigs snapped, which must have been Walter wandering back. I noticed something at the bottom of the packet, that didn't feel at all soft or chewable. I shook the wrapper to see what was inside. A bright white crystal, covered in soil, fell into my palm. It was a perfect oval shape, similar to many that I'd seen in the granite-rich soil on the way up to the glacier. It was hard to imagine how it could have fallen into this packet at its processing depot in Seattle. Walter was back.

'Hi – good walk?'

'Sure. Something… unusual has happened to me.' Walter looked dazed, as if he hadn't slept in ages. He sat next to me and it was then I noticed the light was normal again.

'What happened?' I asked. 'I've just been here, feeling very spaced out.'

'I had to walk – get away. It was like something was telling me to slow down. The whole time I heard … maybe sensed is a better word … that I had to stop this thing I've got about time. It's like I was being told to stop rushing. You know? Like, notice … wake up … all that matters is … now. Just slow down and see.'

I showed him the crystal and told him where it had come from. This simple white object, soiled, as if freshly plucked from the earth, reduced us once more to silence. The late afternoon turned to dusk as we continued to sit and wonder. Instinctively, I hurled the crystal deep into the bush to where I knew the penknife would be. All around us the colours of the forest, its bark, leaves and berries, were radiating an abundant freshness. It was as if we had stepped into daylight after a long hibernation.

■   ■   ■

We walk leisurely back to the car saying nothing; observing, stopping, starting however the whim takes us. We have all the time to find a lakeside spot for the night before it gets dark. A new understanding binds us, never needing to be articulated. Together, we have experienced the varied wonders of this Native American haunt and wilderness; volcanoes and glaciers sliding from snow-covered peaks, forests that have outlived generations of people. Our time around Shuksan has taken us through the territory of the Skagit Indians who, long before the threat of a white invader, survived by their knowledge of the land's resources.

It seems like a perfect moment to be near the stillness of a lake, where secrets can bob below its surface and flow into Skagit River, coursing west towards Puget Sound, seeping into the shallows of the Pacific and beyond, as they plunge into the fathomless depths.

PART 5 HAUTES-PYRENEES INDIA NEW ZEALAND

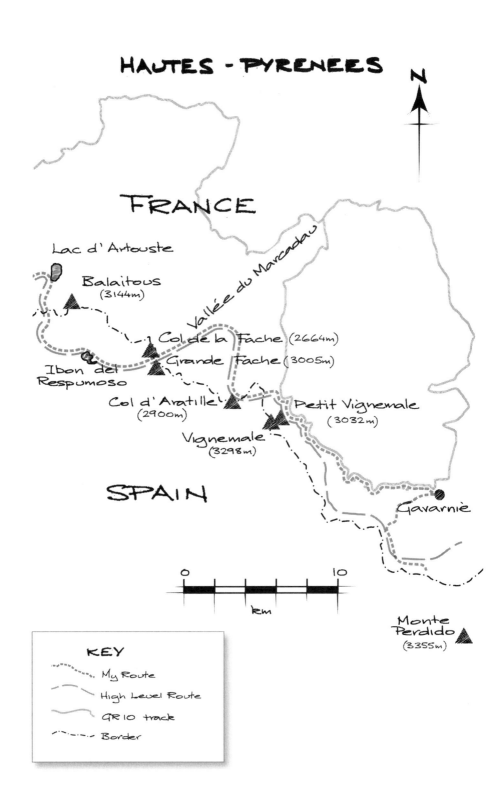

HAUTES - PYRENEES

N

FRANCE

Lac d'Artouste

Balaitous
(3144m)

Vallée du Marcadau

Col de la Fache (2664m)

Grande Fache (3005m)

Ibon del
Respumoso

Col d'Aratille
(2900m)

Petit Vignemale
(3032m)

Vignemale
(3298m)

SPAIN

Gavarnie

0   10
km

Monte
Perdido
(3355m)

KEY

········· My Route

——— High Level Route

~~~ GR 10 track

·–·–·– Border

23 COUNT OF VIGNEMALE COUNTRY: 2003

En route to the rugged higher country of lakes and summits, it is blissful to bask in alpine meadows of wild flowers, listening to the tinkling bells of grazing goats and sheep. The gentle touch of a new season dawning is showing in the Hautes Pyrenees. There are fewer people everywhere and businesses reliant on summer tourism are closing for the season. The damper nights have made the valleys rich in luxuriant greens; oranges and yellows fill the forests. The days are noticeably shorter and the chill from a waning sun drives me into the bivvy earlier. It's no longer comfortable to idle away evenings outside, unless huddled in down, with a thick hat and gloves. I acquired weightier gear for the tougher conditions ahead in an outdoor shop in a tourist town – a robust pack with an inbuilt harness for optimum adjustment, a thicker sleeping bag, more maps and a stove with plenty of fuel.

My route leads on through the highest peaks crowning a harsher terrain of giant boulders and scree. The Balaitous massif is one such area and one of the remotest in the Pyrenees. From the Col de Palas, its stark granite beauty is overwhelming, like a vision from another world. The extensive ridges and the peaks and crags surrounding the fifth highest mountain in the range are intricately connected. The high lonely corries ringed by snow shimmer in the intense heat; the smear of orange and mint-green lichen tints the granite greys.

From this height, the emerald green lakes at the base are inviting, but can only be reached with a risky ankle-twisting descent on a steep slope of loose rocks. There is no one else around. I have miles of space to myself, to wander about freely, wherever the whim takes. Relishing my freedom as I race towards the first of many lakes and smaller tarns, surely, I think, this is the loveliest and loneliest spot so far? A bracing dip in the clear water, the stones and rocks slimy against my toes, relieves my weary feet, aching muscles and sunburnt skin.

The rocky path along scree-covered slopes winds its way from one concealed pool to another. I could spend days, weeks even, in this area alone. Walking through a changing landscape has its highs and lows, moments without colour and then hours of beauty. Skimming the border along the higher reaches of the range already feels more exciting, with constant options to descend into either France or Spain. This is a golden time for exploring.

Lone patches of snow have survived the summer, making the glaciers of the

Vignemale massif dominate the view at each pass leading towards them. Vignemale is only a few days away and the clear, sunny weather is expected to last the week. It isn't hard to understand how that trophy peak captured the heart of the nineteenth-century romantic, the Irish-French aristocrat Count Henry Russell. It was a love affair that grew to such intensity that he leased the summit from the local canton for ninety-nine years and climbed it thirty-three times. He would hold luxurious banquets in the grottos he had blasted in the mountain's slopes, where he lived for months at a time, wrapped in fur-lined sleeping bags. Russell's passion for the new mountaineering craze drove him to make a number of first ascents in the range. His books helped put the Pyrenees on the map for many, eager to hear stories from the heights. Other luminaries of the *Belle Époque* were attracted by the count's zeal for the range, with its wild smattering of lakes and peaks. Tennyson, Flaubert, Victor Hugo, Kipling, Trollope, Napoleon III, Empress Eugenie and the Prince of Wales all followed the count up the valleys. Their transport could vary – sometimes foot, horse or sedan chair.

For now, it's interesting to make my way to Vignemale, the highest mountain on the French side of the range, via Spain. The walkers or mountaineers I encounter here are less inclined to stop and talk than the French, to whom I'm instinctively drawn. It's barely an hour from France, yet Spain feels foreign to me, unfamiliar. I spend my first night in a vast, open valley, nestled behind large boulders, overlooked by the south face of the Grand Fache. The flat space is carved up by small streams and footpaths leading to different peaks and valleys. A rocky overhang shields me from a strong northerly wind tearing though the valley. During the night it is calm again. The clear black sky is carpeted in stars, lorded over by a near full moon and the red glow of Mars.

The ascent to the Col de Fache the next morning is brought alive by snippets of well known history. During the late 1930s, Republican forces fled this way from Franco's militia during the Spanish Civil War. A few years later, during the Second World War, many allied pilots escaped along this same route. Shepherds and farmers understood the mountains and their secrets and provided refuge for some of those caught up in the deadly politics of the times. It's easy to imagine how wild a spot as this can provide infinite possibilities for cover, with its warren of remote routes.

At the Col, I prepare to scramble up the bouldered flanks of the Grand Fache, my first 3000-m (9,843-ft) mountain in the Pyrenees. Two women are sheltering from the sun, already strong, although it's not yet midday. One of them is training her binoculars on two forms balancing their way steadily up the towering pile of large boulders. They're probably no more than half an hour ahead. One, I notice, looks rather comic with a balloon-like stomach, and disproportionately thinner legs, not a very athletic combination. He flops over the rocks, temporarily beached, and then levers along on his belly as his legs kick the air behind him. The steepest section higher up will need a bit more agility than that. As if sensing my audience, he turns around and waves while his friend starts to coo like a bird, at which the women roar with laughter, one of them crying back, 'Attention, doucement!' They see me looking at them and offer to guard my pack if I want to catch up with their husbands. I'm grateful and say that I hope to see them later, to which they both reply without hesitation or a hint of humour, 'Nous aussi.'

It doesn't take long to reach the men. They've taken their time, holding detailed debate as to the best line to scramble upwards. Hands are waving about, pointing wildly, and voices are animated – it's clear how much they enjoy being serious. Their friendship has a long history of one being gruff and the other argumentative, knowing best. They seem only too pleased at following my lead so that one no longer has to negotiate with the other. We have a magnificent climb up a jumble of rocky channels. The view from the top rewards our exertion; shared with a Madonna in a shrine looking out at the Hautes Pyrenees from her summit perch. In the blue haze, the Vignemale massif looms over a horizon of peaks. The contrasting character of Spain is striking from this height, drier and wilder, altogether less alluring to me as a lone walker. We take it in turns to set up our cameras, rushing back into shot before the timer clicks. This needs to be done several times to ensure my two companions fit in the frame either side of me; tricky to achieve as one takes up nearly as much room as the remaining two of us put together.

Back in France, the lengthy descent down glaciated debris from the Col de Fache weaves towards the lush slopes of the Marcadau Valley, famed for their abundance of lizards, native chamois and marmots. Tall willowy pines, water-falls and meadows cloak the valley floor. Stone tracks from ancient trade routes across the Iberian border are still used to transport goods by donkey. In medieval times, this was the border crossing for pilgrims heading for Santiago de Compostela. I camp at an exquisite spot among some giant boulders, at the junction of five valleys. Ponies and cows graze nearby and a stream with its soporific flow of water twists past my bivvy.

The way to Vignemale is a mountaineering treat, a classic route crossing three high passes. The terrain has a diversity of natural features – waterfalls, lakes, a brush with Spain, cairned trails through fine scree, a descent into marshy flats, the silty outflow of glacier towered over by Vignemale's impressive north face, where 1,000m (3,281ft) of vertical and overhanging rock plummet from the summit of Pic Longue. I drink in the extraordinary panorama over a leisurely rest at one of the many sandy banks. Passing the Petit Vignemale, the easiest of the massif's four peaks, I decide to climb it the next day, after trying for the 3,298-m (10,820-ft) summit first.

From the hut below, the view to the Gavernie Cirque is mesmerising as an ocean of clouds gleams pink in a sinking sun. Stars begin to come out over the giant cliffs of Vignemale. The spirit of the count surely lives on in the shadows of nightfall, where he once organised glacier walks and moonlit champagne soirées for his guests. A lively evening is spent in the refuge over carafes of plonk and three courses of hearty food. The consensus is that rope isn't necessary for the ascent tomorrow, because the crevasses on the lower glacier are exposed as well as marked. Being the end of the season, the hazard of fragile snow bridges is limited. Despite the banter, I'm not easy at the thought of being on a glacier alone – regardless of the reduced risk of visible hazards. Two Spanish women agree that I should team up with them.

At dawn, parties of walkers file towards the Ossoue glacier, armed with crampons and ice axes. My crampons are designed for firmer boots, so I lash them on with cord to make sure they don't come loose. Within half an hour of being on the glacier, the boots break free, attached only to the crampon by the cord. As the sun is not yet out to melt the surface layers, the ice is hard, requiring stamping steps to ensure the spikes grip. If the ice gets steeper, the dodgy fit will become dangerous. It would be unfair to press on and hold these women back, so they continue without me as I lower myself gingerly past the yawning crevasse, down towards the glacier base.

The next best option is to race up the Petit Vignemale. It's good moving freely again and I enjoy the view at the top with a retired Irish couple who visit the Pyrenees every year. He has a dry tongue and declares my journey as 'boring; why would you want to do that?' He suggests transport for the less interesting parts 'of which there are many'. This is in no way rude, just honest, and delivered with such sincerity that he makes me think he's got a point. The three of us while away an hour sharing chocolate, in agreement that the Pyrenees are 'unbeatable', as I silently question what makes the commitment to a goal seem worthy, noble even. Thinking in this way reduces my endeavour to an unrewarding grind, nothing but an arduous passage from one coast to another. I banish further thoughts and accept the final square of praline chocolate offered to me.

Edging past the Ossoue glacier, on the way to Gavernie, I peer into one of the legendary grottos of Count Henry Russell. I imagine him there, sporting a tweed jacket and cravat, shuffling about in espadrilles used by the Basque shepherds. Perhaps this was the very cave where in 1884, at the age of fifty, he realised his lifelong dream. There he lay, in his sheepskin sleeping bag, a cigar and mug of rum punch to hand, as lightning forked across his mountain in a storm that felt like an earthquake. One hundred and twenty years later, a squalid disarray of food wrappers, plastic bottles and tissues sprawl over its floor, recently used as a makeshift toilet. It's tempting to feel sad but then I remember that the fire of the count's passion has outlived the rigours of time. These grottos are just one reminder of an enduring legacy. It is impossible not to think of him in this part of the range, triumphant in the freedoms of his hallowed territory, his self-styled Pyrenean playground.

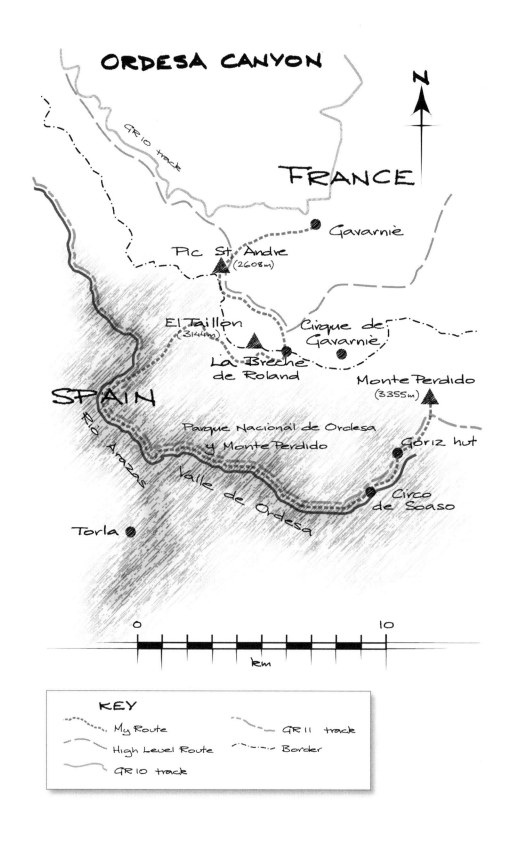

ORDESA CANYON

N

FRANCE

GR 10 track

Gavarnie

Pic St Andre
(2608m)

El Taillon
(3144m)

Cirque de
Gavarnie

La Breche
de Roland

Monte Perdido
(3355m)

SPAIN

Río Arazas

Parque Nacional de Ordesa
y Monte Perdido

Goriz hut

Valle de Ordesa

Circo
de Soaso

Torla

0   10

km

KEY

.... My Route   ———— GR 11 track

— — — High Level Route   —·—·—· Border

———— GR 10 track

24 ANGELS OF ORDESA

It has only been a brief stay in Gavernie and I'm surprised it's a wrench to leave. The most celebrated spot of the French Pyrenees, for all its natural marvels, hasn't in any way captivated me. The stench of dung continually wafts around as donkeys, overburdened by their tourist cargo, relieve themselves along the thoroughfare towards Europe's highest waterfall. Vignemale peeps over Gavernie's famous rock amphitheatre, and in the cirque itself the eye is drawn to an extraordinary gap, the Brèche de Roland. The column of air stands in a formidable barrier of dense rock, like a knocked-out tooth. The gateway to Spain, once an escape route from occupied France, is where I'm heading next. Beyond its threshold lies Europe's little known Ordesa National Park, a geological jewel awarded World Heritage status with its French neighbour.

My hotel owner has invited me to share a final espresso before setting off. She is captivating, with her chestnut hair flecked in henna, eyes heavy with mascara and scarlet painted lips, usually drawing on a cocktail cigarette. In the course of a day she'll change her outfit at least once, into another loud ensemble of colours and fabrics. Looking lost in the faraway past, her deep, throaty voice roams through memories about her rootless childhood, the anchor her hotel has been and the sense of independence it brings to her life. Her companions are three mangy cats to be seen scurrying about the tattered furniture of her apartment through its half-open door. Loneliness pervades her theatrical laughter when she makes light of a history of disappointed love and broken hearts. She lights up over my plans to press on through the remote Ariège, straying close to winter. More than once similarities she perceives in us both are stressed. Of course, the revolving door of hospitality attracts a stream of human traffic into her home, but somehow I imagine my visit will be kept on file. I can hear her indulging the story of 'zee Engleesh woman ... so, so independent. No man. Strong, just like me. Oh yes, how I see myself in her ... '

The way up the Sarradets valley to the foot of the Brèche is a dramatic journey. Steepening scree and boulder fields nestle beneath the rocky ramparts of the Gavernie Cirque and its curious gaping space. A disturbed night in a hut crammed with bunks and snoring bodies makes stepping into the chilly dawn a relief. The careful tread on the glaciers guarding the final approach requires my total concentration. To watch the day wake up at the Brèche is spectacular.

Legend has it that the one-hundred-metre-high gap was hacked out by the dying Roland, nephew of Charlemagne, as he tried to smash his magic sword to stop it falling into the hands of the Moors. But the huge basin gouged by glaciers scouring through the limestone hills does not need the helping hand of myth to make its magic felt. The still, windless, early morning turns gusty the other side of the rock doorway. Peaks higher than 3,000m (9,843ft) span the horizon, bordering an expanse of high-altitude scree desert. Like waves, its hills move in the changing light, interwoven with fawns, greys, browns, oranges and golden yellows. The canyon walls drop down to dense blue-green forest.

Where to begin? All at once I want to see everything, go everywhere. The block-shaped Taillon, the easiest 3000-m (9,843-ft) peak to reach, is to my right, immediately west. I head for it, knowing the guaranteed ascent will secure outstanding views. I look at the map and plan how to break away from the throng of hikers in this populated patch of wilderness. The contours are only a little steeper on the mountain's other side, suggesting a logical circuit of descent. I check with a man guiding a small party whether a path continues that way and he promptly informs me, gesturing a cut neck with a finger, 'to continue is to fall to a certain death'. I show him the map and he agrees it is misleading. 'Remember', he says in a strong French accent, 'it is Spanish, so what do you expect, huh?' This omission of a cliff drop requiring an abseil for safe descent is unnerving.

Once down, I bound off west into the dusty emptiness. The sense of space is all the more exciting because no one else is heading this way. I have never wandered in desert terrain like this. Its sparseness feels alien, making my every step through it seem all the more alive. Every fifteen minutes I stop to take a fresh compass reading to fix my point to the map. Flocks of choughs circle above, their spirited calls a perfect foil to the desiccated expanse. A vulture glides across the sky looking for carrion, natural furniture in a home where I don't belong. The odd cairn has a lonely presence in the vastness. These efforts to imprint a guiding marker through wild land, inherently unruly, look forlorn – but I'm grateful for them. They are the only sign of human traces. I am on my own and uncomfortable with this level of solitary exposure. Comfort zones are bound to expand with experience – so what was unthinkably difficult a month ago would seem more routine now. Yet, being so far off the beaten track is stretching my nerve to its limit. And still, I continue on.

Encountering the edge of a steep slope of scree and loose rock, I pause. I could head back the way I've come – just another two or so hours to the base of Taillon and an easy descent to a more populated part of the national park for the night. To clamber down into a new area of the canyon would commit me to chance; to make a mistake would be serious. It is late in the afternoon, a Sunday too, driving day-trippers homewards for the working week ahead. This is perhaps the remotest edge of the canyon. Down or back? Uncertainty or retreat? Adventure or reason? Unable to resist, I lower myself over the edge and slowly scramble to the bottom.

Looking up the way I've come compounds the loneliness of my venture. I haven't seen another soul for a good few hours. The scale of space between the peaks is hard to take in. The soft undulations of colour rippling into the distance are like the ageless patterns of thick primeval soup. Ordesa canyon is hauntingly beautiful – alluring and hostile at the same time. If the Pyrenees is Europe's last wilderness, then Ordesa is its wildest spot. The sun continues to beat down but there are enough water sources for that not to be a worry. The day is slipping away and finding a way through steep rocky sections takes longer than the map suggests, my progress between short distances on paper is slow. Further on, a meandering stream on a grassy plateau is a useful feature to remember for a bivvy site, should I find nothing better lower down. It might be best to stop for the day now, to avoid anything too strenuous until after some rest. But I am compelled to find out what lies beyond reasonableness.

A short distance lower down, the slope, now covered in thorny bushes, is swallowed by a fifty-foot high cliff. Beyond the drop, the terrain remains steep until the comforting sight of forest at the canyon floor. The initial exposure would not pose much difficulty with light gear but with twenty kilos, including water, agility is limited. There's a metal hand-hold but the only way down is to face into the cliff, where the weight of the pack might topple me over like a turtle. My arms could also give way and I might not have the strength to continue down or climb back up. It is too far to drop the pack – that can be ruled out and I only have small pieces of cord, nothing suitable to lower it. Heading back to the stream for the night just prolongs the standoff. I could return to the Brèche – that is the most sensible idea – and reach the more populated side in darkness. But I don't have the energy to walk all that way. To press on is the least unappealing option. Slowly, I hoist myself over, managing a few steps down before my arms tremble under the strain of the weight. This really is too much for me.

Dangling my legs over the cliff, I wonder what to do next. There is always something de-motivating about retracing steps uphill. Ten minutes pass and there is still no inclination to move or break my inertia. Even if I was able to fly off this godforsaken spot, finding somewhere to sleep hidden from rangers scouting out illegal camping would be difficult. I know that the thirty-minute hike back up the hill to the stream is what I will end up doing. But right now I don't want to do that either.

As I stare into a cul-de-sac of depressing possibilities, a jogger bobs into view along the top of a hill, half a kilometre away. There's barely a moment to wonder why anyone would choose to run on this terrain at this time of day, because someone else then appears, bare-chested, bounding behind like a goat. They stop and bounce on the spot while they confer over the best route down, pointing towards the impenetrable cliff beneath me. Immediately my spirits lift. There really would be no other way to the trees and the road at the bottom except down this track of sorts, which nonetheless requires a leap of gritty faith. Minutes pass and they make light work of covering the distance to me. I try to recall some beginner's Spanish, acquired two months ago, not confident as to how I'll perform under this pressure.

I need not have worried. They jog over fresh-faced, barely panting, and eager to help. One of them speaks perfect English, the first Spanish person I've met in the Pyrenees who can string more than a few words together. He tells me to follow his friend down safely while he carries the pack. Despite his extraordinary positive spirit, it takes him three attempts as he struggles to balance under the weight of the pack and a few seconds to get his breath back at the bottom. Grinning, he tells me they haven't seen anyone else for hours; most visitors to Ordesa come to see the Brèche alone. The three of us express amazement at our chance meeting, very happy with its outcome, and I'm assured I'll be in the valley in little more than an hour. With that, the two friends speed off down the steep slope, disappearing into the thickening tree line.

The knee-straining descent does take longer but the man's optimism helps me keep focused. As the light dims, the lower canyon becomes richer in blues and greens. At the bottom at last, the reassuring firmness of tarmac is a touch of the everyday in such an extraordinary oasis within Europe. The business of the day not yet over, my senses pick up a trail through trees and lush bush towards an idyllic riverside spot, sheltered by pine trees. I have to work quickly to get everything prepared for the night, knowing that as soon as I settle down to eat, exhaustion will take over.

In the last of the light I slump into a ball and look upstream, wondering where I would be now without the lucky encounter with a fluent English speaker, chancing a remote route he hadn't planned to take. Help has taken on many forms in the Pyrenees with an uncanny sense of timing. It has materialised every time I've been most open to danger, like a dogged lurch of faith. Or folly? A branch snaps and I sit up, startled. A deer darts along the river's shallows, gracefully bounding off downstream. So many times in my life, the random kindness of strangers has touched me, as if we are all making sense of this human muddle together.

25 LEARNING THE LANGUAGE: NOVEMBER 2005

Leaving New Zealand to land in New Delhi is about as extreme a cultural shift as it gets. One is a showcase for the values of a bygone age while the other requires a more tenacious approach for the more racy ride. Nothing can prepare a visitor for the sensory bombardment that begins soon after touchdown. The vibrant confusion of splendour and squalor is part of an unavoidable initiation rite for a newcomer, where torments and delights unfold in equal measure. The spectrum of human potential, its greatness and kindness, poverty and disease, spring from the same source. Like a marred jewel, India bewitches because of its flawed beauty. The rich diversity of a home to a billion people is bound to extract a human cost.

A mid-evening arrival after a long-haul flight turned into a tale of self-interest disguised as welcome. There was no sign of the turbulence ahead as two languid customs officials nodded at my passport and gestured for me to continue. Wheeling my reclaimed backpack past placards with a host of names other than mine didn't cause me to flap unduly. A flurry of last-minute e-mails booking a hotel and taxi hadn't inspired my total confidence – as I was repeatedly referred to as 'sir' and had to correct the hotel's confirmation of my arrival date twice. After a second scan of the waiting drivers, I headed over to the 'pre-paid taxi' counter. India was the final destination of my eight-month trip and my guard was down – nothing in the coming weeks could disrupt a smooth ride homewards. Exhausted, after a journey of thirty-six hours, six stops and a resolve never again to be seduced by a marginally cheaper flight, I handed over the required rupees and all sense of responsibility for what might happen next.

Kumar, surprisingly tall for an Indian, shook my hand enthusiastically and insisted I share the front of his beaten-up two-door car. Just as the engine belched into life, he stroked his moustache, then clasped his hands together and started chanting.

'Do you always do this?'

'Oh yes, better to be safe,' he assured me while producing his mobile to reveal the name and London number of a certain Mr Peter Fellows.

'Know him? My great friend. Mr Fellows is a great, great man.' I shook my head, sorry to disappoint.

The horn blasted every time we swerved into another lane, at times forcing the oncoming traffic to veer onto the verge. Cows sauntered across the road with an abandon that would be charming were it not for Kumar's tendency to hurtle towards them. After going nowhere fast, Kumar had had enough. Traffic was busy for this time of night and we were trapped between two auto-rickshaws at the back of a logjam kangarooing along. He reversed without a care for the cars braking behind and swerved into a dirt track, as clouds of dust whipped up around us. A sign claimed this road, cratered with potholes, led to the 'City Centre'. I could only hope for the best, noting with alarm that no one was following us.

As soon as we hit areas sprawling with life, Kumar became vocal, pointing out sights of interest. He was especially excited by weddings, and gawped at the throngs of traditionally dressed guests outside the temples, 'Look, another one! There are hundreds of marriages in this wonderful city each day,' he beamed, as we sped by a blur of garish silks and glittering sequins, attended by costumed horses with feathery plumes. It was surprising how much life pulsed through this vibrant city at the dead of night. I was asked if I was married, to which I instinctively replied 'yes'. This triggered an awkward string of questions. Where was my husband? Does he like India too? What is his profession?

I trained my eyes on the filthy Delhi streets, its air as densely polluted as it had been a decade ago. Since my last visit, there had been a noticeable boom from investment and outsourcing. Silvery office blocks and their luminous windows were stacking up skywards, as Western service industries and computer giants capitalised on India's cheaper workforce. The centre was still a colourful chaos of trade and open-air stalls. Half an hour of being hurled about as Kumar's car roared along narrowing streets, the composure from months of easy, leisurely travel in New Zealand was rupturing. My hotel seemed no nearer either, remaining for a second time, 'not too far.' This became, at my persistence, 'fifteen minutes more maybe'. We soon pulled into a dingy dead end of rubble, looked over by half-built concrete blocks. Kumar cut the engine and announced we had 'at last reached the office'.

'What office?'

'The tourist office where I work. Highly respected. We can organise all your travel, everything, for your stay in India. You will save much time and much money to book now.'

'Now? At one in the morning?'

This surprise detour was unnerving enough. To enter the ramshackle building he was pointing at was another matter, requiring me to give up all sense of personal responsibility.

'Just come in, only for a moment. All the arrangements will be made for you. We are sponsored by the government of India. Very few tourist operators have such a licence, you know.'

The dimly lit back street looked as businesslike as any other residential hub. I was totally disorientated too – we could be anywhere in the capital for all I knew. A lethal mix of mistrust and tiredness switched to rage.

'Get me to my hotel NOW!'

Kumar looked thoroughly taken aback. He tried his best to negotiate with me, shaking his head in disbelief at my obstinate refusal to seize such an opportunity. He was no longer a fitting subject for later parody but someone unpredictable, as he slammed the car door and started up the engine. My heart racing, I remembered how dangerous fear could be. It was vital not to seem nervous. After making a polite observation about a passing sight of interest, an uneasy quiet settled between us as we sped on to my hotel.

We parked up in front of a forlorn red neon sign in the seedy heartland of budget hotels near Delhi's main train station. The entrance vaguely resembled the cropped website picture which hadn't shown the crumbling street lined with corrugated iron shacks and derelict buildings. As I stared lifelessly at the uninviting threshold, Kumar asked if I knew about the nearby bomb blast the week before which killed fifty people? I readily accepted his suggestion to look at a three-star hotel in a smarter suburb not far from where we were.

The farce which followed and my apparent acquiescence might be explained by the exhaustion of forty hours of travel, but the clock ticked on and my resilience hardened as I benignly planted dollars into Kumar's hands on our tour of possibilities, all of them extortionate by local standards. In the end, The Red Castle, with its surplus staff lined up to open the door to hand me soap, to offer tea, to bring an extra towel just in case, lured me to the waiting giant bed. I regretted nothing, not even the fifty-dollar rate, as I fell into sound sleep.

＊   ＊   ＊

My vision to head somewhere hilly was not lacking in scope. It covered a surface area stretching thousands of miles across the Himalayan spine of north India, along its borders with Pakistan, Tibet, Nepal, and Bhutan. My need to narrow the search mysteriously hit the radars of a number of people whose strong sense of direction made up for my initial lack of it. Kashmir, a terrorist trouble spot and long since a tourist magnet, was experiencing a promotion drive at street level. Yo-yoing between different agencies and sweet-talking locals, reminiscing about India's true Shangri-La chipped away at my resistance. Gradually, the idea of having the lion's share of its famed natural wonders to myself seemed so appealing that I booked the next day's flight there. Within hours my dream of waking up on a houseboat to forested mountains and snow-capped ridges was eclipsed by remembering more earthly realities such as marching troops and warnings from embassies. After a restless night of fretful sleep, I asked my hotelier for his opinion.

'Kashmir? Oh no, Madam. I would not allow any member of my family to go there. Look … '

He searched for a newspaper article he'd just seen about a bomb that had killed two people the day before, close to the lake where I would be staying. Accepting another sweet tea, I listened to his views about 'more suitable destinations for a lone lady.' His neck wobbled and finger shook to emphasise the correct places for an aspiring itinerant of India's mountainous regions. Shimla and its crumbling colonial hill station charms would be 'ideal' as a launch pad for the Himalaya – on this he was certain. Due north of Delhi, it had been adopted as the summer capital of the Raj. From Shimla, there would be ample opportunity for climbing excursions. I would then wind up my eight-month trip in the desert for a geographical contrast and a twelve-day meditation retreat. For the first time since arriving in India, I was back in charge of my destiny. All I had to do was book the ticket out of Delhi.

I walked all the way through the new city to the train station, ignoring the rickshaw drivers, badgering for custom, and strangers asking where I was from or whether I was married. In front of the railway entrance, some boys, barely teenagers, were selling padlocks in every conceivable size. Prices were being shouted out as industrial steel versions were touted alongside flimsier ones. Won over by the honed selling skills of the vendors, I suddenly wanted a padlock.

'Hundred rupees.'

'A hundred? Don't you mean twenty? Look, this is the second smallest.'

'OK. For you good price. Sixty rupees. Last price.'

'No, for that one maybe. But this, twenty-five. Last price.'

'No Madam. Forty. Last price. Only for you.'

Hardened by my costly encounters with tourist predators, a close-knit network of taxi drivers, hoteliers, and travel agents, I wasn't going to budge. Just as I walked off, one of them raced up to me with the padlock. The rupees were about to change hands when I noticed this padlock was smaller than the one I'd haggled over. Immediately a spontaneous burst of applause and laughter erupted among the boys, their faces lit up in delightful mischief. I couldn't help but join in. As I laughed, some nearby traders laughed too, until our small area of grubby street was filled with laughter, all of us finding a small moment funnier for being shared. This had been some sort of test and I had passed it.

'You smart. Not like other tourists,' said the older-looking seller. 'Very good. Very good. Everybody falls every time.'

I paid thirty and we were all happy. This had not been a victory over petty bargaining but marked an acceptance of sorts. A line had been stepped over, narrowing the gulf between a fresh-faced visitor from New Zealand and a quick-witted operator of the New Delhi street.

I never bought the ticket to Shimla. Waiting in the tourist queue to buy a ticket was entertainingly spent sharing tales of being fleeced by cunning ruses. One couple had been turned away by a man in uniform at the railway entrance, believing the office was 'closed for repair' and had followed his directions to his 'cousin's' travel business miles away in the Old Town. For the first time, I thought of Kumar and all the others with a certain respect. They had to work hard to learn the language of survival and push its boundaries from an early age. Being comfortable dulls the wit of those who can afford to be ripped off. Feeling the humour of solidarity that my entrée to India was not in any way unique, I accepted the queue's unanimous advice to head to the most peaceful diversion from Delhi – the Himalayan home of the Dalai Lama. McLeod Ganj is a thriving Tibetan community and the headquarters of its exiled government. Kashmir and Shimla would always be there for another time.

▨　　　▨　　　▨

The Himalayan pathways were filled with people who'd normally be in the fields working. Young accompanying the old made their way together along worn, dusty trade routes to cast their vote in the civic hall of the nearest village. This was the run up to election day, the culmination of weeks of campaigning for district leaders to put their vision on the map of one of India's remotest corners. Posters were stuck everywhere: on village walls, carts, on random trees. Beside a photo of a candidate, there would be simple everyday objects like a dog, cat, a pipe, or crown. Illiteracy is the norm in these remote areas and so these essential memory joggers give voice to thousands of people who would otherwise remain unheard. The symbols had to cut through the political hyperbole and capture what these candidates stood for in the minds of those they were hoping to serve. Walking the long way to take part in polling day brought the isolated region to a two-day-long standstill. The energy was in marked contrast to the electoral apathy and disillusionment with politics back home. Corruption is as rife in India as anywhere but this way of transcending the limits of language somehow elevated the political process to a sense of occasion.

As election fever swept through the valleys, the Tibetan prayer flags fluttered. Catching the light, these fabric triangles mark a journey through centuries of cultures and their creeds, unifying the Himalaya's rich diversity.

They are rarely still and their motion now, surrounded by the solid immensity of the steep valley was reminding me that my trip was nearing its end. The two-day journey to Jaipur by bus and train would begin the next day. As I walked back to my hotel, an exotic-looking Indian with long dark hair motioned me over, a steaming cup of tea in one hand.

'Please. Share it with me.'

'That's very kind, why not?'

'You strike me as someone who likes tea.'

The man had a clipped Oxford English accent. He was leaning against a café wall smoking, while his eyes followed the flow of street life.

'Yeah, it's strange being half-Indian when I feel mostly British. My mum fell for my dad while doing the hippy thing through Asia in the sixties. She would drag me to Glastonbury when I was a kid. She's still way more into festivals and all that spiritual stuff than I am.'

We took turns sipping the tea, watching a rich parade of turquoise and coral, stripy aprons and prayer wheels, maroon robes, and baseball boots. Monks, dressed simply with their hair shorn, would carry prayer beads in one hand and a mobile or Walkman in the other.

'Ever thought about doing Vipassana meditation? You should try it.'

'Actually, funny you should ask. I'm leaving for Jaipur tomorrow for a twelve-day retreat. Then I can spend a last week in the desert before flying home.'

'Why not go to Dehra Dun, where I did mine? It's far closer and nicer – in the Garwhal Himalaya. Just show up.'

And so I did. I had not suspected for a moment that a shared cup of tea might serve a greater role than to liven up a lonely evening. It altered the outcome of my time in India and outlook ever since.

26 ENLIGHTENMENT AND THE OBROYS

The retreat is overlooked by rugged mountains and guarded by a river that would repel anything but the sturdiest jeeps. The seclusion is apt for the demands expected of those staying there. All worldly responsibilities are left at the threshold in return for observing strict moral precepts during the twelve days. There's no price tag for this experience and the system depends on donations. Men and women live separately; there would be no stimulants, theft, or murder, and no eating after noon. Reading and writing are banned. Books can be handed in for safe keeping to avoid any temptation. Perhaps the most challenging undertaking of all: no communication of any kind with fellow residents, including eye contact. To break any of these house rules could result in being asked to leave at once.

There is a window either side of the ten-day vow of silence in which talking is allowed and paperwork processed. On arrival, form after form is filled and signed by each resident, checked and countersigned by a vigilant assistant. The spartan regime of living in simple shared rooms with hard beds and two vegetarian meals to be taken by noon each day are explained. A bell chimes the day into segments for meditation and rest, from four in the morning until bed at nine-thirty. The layout is split in two; men live and eat on one side and women on the other. Restless energy can be marched off in the partitioned gardens between the eating quarters and the meditation hall. A strikingly simple pagoda crowns the complex where more experienced practitioners are invited to meditate in a 'cell', facing a shaft of light from a chink in the ceiling.

On the first evening when talking was still allowed, a social division between Hindi and English speakers formed naturally in the women's quarters and lasted throughout. The dozen who spoke Hindi, north India's main language, seemed barely older than teenagers. Despite their reserve, they never disguised their curiosity for the rest of us and would stare unfazed at a returned look. There were also two Australians, a South Korean, and two Indian women of whom the eldest caught my attention as soon as she arrived. She looked thin and delicate in her sari and twitched, a restlessness which never stilled in the coming days. Her hair was swept into a neat grey bun and her large dark eyes burned with warmth and life. The alluring blend of fragility and sparkle made me wonder if her beauty had once been touched by sadness. Our eyes locked as she darted past the open door to my room for a third time making her turn around abruptly and walk in.

'You seem very familiar to me. But we haven't met I don't think,' she said.

'No. Have you done this before?' Of everyone I'd spoken to, only the South Korean had experienced a silent retreat.

'No. I have been meaning to come here over the years. I only live nearby in Dehra Dun. And what about you?'

'Oh, a bit further away, England. I'm a first timer too.'

This delighted her and I heard about a son in the merchant navy who sometimes docked in Portsmouth, just down the road from where I grew up. Our rapport deepened at this and she glowed as she continued to look at me, ignoring the other woman in the room. Her eyes dipped to my bed where my unpacked things were spread about.

'What is that?' she asked, pointing to my head torch.

'Oh this? It's a torch. You wear it like this.' I held it up to my forehead. 'I take it everywhere.'

'No! A torch – that you put on your head?'

'Yes. You simply adjust the strap and carry on about your business.'

'Do you mind?' She looked as excited as an awestruck child as she held it up and cocked her head this way and that, her mouth open and her eyes wide.

'Try it on.'

She pulled at the elastic band, then thought better of it and asked me to show her. 'Like this. The switch is just at the top here – and, here we go … light!'

Never has so little effort been made to inspire so much. The woman's rapture was undiluted as she moved about the room, delighting in the beam that danced about the drab concrete floor. A discussion of costs followed which were converted into US dollars then rupees. Would I have any idea of manufacturing costs or indeed which corner of the world were the parts produced? Seeds of an idea were sowing. Over the days of unfolding silence, during prized time to quieten lively minds, they would germinate, as thoughts of lucrative returns would fill the hours of crossed-legged discomfort. India had not yet discovered the head torch but the look that met mine, as she handed it back, made me wonder when it would.

The long silent hours were filled with passive observation. Vipassana meditation is an ancient technique that the Buddha taught as a cure for unrest. It died out in India and in 1969 was reintroduced by a Burmese guru, a former industrialist with an urbane sense of humour and evident love of food. Every evening we would watch a videoed discourse from the equable Shri SN Goenka. His vision for enlightenment transcends religion and promotes the earthly values of calm and kindness. Over the days he guided us along an inter-woven tapestry of the nature of matter and its relationship to mind. Made of numberless moving atoms, matter is no more solid than water and only seems independent to dulled senses. So if nothing is ever fixed, our interpretation of events is just as malleable and the quest for certainty can only be empty and fruitless.

These ideas are as rooted in quantum physics as the most ancient philoso-phies. This was the first time in eight months of moving through places, their people and values that I had sat still. It was also the first time that I had peered inside an internally shifting landscape. For hours on end, day after day, I saw my mind lurch and lift, hover and plunge as it reacted, warped and coloured. Rarely has it engaged with the unfolding present except during a mountaineering challenge or danger. This sedentary struggle woke me up to how 'now' is all there ever really is; all we can ever claim as our own, as the only true concept of place in time.

Meanwhile, the winter days were shortening and the nights and early mornings were bitterly cold. Yet a life of silence was full. During rest periods each of us would shed our cocoon of wiry blankets and prowl like cats in search of patches of sunlight to bask and stretch. Roaming about the familiar territory each day could still surprise awakening senses. Trees and the life they supported, their bark, leaves and bloom or the birds and butterflies that fluttered among them, strained with detail, tone and texture. The toiling work of hammering and raking through the valley continued outside our walled boundary. Undergrowth would rustle and branches snap as buffalo stamped along a path through the forested hills behind the pagoda. Children would chatter and laugh as they made their way to and from school at first light and before dark, their uniforms visible through the gaps in the bush. Washing clothes and drying them on the line in the centre of our quadrangle quarters during a few sunny hours from noon, was another element to retreat life.

There were two opportunities a day to talk to the teacher, and designated assistants could attend to anything urgent, like the removal of four giant spiders from my cobwebbed room. I grew reliant on the selfless service of an elderly assistant. He dismissed my grovelling gratitude on the second dead-of-night plea for help, declaring 'it was his duty' to protect me from another spider. I had wondered if my shrieks contravened the precept of silence and whether my recoil breached the instruction not to react to pain or pleasure. I sought the counsel of our teacher who solemnly shook his head in answer to both questions and suggested I try 'loving' spiders instead. One day I couldn't find the spider handler and tracked down the gentle cook at work in the kitchen. He followed me to my room and started to chase the spider as it scuttled away from his scooping hands. He hit on a bright idea, gesturing he would be back and returned with a broom, with which he proceeded to thwack the life out of it. The otherwise unassuming man assessed his work and nodded in satisfaction, as I considered how he could so easily reconcile this flagrant breach of one of Buddhism's most sacred edicts.

Apart from my excitable outbursts, there was silence. Yet it was possible to be aware of nearly all the fifty other residents by sensing a mood shift or restlessness. The woman intrigued by my head torch would leave some of the meditation sessions early. She seemed especially affected by the cold and would blow on her hands and rub them together. One evening before the bell marking the evening discourse, she suddenly entered my room. Clearly remembering the ban on eye contact as well as conversation, the woman managed to avoid my look as she moved around in search of something. While gazing at the floor, she gestured to her forehead, which made me wonder if she had a headache. She then spotted my piled up things on a spare mattress and proceeded to lift up various items to check what lay underneath. Now desperate, enough to break the precept, she stared at me while tapping her head repeatedly, until she was sure that at last I had got it. She wanted my head torch.

Reunited with it, the same performance of five evenings ago was relived – the fascination, the careful handling, the trying it on, the adjustment of the elastic, the switch of light. Finally she put it back to where it had been and clasped her hands in thanks. Her encouragement to break a faithfully observed rule was both exasperating and charming, as she then squiggled the air with an imaginary pen. I had handed over the contraband at the start of the course and so I shook my head. She leant towards me and whispered, 'My name is Mrs Obroy. It has been a pleasure meeting you. I don't like this meditation and am going home. You must come and stay. My husband Captain Obroy will pick you up. I will leave my number at the office.' And with that, she was gone.

■   ■   ■

After such an intense social withdrawal, stepping back into a strangely fast-moving world is bound to be overwhelming. There was little time for such adjustment as I found myself garnered with two other people from the retreat to share the hospitality of the Obroys. They were from another social vista altogether – Stephen had grown up in the former Portuguese colony of Goa and worked with street children in Delhi as a social worker. Ritu worked in a bank and was married unhappily to a man she would not leave as their relationship was 'a growing experience'. During the vow of silence, the three of us had each been covertly briefed to await the captain, who dutifully showed up in his car as planned, extending a firm handshake.

A pair of thick-framed dark glasses took up most of his friendly face, a cigarette puffed from the corner of his smiling mouth. A firm paunch ballooning from his otherwise lean frame suggested the captain enjoyed his retired life from the merchant navy. It was eight in the morning and breakfast would be waiting for us. To think we had volunteered to give up food after noon – what was wrong with us? A cassette of a Hindu chant soothed our nerves that were rudely aware of every bump and hole along the road overrun with stray dogs and buffalo. Civilisation was a busy whirl of people, noise and smell. It was a relief to pull into a quiet, tree-lined suburb of driveways and their large comfortable houses.

Mrs Obroy greeted us at the front door as if we were her returning children, hugging us warmly as the captain shook his head at his wife's ability to magnetise people, which was unsurprising as well as marvellous. Over eggs, chapatis, cheese, porridge and cups of sweet tea, we celebrated as though we were old friends returning to the life we had known twelve long days before. The captain explained his wife was not made for 'introspection' and it would have 'amazed' him if she had made it to the end of the meditation. Mrs Obroy added how cold it had been and she had given up hope for peace and calm in an experience undoubtedly rigorous and uncomfortable, 'What was the point in all that? Observe this sensation and observe that. Why?'

'Mumbo jumbo, bloody nonsense,' the captain concurred.

As for him, a retreat could not possibly make up for the balance of a happy life – in his case an evening stroll around the neighbourhood and two whiskies, occasionally three. His weakness was cigarettes, always Dunhill, but the underpinning of his life, holding his week together, is bridge night. It is 'a ritual like a meditation of sorts.' As the maid brewed more tea and served a second round of omelettes, we were taken on a nostalgic tour of his restless seafaring career, distinguished by being the youngest captain in India's merchant navy at the age of twenty-seven. He had travelled the world many times and recalled Alaska and New Zealand as fondly as my own recent memories. We laughed at stories of customs disputes and near collisions with tankers at the dead of night, of quarantine and the colourful haunts in port they'd frequent. Ship hospitality was an important part of his role as captain and one we could imagine him carrying out with dedication.

We then went outside to the patio to soak up the late morning sun where I demonstrated the practicalities of the head torch that had so impressed Mrs Obroy. I watched her face light up in girlish delight as I gave it to her, feeling only the faintest trace of severed attachment as it had served me so well on countless outdoor trips. We drank more tea and accepted gifts of chocolates and shortbread from our hosts, a box each. The dogs were fed by their mistress sporting a curious beam of light that emanated from her forehead while Captain Obroy shuffled off inside, to find some family albums to show us. We flopped in two large hammocks while stories were told about the photos passing between us.

It was only then that the undercurrent of sadness I had barely sensed began to surface. As well as a son and daughter and thriving grandchildren, we heard of the child they lost fifteen years ago. Kamal was one of life's uniquely special people, his short life touching everyone he met. As soon as he could talk he told anyone who would listen how he was going to be a doctor and only help India's poorest people. He might arrive home in a shirt at the dead of winter having given his coat to someone who needed it more and always donated his pocket money. He envisaged a life as a medical volunteer. He wanted to serve others and try to make a grain of difference to the poverty trap. At twenty-three, only months before qualifying, he was killed in a motorbike accident. As Captain Obroy spoke about Kamal, his wife meekly watched and listened, raw pain etched across her beautiful tired face. It was as if her son's sudden and violent death had stunted her life and a childlike spirit of openness and wonder had survived the blight of tragedy. Her husband had found refuge in being her rock but she had yet to find a comforting purpose to mask the unhealed wound. 'All you can do is love,' she told us. 'Be as giving as you can. Kamal taught us that.'

■   ■   ■

My last two days in Delhi made me realise how far I'd travelled since my arrival there some six weeks before. I stayed in the household of the brother of Captain Obroy, who himself travelled to Delhi in order to accompany me as my faithful shopping chaperone, haggling on my behalf for gifts with an authority which got results. I witnessed some of his poker-faced steeliness that had made him a revered ship commander and a mean card player. Some of the hardest and most humourless of traders allowed their prices to wilt in the face of the captain's entertaining bargaining mastery. Thirty-three years my senior and with a love of life more vital than someone half his age, my companion ensured that we ate the most delicious meals, toured the best markets and drank only the best whisky. Observing his evening ritual and topping our glasses up little and often, he shared a stream of stories from years at sea and docking at foreign shores, while flicking his cigarette ash on his brother's kitchen floor with a brazen lack of concern.

We stayed up most of the final night, leaving a four-hour window to sleep before getting up to catch my flight home. Where I had arrived in India jaded and suspicious, I left it feeling grateful and belonging. Waving to the captain from the airport entrance as he drove away, our goodbye felt as uplifting as sad. My time with the Obroys and their special vision of the world would be a lasting treasure. As I had been told so simply, 'we were meant to meet. We will always be in your life.'

27 LAND OF BIRDS: SEPTEMBER 2005

In the beginning, until the first humans landed in canoes, New Zealand was mainly forest, filled with birds and no other mammals but three species of bat. In the ninth century, the first Maori would have encountered many different species of bird, including the giant flightless moa, now extinct. In 1642 the Dutch claimed the land theirs. By 1769 Captain Cook had declared it British and three years later it was christened *France Australe* by the French. The folklore of its Christian settlers enshrines Eden's serpent as a symbol of vice – but they would never have encountered real snakes. The archipelago has always been empty of poisonous or cannibalistic predators. In fact in the two hundred years since colonisation began, the greatest menace has always been man. Despite the bloody human dramas and their environmental fall-out, New Zealand's long isolation from the rest of the world has helped preserve its celebrated wilderness.

It seemed a lucky accident that I began my winter in New Zealand at Milford Sound, sixteen kilometres inland from the Tasman Sea, on the south-west coast of South Island. This area, known as Fiordland, was once gouged by glaciers and is the 'Eighth Natural Wonder of the World'. When the sun shines, water cascades like white sheets down the steep sides of tree-covered mountains into the fiord's pristine waters. When it rains, the land seeps water from every rocky crack and pore. Seven metres of rain a year fall here, the country's wettest spot. Alaska may be vast, untouched and isolated yet this ancient and less remote landscape has a character all of its own. The eye-catching Mitre Peak, at a height of 1,692m (5,560ft), is one of the highest mountains in the world to rise directly from the ocean floor. The bush surrounding its dense rainforest casts its own mood upon the inlets teeming with wildlife.

A fellow American NOLS student had suggested we attempt a winter circuit of the world-famous Milford Track. Overrun with thousands of 'trampers' in season, we had the beautiful route to ourselves. This was where the early Maori had searched for greenstone. The pioneers of the late nineteenth century had also cut a route through the thick bush to the region's main centre, Te Anau, two valleys away. Heavy snow and avalanche-sensitive slopes turned us back half way.

Entranced by the beauty and maverick spirit of the local people, I ended up staying for several weeks. Fresh from Alaska and the Pacific North-West, I had gravitated to another resourceful community living according to the terms of their environment. Only people who work within the National Park area can live there. In return for free board, boat rides or kayaking trips, transient residents help out with odd jobs for four hours a day. I enjoyed the satisfaction of my undemanding work of washing dishes in the only kitchen catering for the fishermen and visitors, and changing beds in the only hostel. Just how neatly could those corners be tucked and how quickly could I unload the industrial plate dryers to fill them again with more ketchup-smeared plates?

Every day became a torment as I set a new deadline to leave, having no real inclination to uproot. Fiordland's geography added to the intensity of being there. There is no horizon, only mountains interlocking around channels of water, directing the eye to their commanding presence. It's as if the earth has been squashed upwards in the competition for space. I hadn't come to New Zealand to live in a community but to play with its ice and snow, to explore its wilderness. Yet to spend time in the thriving social enclave of Milford opened my eyes and fired my imagination. It was full of interesting, well-informed people attuned to New Zealand's rich cultural history with its natural treasures.

After work, if it wasn't raining, a gang would gather around shore-side fires. There would be stories or music; guitars and tambourines, pipes and fiddles. Sina, half Samoan, would enthral us for hours dancing with fire tools, merging into the seamless movement of flame, spinning above the sand. She was so deft and bold that whenever anyone else tried, they tended to burn their hands or drop the fiery batons. I looked forward to washing dishes when Sina was the duty chef. A landscape gardener by trade and dabbling artist, she'd discovered a passion for creating beautiful food. Colour schemes were important to her – but most vital of all for any dish was 'to cook with love.' She was convinced you could taste the difference and that a dish suffers if cooked under stress. Like all the resident staff, she lived in a supplied caravan and welcomed late-night conversation among the art objects she'd made, the shells and pictures. Her wild, unruly hair was wrapped in exotic material and her hands, busily rolling cigarettes after long days in the kitchen, were large strong creator's hands. She would follow the seasons, moving about New Zealand with her working portfolio, her resourceful spirit like an ageless nomad.

There was not one person in Milford who wasn't sensitive to the shifts of light, of a shadow dancing on the water, or a changing sky. One night a cloudless, starlit sky filled with the Southern Lights. It was like watching a milky veil displace countless stars as it rippled out across space. When the lights were at their most vivid and extraordinary, they seemed more like a cosmic dance than an atmospheric phenomenon. The display was dream-like for all of us who'd never seen anything like it.

Wet, grey days became oppressive, driving everyone indoors. Between chores, I'd meander along the forested shallows, absorbed by their haunting quality. There was a wild, Jurassic atmosphere along the delta where magnificent mythical birds should soar above the snow-capped peaks before diving towards their prey below the waterline. Along this shoreline, I'd think about the word *mauri,* meaning the 'life force' of all things. The Maori see it as the essence of survival, employed a thousand years ago by their ancestors, who sought refuge and food in these inlets. They are still full of life now. Thousands of birds with chubby, bright breasts and elegant fantails, ducks paddling in the lush reeds and fern-filled forests harbouring brightly coloured fungi that spill onto the muddy flats.

The rich evolutionary history is enlivened by New Zealand storytelling traditions. Childhood tales are entwined with the mythology of its first inhabitants, a colourful mosaic of Maori terms and tales, to try and make sense of the world. A national identity, so rooted in its landscape, can only make an impact on those passing through it. The stories shared can change long-held perceptions. It's said that when Captain Cook's ship was anchored off the South Island's north coast, none of the gathered Maori saw it. A large sea-faring vessel with a rigging of multi-layered canvas sails had no similarity to the hacked-out tree trunks they paddled. A wise man in the community urged his people to guard against the shape on the water. It was only on his instruction that they at last saw the ship floating on their fish-rich waters. This unknown invader was to change their destiny and the future of these South Pacific islands. This story suggests that vision is shaped by memory; the brain has to experience an image first in order to recall it. There is a gap between what the eye sees and the mind interprets before anything is actually 'seen'. I wonder what else our vision might fail to 'see' or recognise, shaped as it is by a life of cultural conditioning?

By the time I persuaded myself to leave Milford's absorbing charms, I was armed with a list of contacts and prime areas to gain more winter mountaineering experience. More importantly, I had been exposed to a refreshingly creative outlook. New Zealand's short and colourful human history had opened my mind to the pleasures of a simpler life, one with a balance of need and want. I'd seen how possible it is to live by the rhythm of nature's clock. I longed to learn more about man's more primitive state and his connection to the land. An altogether new horizon was opening up quite unexpectedly.

28 STOLEN BOOT

The Southern Alps of New Zealand are renowned for their isolation and exposure to some of the world's most fickle weather. The heavily glaciated mountains run nearly seven hundred and fifty kilometres along the spine of the South Island and the prevailing westerly climate brings prolonged cold fronts to the region from the nearby Tasman Sea. Kiwi alpinists are revered for their skill and endurance; to climb in such remoteness increases the risks. Like the Alps in Europe, these mountains are steeped in stories of daring and Victorian eccentricity. The pioneers smoked pipes and wore tweed and still managed to pull off ambitious feats. The peaks of Cook, Tasman, and Haast are among the best known in this range but are by no means the most demanding. Compounding the challenge of weather and terrain, most climbs require long approaches taking days to reach. Helicopter drop-offs are the costly and energy-conserving option. When an opportunity arose to hitch a ride for a weekend of alpine play, I could barely believe my luck.

After a short flight over alpine wilderness we land on a snowfield. The engines cut and the blades stop. The scheduled stop is for the tourist passengers, a couple and their sporty-looking daughter, not yet a teenager, who leaps off the dangling ladder, looking the part in a tracksuit and baseball cap. It was a tight squeeze in the back and Gavin and I are the last to step onto the landing area the size of a football pitch. There are two inches of fresh snow, pristine white and crunchy. It's certainly the day for such a ride – the mountains sparkle in a bright sun and we can positively hear the silence. Gavin had wangled our free ride through his contacts as a local glacier guide. In return we would ensure the pilot and his crew at base would be well rewarded with beer.

The six of us say nothing as we adjust to the proximity of the icy giants, no longer obscured through the cloudy Perspex of the helicopter windows. Every minute is factored into the cost and the husband and wife start to record the event. A series of pans, tilts and zooms capture a sense of what it feels like to be here. Gavin and I smile at each other, excited too by the perfect scenery. Their daughter sprints away from us all, as if her life depends on it, covering a surprising distance in seconds. Stopping, she kicks up arcs of snow and watches it fall, then spins, arms outstretched before cartwheeling in sheer joy. Her parents take it in turns to smile at the camera, now with a helicopter as the backdrop, while the pilot notices his youngest passenger nearing the other end of the flat space.

'Oi! You're a little too far out there. Just come back a bit please … hey! Come back a bit … '

He doesn't have to shout too loudly to make himself heard. Sound carries on snow. The girl hesitates, then runs a little reluctantly at first, soon picking up an easy speed. The way she moves so effortlessly reminds me of a gull gliding along the surface of water.

'Great snow Mags. Good firm settled stuff, this.' Gavin's Irish accent has softened from three years of living in New Zealand but his features are unmistakably Celtic: red hair, green eyes and freckled face. Tall and sinewy, his every muscle is honed from cutting steps and scrambling through the glacier's churned-up debris five days a week. He's made a pile of snow to see how it holds together and checks what's under the newest layers. An avalanche test assesses the pack's quality and will dictate a route over it. The helicopter is going to drop us off next at Almer Hut five minutes away, before taking the family back via Mount Cook, New Zealand's highest mountain. By dark, we will have reached Centennial Hut, which could take between three and four hours.

'We should have a good run of it. Not too soft for this time of day.'

Everything about Gavin's steady style invites trust. As a Franz Josef Glacier Guide he knows the western area of the range especially well. The Southern Alps drew him to uproot from Dublin to the South Island: his introduction to the icy spires and ridges of shattered rock was 'love at first sight,' inexplicably familiar to someone beholding them for the first time. Working as a guide is demanding, having to navigate inexperienced parties through uneven glacial terrain among a disarray of giant ice blocks twisting down the valley. Routes that might have been relied on for weeks can be ruined overnight by the ice flow's force.

The girl either then forgets, or ignores, the pilot's advice and runs off again, this time not stopping until she's a speck, dwarfed by the nearby faces and their forbidding peaks.

'Hey. Look here! This is not safe. Come back right away!'

She runs back to us within seconds. The pilot reasserts himself, 'Now that's enough, OK, young lady? Stay in this area. We will have to go in two minutes. OK everyone?'

'Yup, it's surprisingly firm, despite the snowfall … ' Gavin says patting it again.

Wanting to be involved, I crouch next to him, prod the snow and agree.

Hopefully its quality will make lighter work of our heavy loads. We are carrying snowshoes and all the gear for ice climbing, as well as gourmet supplies. A snowy missile skims over Gavin's head.

'You cheeky … '

Immediately he pelts the girl back, and she darts about laughing, gathering snow to fire at anyone who catches her eye. I am the next in line, and just manage to splat her back as I step onto the ladder attached to the open door.

Within five minutes in the air, we drop onto a narrow landing space near the hut. Gavin and I jump off, grabbing our packs from the ski basket on the side of the helicopter and we wave goodbye as it rises again and quickly recedes into the white distance. Now we really are on our own.

Our route isn't difficult to navigate and every half hour we swap the lead. The snow is softer in the mid-afternoon heat and breaking trail is more tiring than following. Gavin is easy company and talks like the best of them. Our breaks get longer and more regular. We have to adjust to the weight of spare rope and our packs that are filled with unnecessary extras like books, spare clothes, and wine bottles. I hadn't paid attention to such excess as the hut will be the base from where a helicopter will pick us up again. I'm regretting that now. It has only been two months since I had hauled this amount of gear around for days and my strength has waned. I set my sights on the top of each rise, looking forward to the inevitable decline. In this perfect light, the wind-scuffed shapes of snow cliffs are luminescent sculptures and the insides of crevasses glimmer in every shade of blue.

I think of Troy, Gavin's friend, who'd introduced us after we'd met in Milford. Normally quiet, Troy can astound those around him with an unexpected burst of personality inspired by a hard day's climb. In the two years of taking up the sport, he'd earned a reputation for agility, strength and fearlessness. I went with him one afternoon between shifts. As I belayed below, I watched him swing several times from a protruding rock, before managing somehow to leap onto it with a grace that defied the difficulty of such a feat. Scarcely drawing breath, he then skipped up the rest of the smooth face. When it was my turn to face the same overhang, the 'crux' of the route, my arms shook with the strain of trying to lever myself over it. I sweated, exerting myself, repeatedly trying, unable to respond to Troy's patient encouragement above. There I hung as the minutes passed, defeated. After another attempt, I could only stare in frustration at the obstacle, when a thought lodged: 'Why?' The timing was lethal; the door to doubt now wide open. The most crucial question of all could no longer be avoided: 'Am I really enjoying this?'

The challenge was no longer about fun. My aching body willed me to be lowered as I remembered the times of fear during multi-pitch climbs. The euphoria of finishing them never quite justified the shaking legs and internalised panic along the way. I had banished such feelings with a drive to expose myself to greater heights and routes. Yet here I was at the start of my climbing trip in New Zealand, acknowledging that I really wasn't cut out for it. Looking up at Troy's puzzled face, I called out 'belay' and within seconds was standing on firm ground.

As Gavin and I pant in z-turns up the final steep slope of hardening snow, a man hollers down to us from the hut, asking if we'd like some tea. A fresh brew waits for us in the late afternoon chill, which we enjoy as the sun sinks into a sea of clouds, bathing the peaks salmon pink. We'd imagined that we'd have the hut to ourselves at this time of year but the three-strong party already settled in gives us a warm welcome and we're glad of their company. Sam, who made us the tea, beavers about with an authority that is soon explained – he is an international mountain guide, an elite qualification to acquire. This is a private ski-touring trip with his sixty-five-year-old Swiss father and a family friend. We share an evening in candlelight at the hut's one table.

Their friend joins in occasionally, his head otherwise buried in an absorbing book. Sam's father, introduced as 'Coby, short for Jacob,' has a twinkling humour and strong Swiss-German accent despite having lived in New Zealand for the past forty years. His rapport with his son is strikingly affectionate and they admit to being 'best friends', having shared many adventures together. Sam and Gavin compare notes about the precarious, cash-strapped life working in the outdoors. The subject moves on to what I'm planning to climb while in New Zealand.

'I may try to climb the Hooker Face of Mount Cook in the next two months. What condition has it been in lately?'

'Not too bad. It's not too tricky. You're away from the crowds which is good, making it safer in some ways,' Sam helps himself to more bread, before adding, 'but it's more technical for sure. There's quite a lot of exposure towards the end. Who are you going with?'

'Actually an American I met via the New Zealand Alpine Club's website. He was looking for a partner and has a lot of ice-climbing and expedition experience. I hadn't really wanted to climb Cook. There are plenty of other more interesting, safer peaks which don't have its kudos.'

We all agree Cook is a 'serious mountain,' underestimated by many inexperienced people, attracted by its 'highest' status, at 3,754m (12,316ft). Changeable weather is the most deadly hazard, especially as low fronts tend to linger in the Southern Alps.

'So what experience do you have exactly?' Sam asks. I mention alpine expeditions in Nepal, Alaska, the Alps, the Andes, my walk across the Pyrenees and stress the gulf I feel between being guided and originating independent trips. 'That's really what I'm here to learn. There is no short cut – the only one way to get experience is to make the decisions you pay a guide to make.'

Every mountaineer has had to make that committed leap at some point to become self-sufficient. After a pause, Sam says he remembers that shift well, but his vast experience has taught him to be even more aware of the dangers in remote mountaineering. His voice is now serious. It is clear he is talking as a guide and we are no longer equals. 'And have you met this American?'

'No. We've been e-mailing. He's taking the trip seriously and has really researched the route.'

'You don't know this guy. He says he's got experience but how do you know? What if you find out in a storm that he knows nothing? You mention your month's mountaineering school and your solo Pyrenees trip … sorry my friend, but that's not Alpine.'

I say nothing, unsure how to respond in my growing embarrassment. How naive I must seem in the face of such unquestionable experience and judgement.

'Have you ever been in a storm?' he persists.

'Do you mean bad weather?'

'Bit more than that. Storm. White-out. Days in a tent that could be blown off the mountain?'

'No. I follow weather forecasts before deciding where I'm heading.'

'Until you've been in a storm, you don't know what you really know.'

'I'm sure that's true. But on a short trip, fronts are avoidable.' I'm sounding defensive, so I add, 'Are you suggesting I go out of my way to be in a storm?'

'Put it this way, without serious storm experience, you can't be ready for Mount Cook.'

I sense the edge. I should take Sam's advice at face value, in the way it's being intended, but his concern sounds like a lecture. I look at Gavin hoping he'll know how to lighten things up, but he's pottering cheerfully about the stove, unaware. An awkward silence settles at the table. I offer for a second time to help with supper, but Gavin insists there's no need. Sam brings up the subject again. This time, he is more direct and openly questions my 'readiness' for such an extreme challenge, unguided. I can only agree with him, that in this light, I am not ready. But, I add, I would make a final decision at another time. This doesn't appease Sam, who regards the matter still unresolved. 'Frankly,' he says fixing his eyes on mine, 'without being on equal terms with the mountain, you have no place on it.'

No doubt Sam will remember our talk as a possible life-saving inter-vention. Yet instead of feeling grateful to a well-meaning stranger, my spirits deflate. His cross-examination has left me discouraged, like a ticked-off child. My energy slumps – all I want is to go to bed. There is a necessary risk-taking ethic in the alpine fraternity, matched by skill – but my intention to climb Cook has been assessed as a risk too far.

After supper, Gavin and I look at our maps and make a final plan. We have an early start before the sun softens the snow, increasing avalanche risks. We plan to climb Minarets via the Graham Saddle if the conditions are right. Our backup is to play with skills. As I get ready for bed in my top bunk, I struggle with the gloom of growing self-doubt. Not only an outsider in the exclusive mountaineering community to which I so want to belong – I am tonight a trespasser.

■   ■   ▦

I dream that someone steals my mountaineering boot. The large orange double-layered plastics have come with me on trips to Europe, the Americas and now New Zealand. In the dream I search high and low but never find the missing boot. The theft not only restricts my movement but strips me of my freedom.

Waking up after a short sleep, I have plenty of vigour to leave the hut. It will be a long day but Gavin's assured me that the change of plan, to walk all the way back to the village of Franz Josef, instead of returning by helicopter, is achievable given the forecast and the 4am start. We should reach the glacier by late afternoon, empty of the hundreds of tourists who visit the South Island's biggest attraction every day. We then plan to walk out of the valley along the glacial river's silted banks, to be back in time for a well-earned drink. This route has been a dream of Gavin's since moving to Franz Josef nearly three years ago. It is also regarded by many locals as an 'epic walk out.'

Setting off in near darkness, we quickly warm up as our crampons crunch over the hard ice. The thin orange line across the horizon promises another hot day and so we step up our pace, aware of the pressure to make ground. If I had known we would embark on a twenty-five-kilometre route up and down steep slopes, across glaciers and snowfields before a final scramble beneath the snowline, I would certainly have lightened my load. A rhythm develops as we swap leads. By 10am two facts are emerging – we are not carrying enough water and walking over heavily glaciated terrain of varied gradients is exhausting, slow work.

The ice-blue sky above a cork of thick cloud is dazzling. An uninterrupted skyline of the Southern Alps' most famed peaks and daring routes are unmarred by cloud or crowd. Hours pass as we plod forwards, locked in a world of marvel. At times neither of us can grasp that this space of untouched white is ours. We've left behind De la Beche and the Minarets, skirting around the east face of Mount Von Bulow, crossed the Melchior Glacier and traversed the Sollas Ridge and Zubriggen Col. Mounts Tasman and Cook, Haast and Haidinger, Douglas and Glacier Peak enclose us like an amphitheatre. We head north-west across the Fritz Glacier, looking out to the beautiful views of the Tasman Sea and Okarito Lagoon, with its tannin-tinted creeks harbouring the rare white heron.

By midday, there is still a long way to go. We unrope to front point down to the Baumann Glacier. It would be too dangerous to remain tied together. A slip would pull the other, ensuring we both fall to our deaths. Aware of the twenty-five-kilo weight on my back, I keep my eyes glued to the white square in front and count to keep rhythm, stabbing each axe into the ice before lowering and kicking one crampon before the other. This is standard alpine practice in New Zealand, but I have never been exposed like this without protection. Setting up anchors is time-consuming work and in this larger wilderness, safety risks are continually weighed against the pressing threat of rapidly changing weather and larger distances to cover.

We arrive at a helicopter pick-up point and my nerves are spent. We have a litre of water left between us. It is a struggle not to swill the lot, as we both want to do. My instincts are telling me to wait a couple of hours for the next ride. Gavin's radio batteries have run out and we can't make contact to ensure there will be passenger space. We only have enough fuel left to melt snow for one drink. Unable to shelter from the sun's glare, we debate hurriedly what to do.

If we continue at the same pace, it's reasonable to think we can make the base of the glacier by late afternoon, with enough time to walk out of the valley by dark. Neither of us considers that tiredness and thirst lengthen distance and should be factored into the calculation. Gavin admits he doesn't know what the conditions will be like beneath the snowline, or how long it should take to reach the glacier. He lets me have the final say. I know how much he wants to complete the route, and so agree it would be 'satisfying' to continue.

It takes another two hours to reach the summit of Mount Moltke, requiring a knife-edge traverse of its ridge. No longer enthusiastic, I am aware that I've reached a critical turning point. The beauty is no longer inspiring me.. Tiredness, thirst, fear and a rising resentment are all I feel now, and my energy is steadily slipping away. I call out to Gavin for a hand to help me inch my crampon points along the corniced ridge with sheer drops. At the top, I only half appreciate the extraordinary views of the iced summits. The next five hours are a battle of will as the late afternoon dusk creeps up on us and our situation slides from challenge to exhausting misery.

Beneath the snowline we face an uneven terrain of scree, unstable boulders and a slide down damp tussocks. I add to my tortuous burden by thinking of everything in my pack that would never have been packed for a trip of this scope, had we planned it. There is no longer sunlight to radiate some cheer and we descend in the heavy damp of cloud. I fall well behind Gavin, who's as surefooted as a goat. He waits and I catch up, again and again, as we press on over giant mossy boulders and bush, a landscape of hobbits and goblins. Bracken cuts my hand when I stumble and I start to sob, surrendering to this relief, knowing Gavin is too far ahead to hear me.

We have been moving for fifteen hours. At last, we reach the glacier's edge and finally Gavin looks beaten as we confront a forty-foot ice wall. He tells me that this spot is unrecognisable from its condition two months before, when all it required was an easy six-foot scramble up its icy bank of churned soil and rock – not an exposed climb using two ice tools. Daylight is ebbing away and it'll be dark in half an hour. Gavin dumps his pack and searches for the shortest route before returning to climb the wall, while I slump into a state of unconcern.

He drops a rope from the top to haul up my pack. Being this tired, I can't trust my strength not to fall, and ask him to belay me. At the top we are in near darkness. 'The homeward stretch,' Gavin ventures, trying to sound positive as he looks about for a way through the unrecognisable confusion of ice. Often ladders have to be fixed over yawning chasms to ensure a safe passage. He knows the twists and ruts, gnarls and grooves of the glacier's other side by daylight, but this area is as new to him as it is to me. It is dark now despite the moonlight and we put on our head torches.

Over time, it's inevitable that guides develop an instinct for the safest way through constantly changing ice forms. We don't find this as we falter through the dark, alien terrain of creaking, dripping ice slabs and their ghostly shadows. By day these blocks crash, weakened by the sun's heat and could demolish any life in their way. They could still be unstable and I feel I should move quickly, but my every step meets a stubborn resistance. I kneel and cup my hands to drink from the glacial pools whenever I can, but there is never enough to quench my need.

Gavin has been patient, but at 9pm, when we seem no nearer to the valley head, my slowness exasperates him. My hesitancy on the edge of deep crevasses, requiring an energetic and confident leap to cross, forces us several times to find a safer route which takes longer. At last he cracks, pointing out he'd be in Franz Josef by now if I hadn't been holding him back. Of course, I shout back, a twenty-five-kilo pack and seventeen hours of strenuous movement might be factored into that assessment. It takes energy to maintain a frosty silence and having released tension, we soon work together again. Gavin tries to point to the best hand-holds down the twisted channels of ice. We double back on ourselves, explore this way and that, not stepping on recognisable territory for two hours. Even then, a hacked-out path with an occasional handrail is not easy in the darkness, carrying my heavy burden for an eighteenth gruelling hour.

At 10pm we are off the glacier. By now, I've searched my heart for the value in this feat of endurance. Is it enterprising or is it lunacy? Is achievement ever truly felt if there's been misery in realising it? Does this help to earn one's 'place' on a mountain? How sound Sam's heavy-handed counsel seems on safe, flat ground! I'd need to hunt for the will to make a technically challenging ascent of Mount Cook now, or for a reason to expose myself to the joyless combination of exhaustion and anxiety again.

There is still an eight-kilometre walk through the valley, but the land is flat. Gavin bounds off ahead and it's a relief to move at my own pace. There really is no need to hurry now. The route follows a river along the soft contours of a valley, the flatter scenery as breathtaking as the alpine panorama behind us. Franz Josef Glacier gleams white. The moon is nearly full and the sound of the flowing glacial melt keeps me company as I join a path lined with overhanging trees. Strength surges through me, soothed to be moving rhythmically for the first time in this long day. There are no fears or regrets now, only gratitude for Gavin's companionship and the eventful three days shared. An alpine dream held in my sights for so long has inspired many changes, but adventuring could never be a destination in itself. It doesn't matter what comes next – it's past midnight, already a new day. For now, every bend in the dark track seems to light up, as if a shaft of moonlight is casting a beam to show me the way.

29 FATHER TREE

To outlive more than two thousand years of human history, its wars and famines, empires and cultures, earns an authority over all living things. To have survived since Christ's birth the weathering of age and the deadlier threat of man surely acquires a stature rooted in timeless truth? The New Zealand kauri is one of the world's mightiest trees. The largest are more than fifty metres high with trunks as wide as sixteen metres. Over time, the lower branches are shed as the adult tree grows into a clean, straight, form. Most of the remaining kauri are to be found on the North Island, near the north-west coast. Its ancient forest has been shrunk by fire and chainsaw, either for its precious timber or to clear farmland. Calls for its total protection intensified sixty years ago, after logging for boatbuilding during the war. Waipoua Sanctuary now protects just over nine thousand hectares from further destruction.

Being in the empty forest beneath its luxuriant green canopy in the last light of day is thrilling. New Zealand's oldest pocket of life is busy with movement. Birds fly among the other large trees besides the kauri: taraire, kohekohe, towai and northern rata. Ferns and grasses rustle in a gentle breeze. In my final days before moving on to north India, I had wished to pay homage to the stately kauri by way of acknowledging an inspiring three months spent on these islands. I am taking my time finding the forest's star presence among its other ancient wonders. *Te Matua Ngahere*, the Father of the Forest, is the oldest and second-largest living kauri tree.

Few places in the world equal this isolated corner. Exploring coastal gems in the last week have brought back countless recent encounters with untouched land and wildlife. I loved the wild moody drama of the South Island's west coast, sea waves crashing along white beaches lined with primal forest, home to penguins, seals, dolphins, and birds. A pool of two playful, teasing seal pups, ignored by the enormous hulk of fat and whiskers that was their mother sunbathing on the nearby rocky cliffs, was one unforgettable dawn surprise. For two hours they splashed about and balanced on their flippers, pushing their faces up at me, as if coaxing me to stroke them.

I have marvelled too at the surreal formations of layered limestone that still baffle experts in an age when it seems everything has been explained. The rocks, like stacked pancakes, were formed thirty-five million years ago under the sea by fragments of native organisms, but no one knows how the layers themselves formed. The sea will eventually reclaim them, as the coastline is eroded by battering waves, wind and rain. Every accessible landscape is concentrated with formidable wonders – lakes and rivers ploughing through rainforest, glaciers stretching from altitude to sea level. I also spent weeks in wildernesses where small details amazed me more than the obvious beauty of their nearby mountains or waterfalls. Drops of moisture on leaves and petals, or a carpet of moss can sparkle with colour, transforming in a moment from green to red, orange to white, depending on the light's angle. Fine spiders' webs can mesmerise, draped between blades of grass or branches under the sun's spotlight. Or a lone leaf as it spins beneath a branch, caught in one of their near-invisible fibrous threads.

Enchanted by New Zealand and its people, I even explored the idea of moving here – yet I know that a six-month stay may be wiser. How can my fickle judgement be trusted when Alaska felt like a homecoming and Seattle too, with their thriving mixtures of community and environment on the doorstep? The connections made and memories formed can last a lifetime. I have found it doesn't really matter where home truly is or where it should be, when a common heart-warming thread can weave between places and people, however loosely. Time and again I've been touched by the bonds between people asking the same, ageless question – how to make best use of our limited time with the beautiful and challenging chance of life. The answer had been found by one woman with small blinking eyes and snow-white hair, who gave me a tour of her disused goldmine. Her deep facial lines showed the toil of her fifty-year working life, but she told me firmly, 'It's not been easy and we spent more money keeping this place going than we ever made, with the rising price of fuel ... but I don't regret a day of it. Would I have done something else with my life? It's what I knew and what I loved.'

I was lucky too, to have shared a ride with Alec, the Maori who drove me from Queenstown to the foot of the Routeburn Track. He picked me up outside a hostel at 7am and immediately lifted my depressed spirits. I had been in no way enamoured by one of the most popular tourist haunts here. 'Queenstown isn't New Zealand,' I'd been warned – and how true! There was a toxic energy to its worn out, inter-season feel, yet still the cheek-by-jowl businesses selling adrenaline-fuelled adventure were always trading. The seasonal workers were ground-down and bored, pointing to a placard with rates, too jaded to answer the same questions, repeat the spiel for a thousandth time. They've seen it all – every variant of backpacker, tourist, bungee jumper or well-heeled expat spending their few weeks a year in a hillside holiday home. There are few instinctive smiles between strangers here; most are too absorbed in finding fun. Every spare inch of land around the area's world-class natural assets has been commercialised. Overshadowed by the gothic jaggedness of the Remarkables and the softer, tundra-covered hills opposite, the commercial hub is crammed in front of Lake Wakatipu.

When Alec pulled up in his van, warmly shook my hand and smiled, I only then realised that I couldn't wait to see the back of Queenstown. His greying hair and ready laugh inspired trust as well as his refreshing curiosity and keen ear. A haze of springtime colours flashed past the open window beside him, as his right hand gripped the wheel. The letters L.O.V.E were tattooed on his forearm in grey-blue.

'So, Mags, he simply didn't show up?'

'No. It does seem amazingly casual after a string of e-mails, batting around dates and times. I flew here especially from Christchurch because time's short.' I had put together a proposal to team up with an established adventure business to run life-coaching programmes in the bush.

'That's Queenstown for you. I know this guy. They're all like that. It's a place where you're out for a laugh and a dollar. There's no … what's the word I'm looking for?'

We both thought about this for a moment. Then I concluded, 'I guess it seems worse than it is because the rest of New Zealand is so unusually fresh and undeveloped. But it's more normal where I'm from.'

'Well Mags, I stay for the beauty, not so much the community. One day I'd like Maori neighbours again. Move to the North Island where most of us live. But I've got opportunities here to attend to first.'

'Like what?'

'I guess it's about legacy.' He paused, looking thoughtful. 'Yes. That's the word I wanted just now. Queenstown back there is all about now, now, now. Buy this, have that. I've started to think about passing something on.'

The road climbed and Alec changed gear. Remembering he was a driver with a tourist passenger, he pointed to sights of interest but I was more interested in 'legacy'. At fifty-five and with a big family, he had started to think about how he wanted his life to be remembered. For years he'd dreamed of guiding people into the bush to share his fascination with man's evolving relationship with nature and the stories that had shaped his heritage. His people surrendered their autonomy to the colonising *Pakea*, the source of the land's first voice. Alec also wanted to share Maori knowledge of natural medicines, the plants, leaves and tree barks so little is known about.

'But above all, it's educating people about the essence of being Maori, taking them right into the forest to see where they had to adapt and how they did it. There is a market. Everyone I speak to in this van, like you, wants to know more, about the "real" New Zealand.'

'So, what are you waiting for? You could start tomorrow.'

'Fear.'

The boardwalk rounds a bend. The kauri trees bordering it are so very solid, despite a shallow labyrinth of roots near the soil's surface to extract moisture. They also need a maximum amount of light to sustain themselves and so only grass and fern grow near their base. Rounding another bend, I sense that the forest's trophy tree, *Te Matua*, will soon be visible. A tingling sensation irritates the back of my neck and sure enough, within a few steps, it suddenly looms directly ahead of me.

The extraordinary presence of *Te Matua Ngahere* jolts me to a standstill. Its size overwhelms everything around. Even the trees clustered around its space are like pulled-back drapes unveiling the centre-stage star. Nothing would presume to crowd it, or encroach upon the bold column of light feeding it. The sixteen-metre-wide trunk of the Father of the Forest has a stature to equal its name. Superlatives are often lazy overstatements but I have never seen such concentrated vitality. Overpowered, I walk slowly forward, grateful for the evening stillness and the unhurried opportunity to stand and stare.

A wind rouses the forest, reasserting the kauri's solidity. No force of gale could uproot a tree that has withstood every tremor and hurricane ever to have ripped through its heartland. I remember that the volcanoes of Tongariro which have a similar unchallengeable power, are also spiritually important to the Maori. The National Park is full of chaotic contrasts: active craters and barren lava flows, snowfields and hot springs, beguiling and deadly. Sulphurous fumes cloak the glacier and seep out of indiscernible pores. Hues of blue shroud the holes of worn-out crusty snow, melted around the heat-absorbent rocks. Larger vents stained with reds and yellows belch a thick, rich, mix of toxic gases. A sound very like a whistling kettle can be heard – a reminder of the explosive potential lurking beneath. Evidence of how time sculpts the earth is everywhere; the worn-out craters, once active and deadly, are now valleys, giant creases searing the desert landscape. Herb fields, native beech forests and green lakes inject colour into the pumice soil, where plants struggle to live.

This had been on my doorstep for a few weeks while working at the Sir Edmund Hillary Outdoor Pursuits Centre. In return for helping out in their marketing office, I shadowed some corporate leadership programmes. It was an opportunity to see how this well-respected institution uses their natural resources to develop vision and potential in people. Since NOLS, I was exploring ways to transfer the experience of the outdoors to urban situations. The combination of first-class facilities and bunker-like accommodation for staff and volunteers was unique. During the long, interrupted nights, rats would scrape away or scurry over the corrugated iron roof, or rain pound like hail. It is a thriving and committed community. Groups were tackling the obstacle course or climbing wall, the pulley ride, or the hundred-foot-high trapeze jump that froze the soles of my feet just watching it. Yet I wondered then, as I had many times before during the anticlimax of descending a mountain, about the value of a 'peak experience'. To measure success by results alone is like relying on fast food for sustenance. The satisfaction never lasts.

Alec and I had talked all the way to the Routeburn trailhead. We had let ourselves imagine a time when we might work together, when he could share his ancestral stories, as relevant now as they have ever been. By the time we'd pulled up at the end of the muddy track, the best part of the morning over, it felt sad to part. Alec left the engine running as we wound up our talk. He leant a little towards me as I stood with my pack the other side of the open passenger door.

'You know, Mags. I really hope I'm not overstepping the mark or anything. But there's something I'd like to say to you.'

'Alec, of course. I want to hear it.'

'From everything you've said and from what I can see, you're someone who does a lot of doing. You strike me as someone who sets out to do and goes and does it, then thinks what now, I'll do that, then what? Give yourself some room to breathe, the chance to slow. You have to know what you are first, to know what to do next. Trust me, the doing comes from being.'

It is nearly dark. Sitting now, I can imagine this tree hearing the countless deadly creaks of other, felled trees. It has everything it has ever needed to survive: light, moisture, and purpose, by generating life and supporting it. Thousands of birds will have nested in its bushy heights. *Te Matua*'s presence feels sacred, inspiring veneration.

I get up, a little stiff, and stretch. As I walk off, something makes me turn around for a final glance. The forest has fallen silent, as if the tree is demanding the final word. If it is possible to 'feel' something associated with hearing, then I swear the kauri said, 'Know yourself. Know yourself so well that nothing can ever shake you. Man comes and goes. I am the giver of life, always here, ever true.'

PART 6 ORIENTAL PYRENEES

PYRENEES - ORIENTALES

FRANCE

SPAIN

ARIÈGE

ANDORRA

Mediterranean

Banyuls

Baillestavy

Canigou
(2785m)

Mont Louis

Cerdanya

Carlit (2921m)

Cabane
de Rouzet

Etang
de Lanoux

N

KEY

My Route

GR10 track

Border

Km

0   10   20   30   40   50

30 THE WARRIOR'S WAY: 2003

Giant puff clouds filled the sky, the sun's rays piercing through them like spotlights on the dry canyon country. This bold light made everything in this wild space look unnatural: even the vultures soaring high, watching over their barren kingdom seemed a little contrived. The nearby water source seemed to hiss out of the ground, and irregular rock walls of granite and limestone with their lacerated edges glowed. This place might have had an otherworldly feel, but there was nothing at all unreal about my inertia or lack of will to go on. The outlook for the next month was not encouraging either. Andorra was beginning to seem too high to clear by late autumn's likely snowfall.

Although it couldn't be regarded as an easier route, I considered going to the remote Ariège further east instead. I was missing the lushness of France with its trees and more populated farmland. Looking at the maps again, all options were uninviting; to retrace my steps back to Gavernie, through Ordesa and continue from there, or to round the base of Monte Perdido and press on with the challenging steep descent into the next Spanish valley. The sudden change of weather while starting up the limestone flanks of Spain's third-highest mountain had driven me to retreat. The unsettled prospects for the days ahead were making me cautious. The wildest terrain in the Pyrenees, for all its beauty and scale, was unnerving, especially in cloud; the gorges, so vast and sheer and which carve up the landscape, could swallow me whole. There was nothing for it but to lie down and rest for a while, anything to break this unhealthy state of nerves and sense of paralysis.

I fell into an uneasy sleep on the bottom bunk of a room at the Goriz Refugio, its air stale from the rows of bodies that had filled it the previous night. Waking up, I felt more resigned but still had little idea of what to decide next. Retracing my steps back to the reassuring greens of France now seemed silly. Every faltering step could grind down my resolve, driving me to give up long before the Mediterranean. Once the halfway mark had been reached – still well over a week away, possibly two – I was certain that I would have a release of new energy and impetus. I had to completely focus on reaching that milestone. Combining routes and straying from one country to another would have extended the overall distance too. There was still plenty of time – but an early winter was an ever-present worry. To be committed to Spain with its contrasts and challenges was now inevitable for the next eleven days. I would cross back into France after Tavascan, thereby skirting around Andorra and, at the same time, ignoring the commonly expressed warning to avoid France's wildest stretch of the range, the Ariège.

Supper at the *refugio* was the staple hut formula of soup and pasta. The dining room was crammed with those bent on making an end-of-season dash for Monte Perdido's summit, before the hut closed for winter. Most at my table agreed there was a slim window to climb the 'Lost Mountain', with such unpromising weather expected. I felt uplifted by the room of cheerful people. As we swapped details of our recent experiences, my concerns about which route to follow became less pressing. Earlier I'd asked the hut's guardian if he knew of anyone heading my way eastwards. Most, he said, were either returning to the main car park south at the canyon's base, or back to Gavernie, through the Brèche de Roland. No one had said anything about going to Pineta.

Carafes of Spanish wine were passed up and down the table, as a plain-talking German took a lively interest in my choice of route, known for being demandingly steep and slippery in damp weather.

'I do not accept no one else is going that way. Someone in this damned hut must be going to Pineta!' With that he downed his glass before topping it up again. Trays of steaming bowls of pasta with a creamy cheese sauce arrived at the table, simple but perfect mountain fuel.

'Hey … hey!'

Everyone at my end of the table looked up from their food at the German, whose eyes were boring into the man to my left, who hadn't said much all evening. The only Spaniard at the table, he had had to tolerate the flow of English of which he only spoke a few words.

'You say Bielsa? Yes? … Bielsa? That is right, you, sir.' The German, clearly excited, was nodding as the table waited for an answer.

'Er, me? Tomorrow? That is right. I go towards Bielsa.'

'I believe Bielsa comes after Pineta. Am I right, sir? Yes?'

'Yes. Pineta first. Bielsa along valley. Maybe day after I reach.'

I could have leant across the table and kissed the German for his assertive detective work.

'She … yes this lady here, this Englishwoman, am I right, your accent very London?'

I nod.

'She is going tomorrow to Pineta too.'

My neighbour, whose face was somewhat hidden in a bush of curls, asked a little shyly, 'Is that so? How nice!' But the German wasn't establishing social niceties – he'd hit upon an idea and was determined to execute it, helping a woman in need in the process.

'Yes. That *is* nice. The two of you will go together in the morning, to Pineta. Safe and sound. You will escort her!' After hesitating a moment, he nodded again, smiling graciously as he did so.

'Ah, OK. Sure. Why not? Long way to Pineta. We will go together.' Extending his hand to me, he added, 'I am Santiago.'

'And I am Mags. A pleasure to meet you.'

■   ■   ■

As we edged along the lower buttress of Monte Perdido, losing the paint markings a couple of times, I was grateful for Santiago's solid presence. Navigation could not help a descent that required moment-by-moment attention and careful footwork. When the fog came, the horizon would peep through the thinner patches and vanish again. A glimpse of the steep drop into Anisclo Canyon, its floor hundreds of feet below, was a reminder not to overshoot the route. Gingerly, we faced into the slope, using the fixed chain – uncomfortably wrapped around a forearm – to lower us down the smooth, weathered rock slabs. It was difficult to keep balance with our weighty packs. Santiago moved nimbly despite his heavy build, especially on the steeper sections, where strength eased the continual strain of descent. It was long, hard work. The lower slope of dried scrub and rock was tortuous – so by the time we arrived at Pineta's newly renovated hostel, we wanted to celebrate.

As we were in Spain, supper wouldn't start before nine-thirty. In France, most out-of-the way places would be shut down by that time. This unpopulated valley in one of northern Spain's least-developed spots had a wonderful vitality and Santiago, who spoke little, was fun to be around, with his obvious humour and love of life's softer touches. A visit to a five-star hotel up the winding road, for pre-supper cocktails and rounds of dominos (not played by me since childhood), flowed into an evening of uninterrupted pleasure. Indulging a third marguerita, with a saucer of olives and dim sum smeared in plum sauce, Santiago revealed he was a bank clerk with a nine to five-thirty work routine and lived with his parents and older brother.

The next morning, we were in no hurry to leave. Music was blaring about the hostel and labourers were piling in for breakfast. My new friend delighted me with his attentive efforts with a gimmicky mobile phone charger I had bought on my budget flight to France at the start of the trip. It had a small handle needing to be turned for a disproportionately long time to generate a few minutes of battery life. Santiago was determined to test it, refusing to hand it back until he'd given it his all. At one point, a couple of locals joined us, glued to the bizarre breakfast scene. The manager and his wife then came over too and tables of guests followed, drawn to the ludicrous gadget. For a whole hour the plastic handle was rotated as the men argued over who was next to have a go. Their wrists would then turn hundreds if not thousands of times, my eyes, tired from a late night of Spanish rum, fixed to the blur.

■   ■   ■

The cultural and geographical shifts this side of the border introduced a fresh rhythm to the long journey. Quickly, my senses felt recharged, as well as overwhelmed, by the new cultural flavour and tempo of small Spanish villages, their cafés and supermarkets stocked with different foods. The wilderness had a more barren feel, its rivers ploughing through giant white rocks, as volumes of water churned with a force resembling a chalky soup. Gaining height, the route west of the highest mountains in the range, Aneto and Posets, was beautiful in a different way. This area was more untouched, the enveloping autumn driving away the high-summer tourists. I passed lakes and greener valleys with goats and their tinkling bells, bounding up the pine-filled rocky slopes at first light, descending to shelter by nightfall.

I seemed to be blending more into the landscape, noticing how birds were increasingly friendly and curious. Marmots too, those cuddly rodents, didn't bolt as quickly from the clomping tread of my boots. One afternoon I came across an ideal spot to stop for the night, shaded by bush and pine and in the middle of a network of streams, requiring small leaps to cross. The ground was a patchwork of green and the rocky backdrops nearby cocooned this site perfectly, so tucked away from human traffic, rare here anyway. There was plenty of warm sunshine left to air all my things and there was no need to pitch the bivvy yet.

As I lay on my back, soaking up some sun, the faint jangle of bells had become louder. Forcing myself to stir, I saw that I was no longer alone. Dozens of horned brown goats were coming my way and queuing up on the edge of a stream that separated my resting spot from their line of descent by twenty feet. Hundreds more were racing down to join them. As I looked on at the amassing herd, one of them lunged into the water and made its way across to the bank a few feet away from me, where it froze still, apparently every bit as riveted by me as I was by it. Its curiosity emboldened its companions who, in growing numbers, splashed into the water to join us, in no hurry to move on either. This side of the stream was getting crowded and at some point I would have to make room for the stragglers who were either waiting to get out of the water or starting to cross.

I was sitting up now and still felt at a disadvantage. Dozens, if not hundreds, of goats continued to appear at the top of the valley slope, primed like clockwork to return to their warm, dry shed by dark. It was uncomfortable to be so outnumbered like this – there was only one of me, after all. I stood up. The brazen billy goat who had sparked this stand-off, continued to eye me square on. It was not at all inclined to deviate from its usual route down, to make way for this uninvited stranger. This was the way they romped up and down every day and week, for months at a time. One goat stirred, perhaps bored, and began to press on with its journey. A few followed but not many, 'not enough' I thought, feeling just a little threatened. I began to clap my hands and talk to the horned intruders. I expected them to scatter at the sound of my voice. If anything, they strained a little towards me as if to hear better. Something had to be done.

I turned round and made a dash for my walking sticks lying on the grass, not wanting to expose my back for long. Turning round again, the flock looked three-hundred-strong. About the same number was waiting patiently on the other side of the stream. They had all the time in the world to watch our unexpected encounter. I lunged forwards, just a step. A few were startled, trampling backwards, jolting the row behind into the denser throng, who otherwise remained surefooted. A few wandered off but the rest defiantly stayed. Reluctantly, I started to wave my sticks, managing to scare a third away, but no more. I was at a loss and sat down. Some more lost interest at my passive pose and scattered, filling the valley with the sound of bells.

I retrieved my saucepan to fill it with water from the stream when the latecomers were crossing. I assembled the stove and waited for the water to boil, as the last ones trotted off without a final glance. The clouds were casting giant shadows over my spot and the temperature dropped. In two hours it would be too cold to sit out. I put on another layer and thought of my lingering visitors affectionately, as the evening got darker and a stiller, lonelier mood filled the valley space where they had been.

31 THE MAYOR OF BAILLESTAVY

There's enough wind outside to blow the corrugated iron door off its makeshift latch. Propping my boots against it will stop it creaking open, but not its rattle. Even the metal roof is straining to fly off. Carlit's slate-black granite form, its upper-half hidden in cloud, fills the musty window. An outpouring of scree flows from the cleft of its saddle, layering its boggy base in grey. This marks the eastern outreaches of the Hautes Pyrenees which dwarf the foothills rolling towards the Mediterranean – a direct distance of one hundred kilometres and less than two weeks away on foot.

At first the small refuge in this wild part of the Ariège looked unwelcoming, with its unswept concrete floor and soiled bed with a sagging mattress. Yet the choice of tarns and lakes at its threshold, of strangely shaped rocks embedding the peaty landscape, make it an unquestionably romantic place to stay. This would be France's Lake District but with a rawer, more naked sense of isolation. I haven't spoken to anyone for three days except a terse 'bonjour' to a couple of random, lone men, both with rifles slung over their shoulders. It has been disconcerting to encounter hunters in the remotest places of the range. Guns are commonplace in rural France, where hunting is a socially entrenched sport. There is no such culture in Spain but once, in the heart of 'nowhere', I had to pass a marching file of armed soldiers on a training exercise. It felt very uncomfortable as we tried to pass on a narrow scree path, my eyes never looking up from the ground in front, in case they locked with another's.

After the daily warnings and shaking heads of locals worried by my plans to cross the Ariège in October, I was braced for the solitude but not its wonders, the unexpected shifts of light, colour, sound and shape. My days stripped to the barest tasks of walking, eating and sleeping, are easily filled with surprise. Grass can be pleasingly crunchy underfoot first thing and it moves through a spectrum of colour in the day: angry greens and peaty browns can fire up with the sun's help into tangerine orange or rose-quartz pink, fading into a blanket of mute greys like merging shadows. The bark of plane trees, with its khaki-coloured shapes like desert camouflage fatigues, shredding from a statuesque trunk, is the most elegant wallpaper I've ever seen. Silence itself becomes all the more striking when alone. Sometimes I listen out for its quality, like trying to give shape to an ocean of space. The sound of water flowing under thick slabs of boulder and rock can have such rich variety, treating me, while ground down under the weight of a pack, to a symphony of tones and rhythms.

I am relieved as well as sad to be in the final phase of my adventure. As I near the more affluent and populated shore of the Mediterranean, as the land gets lower and the destination closer, the exotic blue 'finishing line' may not resemble the 'ending' of my imagination. Is that the moment when the future takes care of itself, when I know what to 'do' with the rest of my life, having walked across a hilly route of varied marvels? For all the moments of boredom and pointlessness, aggravations and discomforts, fears and disappointments, horror and exhaustion, I will regret their ending.

There are some old candles in the corner that will make the blustery evening more snug. The sound of stones knocking against each other outside has started up again. Earlier, scanning the gloom and straining to hear where the tap-tap-tap was coming from, it had stopped, as if mocking me. It might be a goat scampering over the loose scree but the rhythm seems too regular for that. I've stopped my imagination from working these strange disturbances into menacing possibilities. No one would be out there in the open, watching me shelter from the windswept bleakness in this little place.

A draped T-shirt and darned socks left to dry over the fire grating have been forgotten by their owner. Perhaps they had also brought the two wine bottles to liven up their stay, a few blood-red drops left at the bottom; ideal candle sticks for the fluttering stumps of wax. The traces of others are comforting as well as ghostly. In Spain, I encountered whole villages that had been abandoned, as if their inhabitants had uprooted and moved on as one family, halting life in its tracks. Those stone ruins, isolated and without road heads, were deserted not so very long ago. Rusting iron window features, often ornately designed, were still on working hinges and faded paint and wallpaper on a partly collapsed wall could be seen through the broken panes. Dusty tables with cutlery and plates draped in cobwebs, fragments of newspaper and books, show the shells of life, its hardware weathering over time. What triggered the exodus of these hidden communities, a day's walk to the nearest road?

The cold and damp weather will decide the way east. The higher ridges have snow and more is likely, making a ridge-top route all the more demanding. Now at Carlit, with the adventure of the higher mountains ending, the valley routes through villages with their Catalan flavour will be a welcome contrast. I am so close to an arrival held in my sights for so long and yet the effort of getting there is just as grinding as it has always been. My impatience to reach it is slowing the passage of time and lengthening distances. Every snapshot of colour and incident must be relished to help drive me forwards, while my inclination is to curl up and sleep like a bear in this unforgiving slide into winter.

■　　　■　　　■

I could spend another night on the ridge above the snowline, overlooking a dense basin of clouds roofing the valley. The days have become noticeably shorter. The late-afternoon view will soon be bathed in a pink-orange glow, but the dark evenings are thick with cold damp, and being driven into the bivvy so early makes for a long night. Restless for the comforts of bustling life and electric warmth, I step up my speed to reach the welcoming light at the valley floor, along the ridge before a track of sorts leads down a slope of prickly gorse into a wood of pine and oak.

It is already dusk and not quite seven o'clock when I come across civilisation. The path passes derelict stone houses and simple, weathered barns of sleepy livestock. An oppressive foggy cold hangs in the air and I'm longing for the first hot water wash in four days. Walking in cloud or into the wind and rain on one's own for hours or even days at a time is rarely as lonely as brushing up against people or communities. The social transition tends to be awkward and the effort of talking unnatural. So I'm prepared for the strange moment of arrival. The path joins a lane winding through a cluster of houses, their curtains drawn, muffling the noise of blaring TV sets. A tall, elegant, square building, the village *gîte*, is unlit and empty. A sign stuck to its door has three words: *Fermé* and *Les demandes* at the bottom next to a telephone number. I make a note of it and walk on past a recently built church. I try opening its door to see if this might be a place to sleep in case there's nowhere else – I don't fancy bivvying in such cold. It's locked.

Further along, a public phone box stands next to a sad-looking play area, a mosaic of worn grass and tarmac. Just as I am within a few feet of its door, a woman with a pram appears, not caring to acknowledge me as she settles herself inside. As the minutes pass, she looks through the glass from time to time to check on her sleeping baby, showing no signs of finishing. It's nearly dark and despite putting on more layers, I am shivering from hunger, now impatient to find somewhere for the night.

Leaving the drone of her conversation, I wander back along the line of houses. Just up from the *gîte*, a storeroom, its door ajar, is discreetly situated next to a house that looks unoccupied. Inside, neat stacks of chopped wood are piled against a wall, leaving a narrow corridor of space covered with wood shavings and leaves. Wedged inside this snug spot would ensure a very comfortable sleep, only one hundred yards from the public toilet. Relieved at the growing possibilities, I head back to the callbox, which is now empty. The *gîte* number rings and rings. The woman returns to make another call and waits, chewing gum, gazing indifferently beyond the pram at the world about her. I give up on the phone and ask her if there's an arrangement for someone to have a key, a neighbourly system not uncommon in more remote places. She points at a nearby door and tells me to speak to the woman inside.

It is now dark as I ring the bell. A small dog yaps as a gruff, stout woman in a pleated tartan skirt and cropped hair opens the door, yelling at the fluffy mutt tearing about my boots. After telling me to try the number again, which I refuse to do, she agrees reluctantly to ring the number of her 'friend' who guards the key herself, shutting the door on me as she does so. Returning, she shrugs her wide shoulders, unconcerned, 'Elle n'est pas là.' She tries to close the door but accepting I won't be got rid of so easily, she softens a little, suggesting I try knocking on the door of a house, 'the last one at the end of the village. Big house on its own. The woman there might know where to find the key.'

Resolving to make a last effort before settling for the woodpile, I reach the last house built into the hillside. Both floors are brightly lit as well as the roof's skylight window. I rap a brass hanger on the front door a few times. There's no movement from inside, so I look for signs of life at the back of the house. Through a neat oval window, its sill crammed with geraniums, the kitchen is like a subject for a still-life composition. The pine table has a terracotta bowl of lemons, and a string of plump garlic hangs above the cooker from a large ceiling hook. A woman breezes into the kitchen with a tray, her grey hair swept stylishly in a bun and an amber necklace decorating a simple blue linen shirt. I think how elegantly she carries her age, as I knock on the window.

At first she doesn't hear. My next effort startles her and she turns round. She can't see anything through the dark so, frowning as if she might have been imagining things, resumes her bustle between the table and an open cupboard. I feel awkward at my intrusiveness, like a ghost peering into another's world. Without thinking how this might look, I tap on the glass again, wanting to explain myself. This time, wide-eyed, she advances towards me and gasps when she sees me there, taking a step back as she does so. I immediately hold up my hands and reassured by this, she opens the window to take a proper look at the unusual sight.

'Madame. Pardon. Je suis désolée …

'Attention! Vous allez bien?'

'Oui … mais … '

'Vous êtes seule? Toute seule?'

'Oui!'

At once her surprise melts into concern. Through the open window, I start to explain about the closed *gîte*, the search for the woman with the key, about my need to stay somewhere for the night. Throughout the narrative, the woman nods attentively, an unruffled vision of calm framed by orange flowers. Despite the unexpected turn her evening has taken, she smiles away more profuse apologies, beckoning me inside where 'we can work out what to do'.

She explains how the woman with the key 'is away for the weekend – so it's pointless trying her number again'. I sip at the tea she made me while she clasps her hands, lost in thought, her busy eyes roaming the floor as she runs through the options.

'Oui … mais bien sûr!'

Immediately her face brightens. Speaking quickly, impatient to put her 'plan' to the test, she declares that if it fails I will spend the night with her – but her house is being redecorated and there's nowhere very comfortable. Her friend, the mayor of Baillestavy, just ten minutes down the valley, can help. 'He always helps those in need – he will know exactly what to do.' Filling my cup with more tea, she heads for the phone, returning five minutes later.

The mayor had to be interrupted from a council meeting, she explains. He would take me to a converted barn, owned by the community, normally closed at this time of year. In fact, she'd been assured she had done the right thing to call him. All the hotels and hostels in the valley are shut and many residents have uprooted for the winter.

I'm ushered outside, where the woman bundles up a canvas covering from an old two-seater sports car. She is unworried by the fruitless attempts to squash my pack into its token boot and, after I squeeze into the passenger seat, she pushes and pants until at last it cushions the remaining space between my lap and the windscreen.

Hurtling along the snake-like bends at uninhibited speed, the brakes are jammed on like afterthoughts. The ride is filled with tales of long balmy summers in the country and weekend retreats for a fast-living set from Toulouse and Perpignan, where they used to mountaineer and climb half the year and ski the other. She was widowed young and never remarried, enjoying her independence too much. Now, 'not far from seventy', she relishes her peaceful life in this valley where she lives all the time. Looking over at me every now and then, her hands instinctively responding at the wheel to every bump and twist, she tells me emphatically how I must continue to live my life of adventure, as she had done.

As we park next to the village café, its terrace crowded with chained tables and stacked chairs, an estate car pulls up alongside. A middle-aged man with greying hair and a moustache dominating a friendly face introduces himself to me as the mayor of Baillestavy. After he unburdens the sports car of its load and with hands shaken, efforts downplayed and every *merci* rejected, I hug this woman for her undaunted rigour, her zesty example of how spirited living should be ageless. The mayor, all six feet of him, smiles over our goodbye, as if nothing would surprise him about this formidably capable member of his community.

As I am taken on my second car journey of the evening – this time up the other side of the valley – the mayor interrogates me about my life. Satisfied with the careful selection of facts for now, he informs that over a shared breakfast in the morning, he will want to uncover more. Meanwhile I learn that he was born in this valley, and works as a teacher. His hand gesticulates while the other steers as he opines about the rural generation vacuum and the need to win back the hearts of disenchanted youths who dream of an urban future. Soon we're parked up next to a slate wall beside a row of cottages. He puts on my backpack and considers whether to do up its waist-belt, then thinks better of it, before leading me through a gate to the door of an exquisite barn, a rustic combination of stone and wood.

A ladder leads upstairs to a sleeping gantry covered in multi-coloured mattresses. A table and comfy chairs encircling a stove occupy the space beneath with a little kitchen at the side. The mayor fusses about, stooping beneath beams, opening and closing drawers. After finding the hot water supply, he turns on the gas and small electric heater, apologising for the dust, its modesty, the lack of a clean towel. If only he'd known I was coming tonight, he would have ensured there was plenty of food and milk in the fridge. Will I be alright? He could return with one of his wife's famous casseroles *aux poulets petits*? No – really? Blankets are here, the toilet out there and tomorrow morning he'd collect me for breakfast, bringing a map with him – and I would talk him through the route which had taken me here, to Baillestavy, from where he has never found a good enough reason to leave. He would show me the best way to reach the Mediterranean, only three days from here – to think, so close! As he extends his firm hand to shake mine and wish me goodnight, I can only return the smile of true warmth, as I note that the mayor of Baillestavy is not just a lucky find, but a true inspiration.

By morning, the aches of a long day have been slept through. My cushioned chamber at the top of the ladder was perfect, and I wake up well after seven to birdsong and a perfectly clear autumn day. The ripened colours are past the early shades of change; the scarlet reds and clashing oranges are more like pallid yellows, languid and falling. On the patio a couple of black and white cats frolic beneath a bare bird table. I brew some coffee, savouring the rich aroma and a new day outside – leaving enough time to pack up for my nine-thirty appointment with the mayor. All my stuff is scattered about the floor, hurled about last thing, as I made every use of the unshared space.

As I open up the backpack, to my alarm something black scuttles out. I squeal, appalled at the thought that an enormous spider has been rampaging about my things. I've endured enough of these encounters to know that any attempt to contain a scurrying arachnid is fruitless, that even the detached contact of a container drives me to panic. Resigned to this stand-off, I pour out the last of the coffee and take my cup outside to wait for the mayor.

The estate roars up the hill, faithfully on time. The mayor strides towards me, looking fresh and ready for breakfast. He wants to know how I slept and whether everything was comfortable but all I can do is enlist his help, again. I don't know the French word for spider and the English is lost on the mayor, an expert in French revolutionary history and geography – but not it seems in spider identification. I describe eight legs and big body but he remains foxed. I draw a diagram, no better than a child's efforts but surely, I think, as he frowns and frets puzzling over it, it can only be… 'Ah, oui, l'araignée! C'est une araignée.'

Almost at once the mayor pales. If 'it takes one to know one' then I suspect neither of us extends a veneration of the natural world to the spider. Showing the kit sprawled over the floor and the offending backpack, we resort to action. He takes a step towards it, his hand outstretched, as I keenly watch. Embarrassingly I squeal again – what if the spider runs loose? This idea occurs to him too. He touches my arm to reassure me, mentions the car, and walks out, returning with a giant pair of hardware gloves. His hands now protected with thick fabric suitable for industrial use, the mayor is ready for what he must do. He picks up the pack and takes it outside. After recoiling twice as he prises it open, perhaps realising the morning is slipping by, he plunges his gloved hand deep inside the pack and takes a look. He upends it and shakes it about, soon exclaiming triumphantly, 'Voilà! Voici l'araignée …' The spider runs onto the patio and beats a hasty retreat, having no idea of the impact it had made.

■   ■   ■

Perhaps because of the drama, and satisfied that he has come to my rescue twice, the mayor seems especially animated, ordering more croissants with coffee and demanding more stories from my walk which began nearly three months before. *L'homme bizarre* arouses particular incredulity, requiring me to answer whether I was exposed to the *devant* as well as the *derrière?* Throughout breakfast, he swivels around to say good morning to this person or that, or wave to every vehicle that drives past our terrace table, a small-scale map of the Pyrenees spread over it. I need to set off to get to my next port of call by nightfall – Ceret, a stylish artistic centre and famed Cubist haunt. The mayor will drive me back to the top of the valley where I can rejoin my way east, saving me several hours of tedious road trudging. Along the way he points to different spots of interest, where he used to play as a boy, or the old route to school.

He turns off the winding lane and selects 4WD mode along a boggy track with overgrown branches and grassy bush. Flooded streams, like small rivers, spill down a slope into our path. It is time for him to reverse the car out of here and for the 'randonneuse' to walk on, along a leafy carpet of oranges, yellows and darkening browns. I will walk up to the ridgeline and follow it for some time before dropping into a valley much further along. I'm helped with the backpack and take my time adjusting it for comfort, not in any hurry to say goodbye. Barely fifteen hours had passed since we had met, two people sparking in happy collision. I had been housed, shielded and fed. 'Thank you' can seem so inadequate, impoverished by another's selfless generosity.

I set off as he gets back into the car and fires it up, waving for a last time as he sounds his horn for a couple of times through the rarely visited woods. A frantic wave back before the car labours backwards, disappearing round a bushy bend. Three days are all that separate me from the Mediterranean and the end of my walk. Yet how much more quickly the threads of chance unravel, having woven so randomly together. Scuffing the leaves, I am struck by last night's transformation from a cheerless arrival, to one of warm-hearted welcome. How deceptive impressions can be.

32 FIREWORKS: 2002

Birthdays are two a penny. The older one gets, the quicker the years pass, and the greater the reluctance to make a fuss. That is, unless you are turning thirty or have moved to a new part of the British Isles, far away from oldest friends and family. Having just relocated four hundred miles from London to Glasgow, and foreseeing a future in the more rugged and inspiring surrounds of the Highlands, it was time to mark my life transition with a party. It would be a rare event to bring together the many different friends made since childhood. For this to coincide with a recent flutter of cyber correspondence with a Nepali film star in need of recuperation, so much the better. It would ensure a steady lifelong supply of laughter at my own expense, to be chaperoned by someone so exotically out of place from my first spartan winter in Scotland.

There would be as little build-up of explanation or ceremony of intro-duction as possible. The party would be held in the ramshackle home of my parents, where I was born. The Jacobean house, with bedrooms as corridors and pre-war sewers unused to servicing large-scale social events, is in the heart of old England. This, for all its ingredients, would be a night to remember.

Newly settled and excited to be in a fresh job in a thriving city, Nepal maintained its presence in my life. The impact of my time there had been like a landslide. Within days of returning, job openings in BBC Scotland had emerged, resulting in a flurry of phone calls and enquiries. Following an informal interview, there was barely a month to dismantle my life and relocate. As I adapted to the swift and decisive changes and wrote to Sonam every few weeks to keep in touch, an e-mail arrived, out of the blue, from Rajesh.

I had scarcely thought about him since our last encounter and was surprised by its openness. His grandmother, who had worked tirelessly on her family's farm since the age of nineteen, and who'd only recently retired due to poor eyesight, had died. This matriarch, in her tenth decade, had lived a life of exemplary resourcefulness. Widowed and a single mother in her twenties, she had been a beacon of independence and strength of character to her family, a shining example to Rajesh and his siblings of how to endure life's unexpected hardships. This invincible woman's passing had made him review the people in his life. Never explaining why, he wanted to re-establish contact. It is an Eastern creed that no meeting in one's life is ever an accident of chance. After a few time-lapsed phone calls, I suggested he take a holiday and come for some invigorating Scottish air, adding his name to my expanding birthday guest list.

■   ■   ■

Those three weeks together were unforgettable, for all their trials and treasures. My high-maintenance guest, to his credit, adapted to the winter chill. Our trip to the Hebridean island of Mull to coincide with Scotland's legendary Hogmanay was colourful and fun. The lock-in culture, and music of fiddles and harmonicas, drums, and pipes delighted the man more conditioned to the hypnotic mystique of Eastern sound or rousing film set songs. He enquired about the materials needed to make his own bothy on his newly inherited grandmother's land. He took a scientific interest in fencing materials, of the grazing cycle of sheep and cows and occasionally managed to imitate the west-coast singsong drawl as well as any native.

His tall, dark appearance turned heads. He was charming and full of smiles and head-throwing laughs, won over by the open-door hospitality and down-to-earth friendliness for which the Celts are so famed. It didn't matter that Rajesh was not used to handling money – he has a team of helpers who take care of such pedestrian matters at home. He was happy to throw himself into the spirit of this hilly island, blown about by the changeable Atlantic fronts, with its refreshing irreverence to the civilian formalities of the mainland, an hour's ferry ride away. We danced and drank and told stories as everyone in Tobermory did, as the passing of another year was marked with merry abandon. He was even recognised by a Ghurka and his wife who worked in my local corner shop in Glasgow. They couldn't believe their eyes. A lot of giggling and blushing and fast flowing Nepali banter later, Rajesh was only too pleased to flourish his signature on the back of a till receipt.

■   ■   ■

Hosting a party is usually a mixed blessing. After the build-up and effort of attending to this and thinking of that, of last-minute panics and changes of plans, the memory of the night often seems compressed into one hour, rather than eight, nine, or ten. Old friends with a long, shared history travelled from far and wide to be there. All corners of the British Isles were represented. The presence too of a guest from a part of the world celebrated for its rich culture and lofty mountain terrain did not go unnoticed. Rajesh, without revealing much about himself, seemed to exude an allure perhaps mistrusted by the men but undoubtedly appreciated by the women. Every time I glanced to observe the general carryings on and check on whose glasses needed topping up, most took their turn to sidle up, intrigued and wanting some shared confidence.

'Mags, this, er, Raj … Raj … '

' … esh ... his name is Rajesh'

'Yes. He's, well, certainly entertaining. Simply charming, fascinating … and not exactly un-good looking!'

He spoke to the Thai cook and her helpers in their native tongue, apologising for being a little out of practice. He made my mother laugh loudly, and often, during supper. He danced with a style that paled the efforts of others, as they shimmied about the disco floor. A shirt was even briefly removed in one rock-and-roll classic. As the champagne and wine flowed, the Thai delicacies devoured, the speeches delivered, everyone at some point gushed that this was one of the 'best' parties they could remember.

The highlight had been carefully rehearsed some hours before the party began. As we all charged about the house setting up chairs and tables, I hadn't held back in delegating some of the workload to Rajesh, who'd scheduled some quiet time for a spot of yoga. My father had planted an ambitious collection of fireworks in various sparse rose beds and patches of herbaceous border, issuing a briefing in strict timing issues – which sticks of inflammable powders should go off first. A few minutes before midnight, donning a white boiler suit smeared with paint and varnish, he ushered us out into the cold, star-filled night. We gathered behind the box hedges, our glasses topped up with fresh champagne. Chatter and laughter rang through the dark as dad, summoning his son-in-law, strode out to the other end of the lawn.

I watched my friends clustered together in couples or small groups and wondered where Rajesh was. He was near enough, at least a few metres away, looking across the garden, as everybody was, watching my father sprint a few paces and crouch, while we all waited for the first explosion.

BANG! The delight and gasps were as immediate as the impact sudden. While a shower of fiery plumes burst into the black sky, smoke wafted about the garden bathing it in pungent, white cloud. The routine and its dazzling display seemed to go on and on and all of us were amazed by the relentless energy of my father and his trusty helper as they dashed from one end of the garden to the other, a catering-sized box of matches to hand. One bang flowed into the next, creating the best amateur firework display I had ever seen. This was a night to remember, a birthday party I could never forget. Everyone had made such an effort to be here, to make the atmosphere what it was.

Suddenly, I needed to share this rising feeling of happiness, of gratitude for everything that had made my life to date. I looked at the profile of Rajesh just a few feet away from me, lit up as another discharge flared into the night. I willed him to notice me, to turn and gesture something that would make me feel that he too was aware – relishing this moment, that everyone who mattered to me most in the world was here, celebrating. There was no glance or contact, no suggestion of personal chemistry. Unaware of me, he continued to look straight ahead. In fact not once during the evening did I ever feel truly connected to this man, who, with his undoubted grace and charisma, touches the lives of millions back home.

We were now being shouted at 'to brace ourselves', that the finale was about to unfold. Staring out into the smoky gloom, the rising sense of anti-climax had to be ignored. This was not the time to indulge regret or disappointment. How could this chapter that began to write itself during a random encounter in Nepali monsoon ever really amount to anything other than what it was – a wonderful, life-enhancing twist? It would be a story that everyone here could carry away with them, of the birthday girl's guest of honour, no more or less. This was the material of real life, my instincts too down to earth, for it ever to take on the shape of romantic melodrama.

Everyone was quiet and expectant. My father dashed for cover and we watched and waited as the ultimate firework was lit and crackled, about to blast into space. No sooner had we started to cheer when it misfired, petering out before shooting sideways and whirling towards the excited crowd, who all ducked. It flashed over us, showering sparks as it crashed into the kitchen wall.

'What a finale,' everyone agreed as we raised ourselves, somewhat baffled but nonetheless delighted for that. Someone proposed a toast to our superb firework technician and his daughter. As I looked at my companion, linking my arm through his, my other hand ready to tilt the glass to my lips, happy feelings for a bright future began to emerge.

After we all clapped and cheered, I thanked everyone for sharing this special evening, 'especially the efforts of one extraordinary individual who has travelled from so far away to be here too.' Smiling we all looked at Rajesh, as we motioned another toast, this time to my most captivating guest.

BOUNDARIES: 2003

The Mediterranean, held in my sights for so long, was barely two days away. After nearly seventy days of walking towards it, the blue streak across the horizon was maddeningly elusive. Expecting it to appear round every bend and beyond every rise made me all the more aware of each passing hour. The coastal terrain is dry and undulating, with a labyrinth of sandy paths winding through hills of olive trees and scrub. The increasing development of the eastern fringes of the Pyrenees is like civilisation jostling for space, lured by the exotic climate and proximity to a warm sea. Such prime land would be pricey and the luxury villas with the lifestyle attached to them reflect the wealth of this exclusive community.

The property is desirable at whatever level. The most affordable have neatly trimmed gardens and sheared hedging, the roofs in shades of pink, orange, and terracotta, contrasting with cool white walls. Those more architecturally distinctive have the space to offset them, driveways the other side of closed gates, many electrically-powered with intercom devices. The garden sprinkler is common in this part of the world and the artfully tended strips of grass are a lurid green despite the minimal rainfall.

For the end of October, while most of northern Europe was experiencing more bluster than calm, the morning was warm and golden. I followed the unsurfaced road past a garden at the end of a row of mown rectangles, hoping this would be a shortcut to the track heading due east. It wound on ahead through gorse fields with their distinctive coconut aroma. Not wanting to waste dwindling energy and motivation, I decided to double-check and peered towards the source of clipping coming from behind the head high hedgerow.

'Bonjour? Excusez-moi?' The snips continued and only stopped when I tried again.

'Oui?' A voice enquired from the bush, before the clipping re-started.

'La route là … vers Banyuls?'

The gardener rose from behind the hedge and peered over the top. A long strand of grey hair was slapped over a bald mound and his cheeks were bright red circles. He dismounted from a stepladder with a jump, appearing the other side of a little gate in a faded blue artisan jacket and shorts. A spray of water was dousing a bed of leafy plants behind him.

'Banyuls, oh, c'est loin, très loin.'

'Oui, mais … les Hauts de Céret … là?'

'Oui. Loin aussi. Quatre heures, cinq heures, là.' He gestured vaguely up the track.

It was hard to imagine how the village, only four kilometres from here, could take four or five hours to walk. Oh yes, certainly it was very far, maybe six hours walk that way. But that would mean an average of less than a kilometre an hour, surely not! Was I alone – it is very dangerous for a woman to be out walking, especially as the weather in the hills is so unpredictable? Best to stick to the main roads. Best to be safe. I pointed out I was merely checking the directions and nothing else, to which he answered that being so close to the border, there were more people here with violent tendencies. A lot of Spanish too.

The skies were cloudless blue and the sun so hot I was dripping in sweat. The day seemed almost too perfect to trust. He was the first person with whom I'd spoken since stepping into this partitioned community with its air of expensive leisure. Countless random people in tracksuits had jogged by with their faithful pooches at heel but there had been no other amblers or dawdlers. Perhaps this typified the world's affluent neighbourhoods. This man and his outlook seemed mean as well as presumptuous. He looked so comfortably proportioned in his well-maintained space, clutching his shears, his garden props.

'I am only trying to protect you, mademoiselle.' he said defensively, looking wounded by my ingratitude.

Something in me was reacting not just to him but his tightly guarded territory, this barricaded environment which projected the very uncertainty it feared. The flamboyant stone figurines and imported horticultural exotica were like hollow attempts to bolster his sense of worth. The time I had spent with the simple purpose of walking from one place to another had shown me that cramming the void with things or pursuits never fills it for long. Grasping the immeasurable value of human kindness had challenged my ideas about what it means to be secure, or the tendency to forget the hidden helping hands guiding the way. Even the encounter with *l'homme bizarre* had as much a role to play in shaping my experience as Philippe had, teaching me about resourceful outdoor living. The paternal mayor and the elegant woman whose spiritedness led me to him, the cuddly form of Santiago accompanying me through a wilder landscape that would have otherwise overwhelmed me, even the enduring presence of the count in these mountains, are all part of the same design. These chance encounters are like layers of fabric, its texture all the richer for the countless flecks of shape and colour weaving into it.

This man's odd concern, his fear, reminded me that this is the very quality that carves up the world and maroons its people. It was that very fear which had made me want to give up, time and again. Every stranger who reached out a hand was how I identified each place I walked through. It is the human face of the environment that makes its geography so memorable.

Dusty tracks lead to rich forests of beech and oak and my last day is mostly spent under a canopy of swaying trees. The wind blows clouds across the sun as each step takes me nearer the widening ribbon of royal blue.

What will mark my arrival at the end of this varied voyage – the photo, the chilled bubbly toast, a phone call home? Or will it be that sweet and fleeting moment of satisfaction that makes the arduous route to arrival worthwhile? This long walk has strayed close to winter and these stately trees sheltering me will soon be bare. The seasonal cycle will begin its journey again as nature winds down to regenerate. The finishing line is only ever half-drawn, opening up further, unforeseeable horizons. That's what makes finding the way so rewarding – life is never a destination to reach but a state of becoming.